Shakespeare and the Sense of Performance

Essays in the Tradition of Performance Criticism in Honor of Bernard Beckerman

EDITED BY

Marvin and Ruth Thompson

DELAWARE

NEWARK: University of Delaware Press

LONDON AND TORONTO: Associated University Presses

Associated University Presses
440 Forsgate Drive
Cranbury, NJ 08512

Associated University Presses
25 Sicilian Avenue
London WC1A 2QH, England

Associated University Presses
P.O. Box 488, Port Credit
Mississauga, Ontario
Canada L5G 4M2

The paper used in this publication meets the requirements
of the American National Standard for Permanence of Paper
for Printed Library Materials Z39.48-1984.

Library of Congress Cataloging-in-Publication Data

Shakespeare and the sense of performance.

Includes bibliographies.
1. Shakespeare, William, 1564–1616—Dramatic
production.   2. Shakespeare, William, 1564–1616—Stage
history.   3. Beckerman, Bernard.   I. Beckerman, Bernard.
II. Thompson, Marvin.   III. Thompson, Ruth, 1927–   .
IV. Title: Performance criticism in honor of Bernard
Beckerman.
PR3091.S34   1989   822.3′3   87-40327
ISBN 0-87413-332-7 (alk. paper)

Printed in the United States of America

Contents

Contributors

RALPH BERRY, Professor of English, University of Ottawa

A. R. BRAUNMULLER, Professor of English, University of California, Los Angeles

JOHN RUSSELL BROWN, Professor of Drama, University of Michigan

MAURICE CHARNEY, Distinguished Professor of English, Rutgers University

THOMAS CLAYTON, Professor of English, University of Minnesota

ANN JENNALIE COOK, Associate Professor of English, Vanderbilt University

ALAN C. DESSEN, Professor of English, University of North Carolina

INGA-STINA EWBANK, Professor of English, University of Leeds

R. A. FOAKES, Professor of English, University of California, Los Angeles

MICHAEL GOLDMAN, Professor of English, Princeton University

ANDREW GURR, Professor of English, University of Reading

JAY L. HALIO, Professor of English, University of Delaware

PHILIP C. MCGUIRE, Professor of English, Michigan State University

HUGH M. RICHMOND, Professor of English, University of California, Berkeley

MARVIN ROSENBERG, Professor Emeritus of Dramatic Art, University of California, Berkeley

DEREK PEAT, Director, Centre for Continuing Education, University of Sydney

J. L. STYAN, Franklyn Bliss Snyder Professor of English Literature and Professor of Theatre, Northwestern University

HOMER SWANDER, Professor of English, University of California, Santa Barbara

MARVIN AND RUTH THOMPSON, Professors Emeriti of English, St. Cloud State University

GLYNNE WICKHAM, Professor Emeritus of Drama, University of Bristol

Foreword

No one was more interested in bringing the academy and the theater together than Bernard Beckerman, who was himself a living representation of the rapprochement that *is* possible. Scholar, teacher, director, administrator, he knew the difficulties but stressed the possibilities for more fruitful communication between the two active enterprises. He saw a communication that could be mutually enriching, and thanks to his own work—in the theatre, in the library, and in the classroom—we have a superb fund of scholarship, criticism, and understanding that scholars and theatre professionals all over the world have found eminently useful.

The present collection of essays by his friends and colleagues is in every sense a fitting tribute to the memory of this generous and learned man. How he would enjoy reading each one, arguing with this or that point, praising new knowledge and insights, adding something here or there from his own extensive experience. How delighted he would be to follow Derek Peat's presentation of evidence concerning the Lord's Room or Andrew Gurr's discussion of staging plays at the Globe and other Elizabethan theaters. J. L. Styan's definition of different types of space would have fascinated him—and doubtless would have evoked further exploration of the issue. Fervently interested in the original staging of the plays, as his *Shakespeare at the Globe, 1599–1609* demonstrates, he was not a mere antiquarian. He understood that today's performances must speak to today's audiences. But how? That was the question.

Alan Dessen focuses the question acutely, as in a different way so do Hugh Richmond and Thomas Clayton. The problem of "authenticity" seems crucial. While it resists easy definition, the writers in this collection make good progress in helping us understand the gains and losses in "modernization." Glynne Wickham's experience in directing both *Love's Labour's Lost* and *As You Like It* has led him to some surprising conclusions about the relation between the two plays, conclusions that not everyone may accept, but many will find stimulating for further investigation.

Practical matters involving staging necessarily concern not only actors and directors but editors, too, as A. R. Braunmuller shows. An early practitioner of performance criticism, R. A. Foakes demonstrates the importance of stage imagery for anyone who wants to visualize or perform a Shakespearean play. What happens when stage directions are absent has led Philip C. McGuire to inquire into an important situation in *A Midsummer Night's Dream:* just what does Egeus do at the end of the play? Soliloquies, asides, and other nondialogic speech are extremely complex parts of the script that require careful attention, as Maurice Charney shows. Distinguishing between acting styles, particularly as dictated by differences between Marlowe's and Shakespeare's characters, is also vitally important, as Michael Goldman argues; otherwise we are apt to perform Marlowe's work as if it were Shakespeare's—to the advantage of neither.

A vital consideration is of course language, and here Inga-Stina Ewbank, Ralph Berry, Homer Swander, and John Russell Brown offer incisive accounts of how language operates in Shakespeare's plays. Professor Ewbank analyzes Shakespeare's adaptation of Greene's novel, *Pandosto,* to show how the dramatist transforms not only mode but also language, and she goes further to see how these effects work in two modern productions. Berry's suggestion that soliloquies help "bond" actor and audience is an astute observation; he also considers what happens to characters who lack soliloquies. Swander's essay, especially as it focuses on the epilogue to *The Tempest,* extends the point and develops it. Both more general and more specific (in his examples), Brown shows how the gap between text and theatrical understanding must be bridged—and how it can be. Marvin Rosenberg carries the arguments still further by examining the way subtexts operate—what underlies the words in the text and shows the actors how to say them.

No collection of essays on performance criticism would be complete without a detailed examination of Shakespeare's plays in performance, and Thomas Clayton's essay provides a detailed and extensive critique of a number of recent productions. Fittingly, it begins with an excerpt from one of Bernard Beckerman's last published essays and extends the implications of "balancing" that Beckerman talked about. Practical criticism in turn leads to theoretical considerations, and appropriately the discussion of a number of fundamental issues concludes Clayton's essay and the volume proper. Neither his essay nor any of the others collected here presumes to be definitive; that is not the way criticism works. But each one in its way makes a contribution to our understanding of what happens or does not happen when we see a Shakespeare play performed, and for these contributions we can only be grateful.

Jay L. Halio

Shakespeare
and the Sense of Performance

Performance Criticism

From Granville-Barker to Bernard Beckerman and Beyond

MARVIN AND RUTH THOMPSON

The authors of the fine essays that follow and the distinguished scholar to whose memory they are dedicated, Bernard Beckerman, have in common the fact that they belong to the single most important tradition in contemporary Shakespeare studies: performance criticism. The names represented here are those of persons who were warm friends and admirers of the late professor Beckerman, and beyond that they are in every sense important in their own right. With Bernard Beckerman, they helped bring the very tradition itself into being.

As editors, we are privileged to have had a modest role in preparing the book. Here, beginning with a definition, is our understanding of the critical mode with which these studies are concerned.

As it refers to the plays of Shakespeare and his contemporaries, *performance criticism* is a term used to draw attention to stage-centered criticism. Because this kind of scholarship has acquired a history of its own, and because it now embraces so many approaches, the term itself should not be defined too narrowly. However, the following six characteristics seem to apply:

1. *Performance criticism is an approach by which the text of a play is closely related to what can be known or considered about the conditions of the stage;* in brief, it is a close and steady relating of the verbal and the visual as drawn from both text and stage. As to the play itself, one need no longer work from the formal elements of language, character, plot, and theme; but as to stage, one would hope somehow to take into account these following: (1) the physical nature of the stage, (2) the business of the acting, and (3) what can be known about or estimated of the nature of the audience and its probable response. (As to this latter there will be *some* response, necessary to consider, if hard precisely to account for.) Over a period of years the direction of influ-

ence seems to have moved from text to stage and back again to the complete play, that is, to deducing ideas about stage matters from the plays themselves for the ultimate enrichment of the latter. But however arrived at, such knowledge seems to be of increasing value in itself, either in single detail or in various combination, as well as richly suggestive of further amplification. The important thing is that constant interchange and cross-reference between text and stage work toward giving to the play the fullest and most accurate meaning possible.

2. *Performance criticism is an approach that considers a play at its own moment in dramatic history,* for example, *Richard II* as it reflects Shakespeare's skill around 1595, roughly at the same time as *A Midsummer Night's Dream* and *Romeo and Juliet,* rather than *merely* as one of the history plays.

3. *It is an approach that draws attention to the forward movement of the play as it progresses through time.* As with music, so with drama. Both exist in temporal space and to examine a play as it might be acted on stage is to remind oneself of how it moves through moments of time, from beginning to end. And this is true even when one may want to focus on a single scene or action such as Hamlet's meeting with the players, in particular when he discusses with them the conditions of the theatres in London. Although it has been argued that at this point in the play the forward momentum comes to a complete stop, one must insist that even such a marked pause in the larger action is like a measure of rest within a musical composition. When the demands of text and stage are considered together, the underlying "beat" is there after all, even if momentarily unheard.

4. *It is an approach that stresses the nonillusory rather than the realistic.* This is true for at least four reasons: place is most often indicated, rather than carefully defined, by the relatively limited number of specific verbal clues as to where the action may be set (and they, whether as stage direction or, more often, as derived from within the spoken language, come at us rather quickly); place may be indicated by a limited number of stage properties (a chair, a bed, a bank of flowers, etc., as well as costume); the action itself is, by our standards, fast (even if the sense of "two hours' traffic" were stretched a bit), so that changes in scene are necessarily fluid and, as such, tend to be suggestive rather than realistic; finally, the succession and variety of stages used by the Lord Chamberlain's/King's Men is wide, ranging from that of public theatres like the Globe, to that of Blackfriars', to improvised stage areas—much less definable—of performance at Court, at the Inns of Court, or on tour at the Universities, Great Houses, and Innyards. All this would argue that the company would be adept at having to suggest or improvise place, rather than carefully to define it.

5. *It is an approach that works toward defining a sense of the authentic.* Again it will be hard if not impossible to establish authenticity when certain textual problems are unsolvable and when a variety of first stagings are lost in the mists of early performance history. But it is necessary for us to work toward such a goal for at least three reasons: (1) in order that we can judge any present-day performance for its approximate authenticity; or, more often, (2) in order that we can better judge a performance for its "translation" into modern stage idiom; or, finally, (3) in order that we can apply knowledge of historical performance since 1660 for our more complete understanding of the possibilities inherent in any given play. As to this last point, our accumulated historical knowledge about both text and performance helps us to work toward the "authentic" in the larger sense. As is true of a cantata or major choral work by Bach, so with a play by Shakespeare: one is never quite finished with it. Such a work has its own organic, living growth, and as each age interprets it, successive performances of a play take us a bit closer to the larger—if forever elusive—authentic.

6. *Finally, of all approaches, performance criticism seems more nearly capable of self-correction, in that the demands of text and stage are considered together.* It serves—by matching critical theory against our growing knowledge of stage practice—to limit error and thus to establish greater accuracy of fact and informed speculation than would a more single-minded approach or an openly experimental one.

An illustration in summary of the above six points—an illustration deliberately chosen for its obviousness—would be Hamlet's advice on behavior proper to the clown. A traditional reading would be that Hamlet's language of precision helps to define his own character at this moment of the action as well as touching obliquely on larger matters of the play. Familiar enough. But the speech gains further significance when considered as being set against the stage of the Globe Theatre itself—on the general physical nature of which there is some broad agreement—with choices for movement, treatment of space, and general staging that are, to *some* degree at least, limited; with certain responses probable from the players-as-auditors together with responses of the larger audience itself. When all these items are brought into focus, with names like Tarlton, Kempe, and Armin hovering in the historical air, one must consider— under the broad aegis of performance criticism—how such matters as gesture, space, grouping, movement, role, stage properties, costume, directoral hints, aesthetic distance, speaking style, silence, ceremony, and pace of scene and episode would likely have been dealt with then, as well as to speculate on how such information can be reflected by or "translated" into present day performance. A number of our contributors have elsewhere touch d on the matter of Hamlet at this moment in the play, obliquely if not directly. It is a tantalizing prospect to imagine our contributors gathered together in some pleasant late afternoon room with good wine, a bit of food, and enough leisure at hand to discuss Hamlet and this particular one of his various problems in an attempt to define, deal with, and, in the style and most generous tone of modern-day *sprezzatura,* resolve it.

But this is more than a pleasant bit of dreaming: in a true sense it is what our book is about.

To go beyond definition and to set the essays of this book within their larger perspective, we offer materials for a brief history of performance criticism or, to be more precise, of certain moments crucial to its development. To begin, we argue that the true origin of performance criticism goes farther back in this century than is usually assumed; that its continuation into the present is far more influential in all kinds of Shakespeare studies than has been recognized; and that everywhere, infusion of ideas drawn from stage practice—both historical and contemporary—is proving increasingly important to what the larger movement has achieved. There are two periods that we see as important for establishing the movement: first, those several years culminating with the late 1920s and the early 1930s; second, the important decade and more beginning with the early and mid-1950s. In general the way in which the business of the stage is brought into the larger criticism is accomplished by the critics calling increased attention to stage imagery, at first narrowly, but now more broadly considered, and to matters derived from it. Readers will recognize our indebtedness on this and other developments and trends to various scholars, among them, John L. Styan, Ann Pasternak Slater, David Bevington, and Ralph Berry.[1]

Chief among the important names of the movement's early years are Harley Granville-Barker, who comes to criticism from theatre, and Muriel C. Bradbrook, from the academic world. (We would note that both of them—like Bernard Beckerman later—began their active careers at a very early age, a fact perhaps related to the breadth and inventiveness of their various critical discoveries.)

Although there were earlier important commentators, Harley Granville-Barker (1872–1946) was the first major figure in Shakespeare criticism to have brought to his work the combined skills of the actor, the playwright, and the producer. His career as critic began in the early 1920s, but his many activities before that were so various and wide-ranging as to make him both the link to the Victorian period and the innovator who made the final break with it. As such, he is indebted both to producers like William Poel and to A. C. Bradley at his critical best, testing the ideas of the latter against developing stage practice. With some few exceptions, the ideas and the methods of Granville-Barker in his collected *Prefaces to Shake-speare* remain constantly valuable.[2]

Because his activities as a man of the theatre are so crucially reflected in his writings, more so than is true of any other major critical figure, it is necessary to consider them here, if briefly.

As actor, he played within fifteen years (1896–1911) something like forty roles, many of them in important plays. As playwright, he wrote six plays of his own between 1899 and 1923 and collaborated on as well as translated many more. As producer or coproducer, he was responsible for upward of one hundred plays between 1900 and 1914—and more than that through his later career[3]—among which he accomplished in three plays (1912–14), *The Winter's Tale, Twelfth Night,* and *A Midsummer Night's Dream,* productions that were more certainly in the style and spirit of Shakespeare than were any stagings since the time of Burbage and the Globe itself. For these three plays he employed methods whose significance would prove central to his mature criticism: he included the full text; he used an approximation of the thrust stage; he simplified stage business and costume; and he speeded up the pace and played the action with next to no interruptions. This was a revolution in the full sense of the word; if in previous centuries men like Pope, Johnson, Coleridge, Hazlitt, Lamb, and others had saved the text of Shakespeare's dramatic art for us and refined our conception of it, it was Granville-Barker alone who restored something like the essential Shakespeare to the stage. Thus, when in the studies that grew into the *Prefaces* he repeatedly asked the question, "How should this be played?" he struck off answers that reflected to some greater or lesser degree every one of the six characteristics of performance criticism listed earlier in this introduction whose definitions we had derived by examining the full range of the tradition.

Second, and perhaps of equal importance, Granville-Barker warned against mere antiquarianism. As early as 1912 he wrote, "We shall not save our souls by being Elizabethan. . . . To be Elizabethan one must be strictly, logically or quite ineffectively so. And even then it is asking too much of an audience to come to the theatre so historically sensed as that."[4] His successors would make constant refinements and changes in his approach, itself doubly grounded in sound theatrical practice and critical good sense, but of Harley Granville-Barker it is perhaps fair to say that in his criticism the glory of Shakespeare's language—long recognized, of course—together with the incredible richness of character, action, and theme is for the first time fully matched against the demands and the exciting possibilities of his stage.

If Granville-Barker had created an entirely new kind of criticism out of current theatre experience, there was another group of scholars, chief among them Muriel C. Bradbrook, who were to develop the critical implications derived from research on the nature and physical conditions of Shakespeare's own theatre. Like Granville-Barker, Muriel Bradbrook had begun her work at a very early age. *Elizabethan Stage Conditions* (1932) was the result of work she had completed the previous year as an undergraduate at Cambridge in competition for a prize.[5] At the age of twenty-two, as a student, she had initiated a major summary statement of the value to critical scholarship of research by persons like Lawrence, Thorndike, J. Q. Adams, and E. K. Chambers. Her resultant short book is thus a pattern for bringing together into practical criticism the results of scholarship on the stage. Where Granville-Barker had argued against antiquarianism, she warned against trying for too precise an interpretation of the newer stage scholarship.[6] Her contributions on such matters were so sound that when she examined the materials of her book for its reissue in 1962 she could, as a mature scholar, stand by the historical accuracy of her earlier observations. She added only that subsequent historians of stage and theatre conditions had brought in new conclusions on pageantry and the arts: these included such persons as G. R. Kernodle, Walter Hodges, Richard Southern, Glynne Wickham, and Richard Hosley. Finally, she added new emphasis to our general indebtedness to Granville-Barker.[7]

Between those two dates, 1932 and 1962, a good many things happened, too many to touch on in detail, but it was in the early 1950s that criticism managed once and for all to merge the concerns of stage and study. For example, two articles of those years seem both reflective and prophetic of growing interest in the audience and in the problem of stage business and imagery. In 1953, Warren D. Smith in "Stage Business in Shakespeare's Dialogue"[8] noted that the indications for stage business within the dialogue of the plays both of Shakespeare and his contemporaries outnumber by a ratio of ten to one the number of marginal notations in the basic text. In the Shakespeare plays, for example (Kittredge edition) there are nearly three thousand directions for stage business (action performed without shifting position) compared to fewer than three hundred in marginal notations. More important, most of these directions seem to be cues not to the actors but to the audience as if to draw the latter's attention to actions that have already taken place, not only broad actions but also facial expressions, weeping, behavior like that of Lady Macbeth wringing her hands, and so on.[9] These are illustrations of how Shakespeare is everywhere concerned with keeping his audience informed of stage business that for one reason or another might not have been easy to see. At the same time R. A. Foakes in 1952 called for a critical approach that would take account of stage imagery as distinct from the merely verbal.[10] And in the consideration of stage imagery there had been need for a sharpening of focus. For example, in 1933 L. C. Knights in refuting Bradley had made the extreme claim—no longer held today—that the play be considered as a dramatic poem and in the process drew attention away from character study to language, making visual imagery itself of dramatic concern.[11] In addition, of course, the impressive work of Caroline Spurgeon (1935) drew immediate attention to imagery (even if her ultimate concern was with the way Shakespeare as artist worked and with the "furniture of his mind").[12] But if such growing interest in imagery was pursued by a great many writers, including the New Critics, not all of them had seemed sure of the direction of their treatment. Hence, the value of R. A. Foakes's article was its asking, once and for all, for sharper definition of stage imagery.

A number of major studies were begun within that crucial decade that would focus various interests related to audience, stage, and stage imagery into something like a recognizable approach. For example, by 1953 John Russell Brown began to publish a series of articles that grew directly out of his work and association at the Shakespeare Institute at Stratford-upon-Avon with scholars like R. A. Foakes, C. J. Sisson, and Allardyce Nicoll. These articles, which had wide dissemination and influence, were the direct result of exciting years in Stratford when stage and study were brought together quite literally. His essays became part of his influential *Shakespeare's Plays in Performance* (1966), a book rich in suggestion for consideration of actors, stage, and audience, as well as in the critical language that could reflect such interests.[13] Another important work of this decade was Maurice Charney's *Shakespeare's Roman Plays: The Function of Imagery in the Drama* (1961), in which he developed in detail what he called the "presentational imagery" of gesture and the visual that went beyond the merely verbal.[14] A third work that dealt with the primary relationship of actor and audience was John L. Styan's *Elements of Drama* (1960), in which the author worked toward a method and language of analytical criticism based on stage-centered study of Shakespeare but reinforced by reference to other drama as well.[15]

Thus throughout this very important decade, such works as these gave genuine impetus to a synthesis of the central concerns of text and stage. Brown, Charney, Styan, and Bernard Beckerman, whom we shall turn to shortly—together with Nevill Coghill in *Shakespeare's Professional Skills* (1964)[16]—demonstrated the multiple effects of theatre, audience, visual meaning, and stage imagery as devices for unification. These scholars and others—like Walter Hodges and A. M. Nagler, who dealt more specifically with the playhouse structure, or A. C. Sprague and R. Watkins, who studied the problems of playhouse productions and the players—had established with their various pioneering approaches the foundations for a new kind of criticism.[17] Whatever other related approaches might be further developed—concerns with styles of acting, with the effects and dramatic meanings of properties, costume, space, gestures of all kinds, action and placement of action, ceremony, silence, iconography—performance criticism had by the mid-1960s come of age: increasingly it was to become part of the permanent core and source of a wider body of Shakespeare criticism.

Bernard Beckerman (1921–84), to whose memory this collection is dedicated, epitomizes the decade we have been considering. Everything seems to be reflected in him: like Granville-Barker, who had been above all a man of the theatre, he based his own criticism on actual work with the stage; like Muriel Bradbrook, he reflected the informed attitude of the academic world; like those scholars of the 1950s who developed critical language, both for matters dealing with the theatre audience and for visual imagery, he was a synthesizer, the single person who seems to have been able to bring together and summarize material from all areas in his work.

In the years immediately following World War II, while still very young, Beckerman began work in the theatre as a director. From 1950 to 1965 he directed fifteen plays of Shakespeare for Hofstra College, all but two of them produced on the J. C. Adams full-scale model of the Globe. Thus his preparation for critical work was in its own way unique: no other critic of that important decade, or in fact of any period since 1660, had such immediate personal experience with an approximation, at least, of Elizabethan stage conditions. He combined the results of such practical knowlege in his dissertation in 1956 at Columbia University: *The Production of Shakespeare's Plays at the Globe Playhouse, 1599–1609,* which was published in 1962 as *Shakespeare at the Globe: 1599–1609.*[18]

In that book, he deals with the larger problems of repertory, dramaturgy, the stage, acting, staging, and style; throughout, he touches on matters that concern us at every level. His book thus stands as a summary of the full tradition. He counts scenes, movement, entrances, exits, asides, kinds and numbers of stage properties, types of form and structure as they reflect stage business, number of people on stage in given circumstances, authority figures and their function, kinds of climactic plateaus, endings, and the like. He searches everywhere, but his chief sources are text and stage: the fourteen Shakespearean and fifteen non-Shakespearean plays of the period 1599–1609, and the conditions of staging them at the Globe.

Even his appendixes are revealing of this twin concern. He deals with the number of plays, length of performance, summary of court performances; with types of locale that are particular, general, neutral; with disguises and their suggested effects; with properties required, such as tables, chairs, beds, scaffolds, tombs, tents, trees, rocks; with formal scenes (requiring more than five characters) that involve visual imagery, such as single combat scenes, banquet scenes, procession scenes, and the like.[19]

The numbers and kinds of such items he touches on here and

throughout the book are truly impressive for the breadth of concern they imply. The result is a compendium of stage and study that sums up achievements dating from Granville-Barker's first lectures some forty years earlier up through the period of the 1950s; like the *Prefaces, Shakespeare at the Globe (1599–1609)* was to be found on everyone's desk.

Bernard Beckerman's contributions to performance criticism do not, of course, begin and end with *Shakespeare at the Globe*. Over the next twenty years, as his bibliography shows,[20] he lectured and published widely on Shakespeare and other dramatists and on their dramaturgy. He was by no means alone. During this period, studies and approaches by his fellow scholars proliferated to the point where their cumulative impact itself becomes important. Significantly, a good number of those scholars who helped determine the nature and direction of performance criticism are contributers to this present volume. And the body of knowledge they represent and that they helped create is permanent: with a history of some seventy years to its credit, the tradition can serve as source material for today's burgeoning scholarship as well as for whatever new approaches may develop.

And here a note of personal indebtedness: As editors we looked for evidence that performance criticism had established itself within the academic world as well as within the larger critical tradition. To that end we were fortunate that John Styan provided us with a list of books which, as of 1987, he recommends to graduate students at Northwestern University who are reading for his course, "Shakespeare and Performance." All the names are here: a good many that we have referred to above as well as others we all know well. Professor Styan has grouped them under eight headings: (1) the playhouse; (2) the stagecraft, (3) the conventions, (4) audience manipulation, (5) performance criticism and theory, (6) metadrama, (7) production history, and (8) editions that include production material (see Appendix). A quick check by decades since the 1940s shows the following: for the 1940s and the important decade of the 1950s, he lists ten major books (chiefly having to do with the playhouse and matters of performance); for the 1960s, thirteen (scattered among all the headings, with the exception of the playhouse); for the 1970s, twenty-six (scattered, with the exception of the playhouse); and already by the mid-1980s, eighteen (again rather broadly scattered). Of course by the present date of publication there are many more, with new listings appearing literally by the month.

The scholarly works thus represented, both in books of criticism and more recently in editions that include production history material—not counting the vast bibliography of articles—stand as an impressive achievement indeed. As the essays in this collection suggest, the tradition of performance criticism seems capable not only of generating valuable new theories, but also—with such prospects as that of the Bankside Globe[21]—of paving the way to exciting practical discoveries.

Notes

1. John L. Styan, *The Shakespeare Revolution* (Cambridge: Cambridge University Press, 1977), especially chapters 4 through 12 and the conclusion; Ann Pasternak Slater, *Shakespeare the Director* (Totowa, N.J.: Barnes and Noble, 1982), especially the introductory chapter with its extensive notes; David Bevington, *Action Is Eloquence* (Cambridge: Harvard University Press, 1984), also containing a valuable, heavily annotated introductory chapter; Ralph Berry, *Changing Styles in Shakespeare* (London: George Allen and Unwin, 1981), especially valuable for his treatment of how, since 1947, directors have had a major influence on the tradition.

2. Harley Granville-Barker, *Prefaces to Shakespeare*, 2 vols. (Princeton: Princeton University Press, 1946–47). For a complete list of published works by Granville-Barker see Dennis Kennedy, *Granville Barker and the Dream of Theatre* (Cambridge: Cambridge University Press, 1985), 220.

3. Kennedy, *Granville Barker*, 207–14, gives a complete list of productions.

4. A letter by Granville-Barker to *Play Pictoral* (1912) as quoted in Kennedy, *Granville Barker*, 130.

5. M. C. Bradbrook, *Elizabethan Stage Conditions: a Study of Their Place in the Interpretation of Shakespeare's Plays* (Cambridge: Cambridge University Press, 1932). Interestingly enough, she notes that E. K. Chambers, in the introduction to his massive *The Elizabethan Stage*, 4 vols. (Oxford: Oxford University Press, 1923), had disclaimed any critical intention for his treatment of the plays themselves beyond what they could contribute to our knowledge of the theatre. In fact, he repudiates "their literary aspect with which I am not concerned," as quoted by Bradbrook, 3.

6. Bradbrook, *Elizabethan Stage Conditions*, 146.

7. Bradbrook, *Elizabethan Stage Conditions*, viii–ix.

8. Warren D. Smith, "Stage Business in Shakespeare's Dialogue," *Shakespeare Quarterly* 3(1953): 311–16.

9. Ibid., 312–13.

10. R. A. Foakes, "Suggestions for a New Approach to Shakespeare's Imagery," *Shakespeare Studies* 5(1952): 81–92.

11. L. C. Knights, "How Many Children Had Lady Macbeth?" (1933), in *Explorations* (London: Chatto and Windus, 1946), 1–39.

12. Caroline Spurgeon, *Shakespeare's Imagery and what it Tells Us* (Cambridge: Cambridge University Press, 1935).

13. John Russell Brown, *Shakespeare's Plays in Performance* (London: Edward Arnold, 1966).

14. Maurice Charney, *Shakespeare's Roman Plays: The Function of Imagery in the Drama* (Cambridge: Harvard University Press, 1961).

15. John L. Styan, *Elements of Drama* (Cambridge: Cambridge University Press, 1960).

16. Nevill Coghill, *Shakespeare's Professional Skills* (Cambridge: Cambridge University Press, 1964).

17. Walter Hodges, *The Globe Restored* (London: E. Benn, 1953); A. M. Nagler, *Shakespeare's Stage* (New Haven: Yale University Press, 1958); A. C.

Sprague, *Shakespearian Players and Performances* (Cambridge: Harvard University Press, 1953); Ronald Watkins, *On Producing Shakespeare* (London: Michael Joseph, 1950).

18. Bernard Beckerman, *Shakespeare at the Globe; 1599–1609* (New York: Macmillan, 1962).

19. Beckerman, *Shakespeare at the Globe,* 217–31.

20. See the Bibliography of his publications, provided for us by Gloria Beckerman, which appears at the close of this volume.

21. And here the advice of such scholars as John Orrell, Glynne Wickham, Andrew Gurr, Muriel Bradbrook, and others—cited at various points above—will be of invaluable help in the design and reconstruction of Shakespeare's Globe.

Hamlet and the Audience

The Dynamics of a Relationship

RALPH BERRY

The extended ingratiation by which Hamlet develops his special relationship with the audience rests on two factors: the persona of the actor
and the sequence of major soliloquies. The persona is, I think, more
important than technique. Hamlet is not, oddly, a part that demands great
acting. But it does demand the essential star quality of magnetism. An
actor, perfectly competent in a general professional way, who essays
Hamlet without charm can be merely embarrassing. The part is written for
a star actor, who may be a third-rate star, but not for a *good* actor. From
his base of personal magnetism, the actor woos the audience in seven
soliloquies. In general, the soliloquy is a device for bonding actor and
audience. Those characters to whom it is granted are on a different plane
from those lacking one. It's a rule that soliloquies never alienate audiences.
The device is too intimate, fascinating, absorbing. And in *Hamlet,* the
soliloquy sets up a particular kind of relationship.[1] The audience becomes
a counselor, perhaps even a psychiatrist, as Hamlet brings to it his problems. "Am I a coward?" Enmeshed in the self-analyses of this fascinating
young man, the audience—like a good counselor—may not interrupt but
listens, intent, to every word. For seven sessions, Hamlet pours out his
fears, doubts, and resolutions, and to all of them the counselor-audience
gives sympathetic ear. It is of course on Hamlet's side; it assents to his
perception of affairs. And this remains broadly true throughout the first
four acts.

The shift in this equation of forces occurs at what is surely planned as
the interval. Traditionally, and with good reason, stage directors take an
interval after act 4, scene 4, which ends on Hamlet's last soliloquy: "O,
from this time forth, / My thoughts be bloody, or be nothing worth!" Mark
the theatrical implications. If the interval is at all prolonged and the
playing of the next few scenes somewhat stately, it will be close on an hour
before Hamlet reenters during the gravedigger scene. The actor will have
spent the time resting in his dressingroom. He may quite possibly have
taken a nap. (Albert Finney did regularly during his National Theatre

24

Hamlet of 1976.) The actor, naturally, needs a rest from the audience. All his energies will be required for the fencing match. Less obviously, the audience needs a rest from him. Hamlet has, after all, been somewhat overexposed during those four acts. And it is a catalogue of failure that he has to tell. The sympathies of the counselor-audience have been very fully exploited; they might be wearing thin. So the audience, in the interval and following scenes, takes a break from the tribulations of Hamlet.

* * *

Ophelia takes up the running. Effectively, she is a support actor. Ophelia is there to divert the audience during the extended interval, while the star is resting. What is the reality of her appearances? Ophelia delivers an aria: two arias, strictly. That is how the actress approaches her task and how the audience sees it. And however her scenes are played—fey, pathetic, sexual, disturbing—there will be general agreement that enough is enough. There's an odd suggestion in her role of a difficult child staying up late, solemnly performing before a stage audience of adults. Such a performance never "fails"; that is not possible, in its circumstances. But there may well be a general feeling at "good night, sweet ladies" that, as Mr. Bennet put it to his daughter, "You have delighted us long enough."

In my experience, Ophelias are seldom genuinely moving. More often, they are slightly embarrassing, even boring. This is not a reflection on the competence of unnamed actresses. It is rather, as I see it, the essence of the part. Hamlets rarely fail; Ophelias rarely succeed. No deep bonds have been established between Ophelia and audience. She has no soliloquy or aside, for example. No one goes to the theatre to see *The Tragedy of Ophelia*. Ophelia is not, I think, loved. It is not that she is unlovable, but not enough of her is exposed before the audience for it (and Hamlet) to love. In any case, the appeal of madness to the general audience cannot be large. One would as soon not be present; the stage offers a court, not an asylum, and an air of painful indecorum prevails. Hence the audience is glad enough, at her exit, to put Ophelia out of mind.

Is this too brutal a formulation? Not, I think, if we reinforce it with the principle that Hamlet generally imposes his viewpoint upon the audience. He sees Ophelia as an adjunct to his own psychodrama. At all their meetings (shown or reported), Hamlet is absorbed in his own feelings, not hers. His moods with Ophelia range among engagement, detachment, and hostility. Their encounter (following "To be or not to be") reads like the end of an affair, rather than an episode in its development. It is clear that Hamlet sees Ophelia as absorbed into the maneuvers of the oppositions. During the play scene, he treats her badly; but his behavior is I think excused if not condoned by the audience, for the focus is on Hamlet's manic excitement rather than Ophelia's distress. By the time Hamlet sees her corpse he has, fairly obviously, forgotten her. The funeral brings her back to mind; he says, "I loved Ophelia"; but his emotions toward her are essentially unexplored. (She figures in no soliloquy.) On the whole, our feelings for Ophelia appear to parallel those of Hamlet for her: charming girl, sad fate. The audience-counselor accepts Hamlet's perception of his relations with Ophelia. There are no solid grounds for gainsaying him. It's his play, after all. No Ophelia is going to steal it from him. When the Queen's lyric lament ends, decorously, the life of Ophelia, the audience is being emotionally cued for the return of the star. Subliminally, the audience responds to the play's promptings and sends out its own impulses: *bring back Hamlet.*

* * *

He comes back, to the infinite pleasure of the audience. As everyone remarks, he seems older. He is. Hamlet turns out to be between twenty-eight and thirty, his age being fixed by the reminiscences of the First Gravedigger. This is surely the great turning point in the audience's relations with Hamlet. The stealthy drip of information about Hamlet yields a fairly straight answer to that fundamental question, one that people habitually pose, answer, and reflect on all their lives: how old is he?

The essential answer is marked. *Hamlet is older than we thought.* All our responses in the early scenes are based on the assumption that "young Hamlet" is indeed young, say in his early twenties. The appeal is to our sympathies. Poor young man! What cruel dilemmas he must face! And the crafty vagueness of the early information sketches a kind of alibi (in the correct sense) for Hamlet. Claudius's "For your intent / In going back to school in Wittenberg" leaves in the air the suggestion that Hamlet was abroad, in Wittenberg, when his father died. That, as Bradley showed, would supply a sound excuse for his not being chosen king of Denmark. But Claudius's line is perfectly compatible with Hamlet's being in Denmark when the new king took over. And not until the later stages of the play do we grasp fully that Denmark is an elective, not a hereditary, monarchy. Buried in the play's hinterland, therefore, are the two supreme questions: where was Hamlet at his father's death, and why was he passed over, or outmaneuvered, for the succession? My point in registering these Bradleyan questions is not to pursue them, but to stress that they can be allayed or neutralized on the assumption of Hamlet's youth. There are good objective reasons for the Danes' preferring the experienced Claudius, as ruler, to a twenty-year-old Hamlet. Those reasons look far weaker, and the consequent queries much sharper, if Hamlet is approaching thirty. What was the prince and heir presumptive doing abroad at that age? Isn't he rather old for graduate study? Why, if at home, did he allow Claudius to pop in "between th'election and my hopes"?

The discovery of Hamlet's age, in 5.1, must adjust the audience's perception of Hamlet and thus its relationship with him. It is not a matter of the audience-counselor reflecting consciously: you didn't tell us that in our first session. But the vestigial memory of the first soliloquy is part of its response. Is a twenty-nine-year-old permitted quite the totality of grief and prostration that a twenty-year-old is? If the audience knew the facts in 1.2, would it not feel that Claudius had a case when he urged Hamlet, in effect, to pull himself together and grow up? The play makes excuses for Hamlet, and so does he, by that subtlest of devices: advancing all manner of criticisms that could be leveled against him, save the right ones. By 5.1 it is time to put the excuses aside.

The successive layers of consciousness and repression of which the play is composed are the mind of Hamlet. In act 5 dawns the realization that he is approaching thirty and that time is running out. That consciousness is forced upon him, and upon us. It is the Gravedigger who blows the gaff. Thereafter the reminder of age, and of mortality, takes Hamlet nearer to the fact of death and the imperatives of his diminishing space. The gravedigger scene is, as it were, a soliloquy for three instruments. It is a meditation on mortality. After the violence of Ophelia's funeral, it leads to the final scene, on which the basic observation is that Hamlet has become fully adult. In a word, he acts his age.

* * *

The reality of this in stage practice is worth pursuing. We know Hamlet's age. What of the actor's? It's a reasonable bet that for the Elizabethan audience the actor could scarcely have looked younger than his age as stated. Acting has generally been a rough trade; and Burbage himself was thirty-three in 1600–1601, the date to which *Hamlet* is usually assigned. From Betterton on, there has been a long line of over-age Hamlets, ending I think with Michael Redgrave's, who was fifty in 1958. For today's actors, the upper limit is around forty (Olivier in his film, Finney in 1976). They are allowed to exceed Hamlet's stated age by a decade. The modern convention is certainly healthier than the older one, in that it avoids manifestly elderly Hamlets. Yet the underlying problems have still to be faced.

I take as exemplary Joseph Papp's reported remark to Kevin Kline, the latest Hamlet of substance (New York Shakespeare Festival Public Theater, 1986): "You're not getting any younger, Kevin—what about Hamlet?" The germ of the part is all there, in that question. The actor is not getting any younger. If he has the opportunity—like Hamlet—he cannot delay much longer. "An actor," said Michael Goldman, "is a man who wants to play Hamlet."[2] Kline, as it happened, accepted the challenge at the age of thirty-eight, a good age. What does it *mean?*

The effective reality of the actor's age has changed. For Burbage, that reality was limed sack, substandard food, rough conditions, health care in which one's best chance lay in avoiding the physician: a man as robust as he must have borne his age successfully, not dismissed it. For today's actors, an extension of half a dozen years to their "young Hamlet" period is easily possible. They take good care of themselves: the Kean-Barrymore self-destructive syndrome is not the mode. They observe proper diet, exercise intelligently, and take the best medical advice. When they break out over a weekend, they might take a second glass of white wine. That is the way the best and most ambitious actors play it. At all except the very closest quarters, a contemporary actor is well placed to keep his age at bay, a secret from the audience. I hazard that today Hamlet might ideally be cast at around thirty-five, or a little over. The Elizabethan/Jacobean Hamlet could well be cast precisely at the age as stated, twenty-eight to thirty. The reality is always the same: Hamlet's age comes partly as a revelation, partly as a recognition of something we really knew already. It is anagnorisis.

* * *

The final scene is therefore Hamlet's coming of age. It is his rite of manhood; and that is as true of the actor as it is of the Prince. There are no more soliloquies, no more complaints and appeals to the audience. He just has to do it. In part one, Hamlet confided in us, the audience; now he confides only in his friend. The special relationship with his counselor is over. Only his executor now matters. As a man should, Hamlet makes his posthumous arrangements: Horatio takes possession of the document that damns Claudius and is given as much of the story as Hamlet thinks fit together with the bill of indictment against Claudius. Hamlet makes public amends to Laertes, in his graceful apotheosis as Renaissance Prince, before going on to assert his superiority in the noble art of fencing. At the climax, Hamlet accomplishes his revenge and does what he can to bring about a smooth transference of power to Fortinbras. These are the actions of an adult, and they are social. The alienated individual of the first four acts is transformed into the public figure of the finale. What the audience has lost in intimacy it gains in respect. It is the triumph of a public figure that we applaud.

Notes

1. *Hamlet,* ed. Harold Jenkins, New Arden edition (London: Methuen, 1982). All references are to this edition.
2. Michael Goldman, *Shakespeare and the Energies of Drama* (Princeton: Princeton University Press, 1972), 74.

From Narrative to Dramatic Language

The Winter's Tale and Its Source

INGA-STINA EWBANK

> For you there's rosemary and rue; these keep
> Seeming and savour all the winter long.
> *The Winter's Tale,* 4.4.75–76

The bittersweetness of Perdita's offering catches the experience of writing this essay. Bernard Beckerman taught us always to remember the theatrical nature of Shakespeare's texts, and his influence on Shakespeare scholarship—as on the study of Elizabethan drama generally—will keep "seeming and savour" for many long winters. For myself, the memory of a particularly happy winter spent, in 1984, as a visitor in his department at Columbia is inextricably woven into this encounter with *The Winter's Tale.*[1] For, with a kindness as inimitable as his theatrical scholarship was rigorous, Bernie would steer the discussion—whether it took place in the corridors of Philosophy Hall or in the cut and thrust of the Columbia Shakespeare Seminar—away from the sophistries of Shakespeare in the study toward the realities of Shakespeare in the theatre. This essay began as an attempt to explore how Shakespeare translates his source language from the narrative into the dramatic mode; and it is under Bernie's influence that it goes on to ask whether what I, in my study, think of as dramatic is also what directors and actors have found effective in the theatre. So, without claiming to be a worthy testimony to that influence, the essay pursues the two aims—in the end, I hope, seen to be interrelated—of testing the impact of Greene's language on Shakespeare and of Shakespeare's on some modern directors.

The first aim was prompted by a kind of unease with much of traditional source study. Lists of "parallel" passages and "borrowed" words or phrases tell us very little of how the language of a source text affected Shakespeare's imagination. If Shakespeare was very familiar with his source—and the Arden editor speaks from a consensus of opinion about Shakespeare's having "had *Pandosto* at his elbow when he wrote"[2]—how and why did he, then, absorb, use, or reject its verbal texture and struc-

29

tures? The answer to this question would seem to lie not simply in a comparison of the verbal tissues of the two printed texts but in an attempt to trace impulses from Greene's text in the whole organism of Shakespeare's play.

The second aim then follows naturally, as that organism fully lives only on stage—but here the problems of performance criticism begin to rear their heads. Which stage? And which performance? Simon Forman's somewhat bizarre account of the *Winter's Tale* that he saw on 15 May 1611[3] tells us little about the life of the play at the Globe. From Dennis Bartholomeusz's careful tracing of the play's performance history[4] there emerges, among much else, the sense that *The Winter's Tale* is particularly open to "translation" by those who stage it—in the modern theatre, that is, by the director and the designer. In the end, believing that a study of minute particulars would be more helpful to my quest than a general survey, I decided to examine two Royal Shakespeare Company productions: Trevor Nunn's of 1969 and John Barton's, with Trevor Nunn, of 1976 (hereafter often referred to, for shortness, as respectively "1969" and "1976"). I chose those two because I had seen them; because there were authoritative reviews available;[5] and, not least, because I was able to consult the prompt books of both productions in the library of the Shakespeare Centre, Stratford-upon-Avon.

Of course, even with all these aids, it is impossible fully to recover *how* the text was acted and spoken. What can be recovered with certainty is *what* was spoken—or, rather, what was *not* spoken. Hence my quest came to concentrate on cuts in the text and why they might have been made. If this sounds a negative method, it proved at once revealing and chastening, as one example will show. I had always thought of the first scene of *The Winter's Tale* as peculiarly important because it establishes the language world of the play. In introducing the two kingdoms, the two kings, and their two sons, it also introduces a speech mode of hyperboles and conceits that more than hints at a slightly hysterical, overstretched ethos in the two courts. The figures of the language translate the overall artifice of Greene's romance into a precious style for the courts of Leontes and Polixenes. "Believe me," says Archidamus, with a balance of clauses as neat as any in Greene's version of euphuism, "I speak as my understanding instructs me and as mine honesty puts it to utterance." Both 1969 and 1976 remove that self-conscious balance by cutting the second clause. Both also cut much of the elaboration from the dialogue as a whole, including (1969 only) the lovely absurdity of Archidamus's proposal for preventing the Sicilians, when they come to Bohemia, from finding that court inferior:

> We will give you sleepy drinks, that your senses, unintelligent of our insufficience, may, though they cannot praise us, as little accuse us. (13–15)

One reason for these cuts is presumably that the rhythms of such patterned prose are alien to the modern actor. The similarly structured dialogue between Polixenes and Camillo that forms the second scene of act 4 was similarly cut in both productions, leaving only really those lines which were necessary for the plot. But a more important reason would seem to be that, in the directorial conception of the play, these lines are simply not needed: other, nonverbal, means are used to establish the play's world and define its themes and meanings. This begins to become obvious when one notices that both productions omitted the last eight lines of 1.1, ending the scene on Camillo's reference to Mamillius as "a gallant child" and so leaving out the passage, both ominous and thematically rich, about the old men who, "if the king had no son," would wish "to live on crutches till he had one."

It becomes even more obvious when one notes the part played by the visual design of each production. In 1969 *The Winter's Tale* was acted in a white three-sided box set, a nursery that explained Leontes's psychology and motivated his jealousy.[6] Before any line of the first scene was spoken, part of Time's speech was heard, coming out of the darkness, while centerstage flashes of light revealed a rectangular box containing the anguished and virtually crucified figure of Leontes. The same box later held Time for his speech in 4.1 and, in the last scene, Hermione's statue—thus writing large the thematic connections within a play *seen* to be about Time as Destroyer and Healer. In 1976 a kind of "Lapland" decor—the stage enclosed with curtains decorated by primitive symbols; floor and furniture covered in rugs and furs—established for the audience a tribal world in which behavior might well be incalculable. Here Time the Destroyer had been given local habitation as a bear. The figure that ritualistically took Antigonus off to his death wore the robes of Time and carried an abstract bear-mask; still there, lowered. The opening moments of the play quite literally activated the visual symbolism. On "It is a gallant child" Mamillius charged Archidamus with a toy spear; and at the end of Polixenes's first speech a veritable bear chase developed, with Polixenes draping himself in one of the furs on stage and becoming the hunted prey, "speared" by the little prince.

From this example alone, it would seem that my two aims are held together insofar as they involve exploring the anxiety of influence, albeit two very different kinds of anxiety.[7] The Royal Shakespeare Company has created a theatrical tradition for which we must be grateful. But, like all traditions, it limits even as it strengthens, particularly as it presents each director with what Roger Warren has described as "the constant temptation to avoid last time's solution, however successful."[8] Each individual talent within that tradition, when confronted with a play in the Shakespeare canon, is bound to be conscious of a performance history. It is natural for Bartholomeusz to define the 1969 production as representing "a sharp and radical change in style"[9]—a change, that is, from the last time that *The Winter's Tale* had been played at Stratford. That was Peter Wood's pictorially beautiful production of 1960, which preserved Shakespeare's text almost intact and presented its human content almost naturalistically: Leontes (Eric Porter) and Paulina (Peggy Ashcroft) were allowed to achieve "the successful union of powerful realism and credible grandeur."[10] As against this, Trevor Nunn in 1969 projected a symbolical vision where the white nursery and the box of Time spoke more eloquently, at times, than the characters. It was for the 1976 production to insist even more radically on translating Shakespeare's words into visual symbols—and, having done this, to dispense with a good many of the words, thus communicating with the audience through emblems as much as (and sometimes more than) through language. The effect of this reaching, as it were, below Shakespeare's words is also in some ways—amazingly and obviously wholly unintentionally—a return to Greene's rather than Shakespeare's tale. But to see this we need now to turn to the anxiety of influence in Shakespeare's encounter with *Pandosto*.

Whatever attracted Shakespeare to *Pandosto* in or about 1610, it is clear that Greene's narrative, with its single-mindedness of plot and with its themes founded on simple antithetical contrasts, helped him to a new purchase on the tradition of romantic tragicomedy which the King's Men were developing from about 1608 onward. In *Pericles* he (and, as the Oxford editors would have it, George Wilkins[11]) had adapted for the theatre the pattern of romance narrative; in *Cymbeline* he had experimented with interweaving several kinds of story material. In *The Winter's Tale* he found a new way of combining scope in time and space with intensity in human relations. It is of course impossible to say exactly what was the contribution of *Pandosto* to the matrix from which the play emerged; but it is possible that in the pattern of *The Winter's Tale* there is a translation, into structure, of Greene's style. Greene's energies, one feels in reading *Pandosto,* have all gone into the language, so that the dominant impression is of a style in which irrational human acts are rationalized by the symmetries and antithetical balances of vocabulary and syntax. This style Shakespeare has absorbed and transmuted, not so much verbally (a point to which I shall return) as structurally: into that two-part structure of parallels and contrasts which, as such, has so often been commented on.[12]

One of these contrasts is court versus country; and while enlarging and enriching the pastoral element in his source Shakespeare may even, with part of his mind, have been defying Fletcher who, in his preface "To the Reader" in *The Faithful Shepherdess* (1610), had defended his own unsuccessful version of pastoral and scorned the popular notion of "country hired shepherds in grey cloaks . . . Whitsun-ales, cream, wassail, and morris dances"—a table of contents, almost, of *The Winter's Tale,* 4.2. Against Fletcher's now famous definition of tragicomedy—

A tragi-comedy is not so called in respect of mirth and killing, but in respect it wants deaths, which is enough to make it no tragedy, yet brings some near it, which is enough to make it no comedy[13]

—Shakespeare, apart from adding to his source the mirth of Autolycus and the killing of Antigonus, flaunts two "real" deaths and a mock one, followed by a "resurrection." As so often in Shakespeare's works, the anxiety of influence resolves into a delight in both using and challenging tradition.

The same could be said of his encounter with *Pandosto* as such. As it was a popular work,[14] and as he followed the narrative outline quite closely,[15] Shakespeare must have known—maybe even have counted on the fact—that to many in his audience the experience of seeing the play was partly one of recognizing samenesses and differences. Translated into modern terms, it must have been rather like watching a film when you are familiar with the novel on which it is based.[16] This dimension obviously does not exist in a modern audience's response; and so, it might seem, it need not present a problem to modern directors. Nevertheless, a combination of affirmation and denial of its source *is* part of the art of *The Winter's Tale* and does raise problems, in the theatre as well as on the printed page. The self-consciousness of Shakespeare's dramatic technique in the play has received much attention: the way it thrusts at us its anachronisms, its geographical absurdities, its reminders that it is both a tale and a play.[17] Part of that self-consciousness, it seems to me, is a conscious playing with mode and genre themselves, in this tale of a bygone age, as if to show that he could make his drama more narrative and his narrative more dramatic than Greene's romance, and that, in doing so, he could also make his romance both more marvelous and more real.

Greene's process of storytelling pays little attention to formal structure but much to the genre implications of the events related. After the title page's promise that *Pandosto* will demonstrate "The Triumph of Time" (more truly fulfilled by Shakespeare than by Greene), and after the initial announcement of the theme as "the infectious sore of jealousy,"[18] the story rambles on, jerked now and then by turns of Fortune's wheel (as on p. 3). But the narrative transition from the deaths of Bellaria (Hermione) and Garinter (Mamillius)—signified as "this tragical discourse of fortune" (30)—is made by the narrator admonishing himself:

> But leaving him /Pandosto/ to his dolorous passions, at last let us come to shew the tragical discourse of the young infant. (32)

The reunions at the end are described, as heard of by Egistus (Polixenes), as "this most comical event" (85); while the death of Pandosto is reported in a syntax that makes him appear a victim more of the decorum of genre than of conscience or moral retribution:

. . . he fell into a melancholie fit, and, to close up the comedy with a tragical stratagem, he slew himself. (85)

The narrator, the reader is reminded, controls the tale. The dramatist does not foreground genre but the emotions underlying genre, and so—even while the language that marks the turning points in the structure has the symmetry and antithetical balance of Greene's—he lets the characters appear to control the tale. If the tragedy of *The Winter's Tale* begins with Leontes,

> Too hot, too hot!
> To mingle friendship far is mingling bloods,
>
> (1.2.108–9)

and the comedy with the Shepherd,

Now bless thyself: thou met'st with things dying, I with things new-born, (3.3.108–9)

it is also possible for Leontes, unlike Pandosto, to live on to an experience of wonder beyond any definable genre. Playing with genre, Shakespeare creates endless problems of motivation and tone for actor and director, and I shall return to some of those.

Problems of tone result, too, from Shakespeare's playing with narrative and dramatic modes. Shakespeare's play has far more narrators than does Greene's tale, with its single, omniscient teller. Each is particular about what he tells, and how, beginning with Mamillius choosing "a sad tale" as "best for winter" (2.1.24). The last words we hear from this little prince are the beginnings of his never-finished tale. The Clown in 3.3 is acutely conscious of the difficulty of conveying to his father what he has seen and heard; his speech, lines 86–99, dramatizes the problem of fitting into a consecutive narration two events happening simultaneously: a problem that never arises in Greene's Antigonus-less and Clown-less account of how the small boat carrying the baby princess simply "was driven with the tide into the coast of Sicilia, where sticking upon the sands it rested" (32). The Clown's narrative is both dramatic and metanarrative. It is also, because of the speaker and because of the way he dashes between the shipwreck and the "land-service" of Antigonus being eaten by the bear, such obvious comic material that, judging by the fact that it was left uncut in both 1969 and 1976, it offers no problem on the modern stage.

Other scenes have proved more difficult. One such is 3.1, where Cleomenes and Dion on the way back from Delphos rehearse what they are going to "report" to Leontes and his court. It is a brief scene, but it interrupts the onrush of Leontes's mad vindictiveness and so has often troubled directors. For his 1986 production with the Royal Shakespeare Company at Stratford, Terry Hands set it at the back of the stage, with the disruptive main action continuing silently in front of it, literally fore-grounded. The effect of an oasis, a moment of stillness and awe, was thus lost. Both the 1969 and the 1976 productions, on the contrary, seized on this opportunity. Both cut the lines (4 and 5) in which Dion selects what has been most important in his experience and struggles to find the right language to render it:

> I shall report,
> For most it caught me, the celestial habits
> (Me thinks I so should term them). . . .
>
> (3.1.3–5)

But both retained the rest of Dion's speech, in which report dissolves into exclamations, as well as the chiming-in of Cleomenes, with its rapt memory of wonder:

> and the reverence
> Of the grave wearers. O, the sacrifice!
> How ceremonious, solemn and unearthly
> It was i'th'offering!
> *Cleomenes.*   But of all, the burst
> And the ear-deaf'ning voice o'th'Oracle,
> Kin to Jove's thunder, so surpris'd my sense,
> That I was nothing.
>
> (3.1.5–11)

In *Pandosto* the scene in the temple is narrated, and the Oracle is allowed direct speech:

> They had not long kneeled at the altar, but Apollo with a loud voice said: 'Bohemians, what you find behind the altar take, and depart.' (26)

When Shakespeare chose to evoke the mystery of the Oracle through Dion's and Cleomenes's memory (characteristically turning a nonspecific "loud" into a felt "ear-deaf'ning"), then he opted for narrative—but a narrative far more dramatic in its impact than the dramatized speech of Greene's Apollo. The language of the scene also prepared his audience for the final great revelation in the play, of which Leontes might well have reported that it "so surpris'd my sense, / That I was nothing."

I do not wish to suggest that Shakespeare was simply rejecting Greene's narrative strategies. If boundaries between modes of presentation are often blurred in *The Winter's Tale,* so they are in *Pandosto,* where the narrative is forever breaking into semidramatic monologues and dialogues.[19] In at least one notable instance Shakespeare seems to have affectionately drawn on the mixed modes of his source.[20] The reunion of father and daughter is made by Greene as nearly dramatic as possible. He tells how Pandosto

> suddenly leapt from his seat and kissed Fawnia, wetting her tender cheeks with his tears, and crying, 'My daughter Fawnia! ah sweet Fawnia! I am thy Father, Fawnia.' (84)

Shakespeare's presentation of this scene (which in his case also has to contain the reunion of the two kings) through the staggered arrival of three Gentlemen narrators is famous. Each Gentleman in turn asserts that what he has witnessed is beyond description ("a sight which was to be seen, cannot be spoken of": 5.2.40–41); and yet each, while emphasizing that the "news, which is call'd true, is so like an old tale that the verity of it is in strong suspicion" (26–28), has a stab at telling. In the breathless wonder thus communicated there is a tonal mixture such as can only be found in Shakespeare's last plays; but one ingredient is surely the faint absurdity of the source. Sifted through the Third Gentleman's narration, Leontes's emotion is as undignified as it is moving:

> Our king, being ready to leap out of himself for joy of his found daughter, as if that joy were now become a loss, cries 'O, thy mother, thy mother!' then asks Bohemia forgiveness; then embraces his son-in-law; then again worries he his daughter with clipping her. (47–52)

And, although we are ready to credit "the noble combat that 'twixt joy and sorrow was fought in Paulina," there is a touch of the ludicrous about the image which the same Gentleman uses to describe it:

> She had one eye declin'd for the loss of her husband, another elevated that the oracle was fulfill'd.[21] (71–74)

This scene has clearly been a challenge to directors. The 1969 production broke a long tradition of doing it comically: it was staged with what Dennis Bartholomeusz describes as "grave, formal reverence."[22] In 1976 awe prevailed, with the three gentlemen entering backward, as if the scene they had witnessed was just offstage. Textually, the gravity was achieved by heavy cuts. A good deal of the narrative self-commentary was removed in both productions, such as the Third Gentleman's

> I never heard of such another encounter, which lames report to follow it, and undoes description to do it. (54–56)

So were some of the descriptive passages where the comic hovers around extremes of emotion, as in the meeting of the two kings:

There was casting up of eyes, holding up of hands, with countenance of such distraction, that they were to be known by garment, not by favour. (45–48)

Both, perhaps to avoid spending time on matter already known, cut the account of Antigonus's death, and 1976 also went on to cut the entire description of Paulina's split response (omitting altogether lines 58–76). In the latter production, the statue scene was particularly rapt and trancelike, with Paulina's incantation spoken most movingly[23]: and possibly the directors wanted to avoid any suggestion of sending up Paulina in the scene before. In all, it seems that the extraordinary combination of woe, wonder, and laughter, often in one and the same scene, which makes *The Winter's Tale* both so unearthly and so human, is difficult to realize on the contemporary stage.

As language seems to be at the heart of this problem, we must turn now to look more closely at the actual fabric of the language, not just its mode of presentation. By 1610 Shakespeare had little to learn, from Greene or anyone else, about dramatic language; but we can learn something about it from his encounter with Greene's language and from the relation of that encounter to the theatre language of our time. I have already suggested that the style of *Pandosto* beats as a kind of undertow through the structure of *The Winter's Tale,* and that it crops up not only in courtly dialogues, such as 1.1 and 4.2, but even in the distorted symmetries of Leontes's jealous speeches and the antithesis of the Shepherd's discovery—enough, I trust, to indicate that Greene's language was in Shakespeare's ears when he composed the play, *and* that, critically, it won't do just to use *The Winter's Tale* as a stick to beat *Pandosto* with.

For, of its kind, *Pandosto* has virtues, and I cannot imagine Shakespeare's not being moved by Bellaria's lament for her lost child (even if he does not echo it):[24]

Alas, sweet unfortunate babe, scarce born before envied by fortune! would the day of thy birth had been the term of thy life; then shouldest thou have made an end to care and prevented thy father's rigour. Thy faults cannot yet deserve such hateful revenge; thy days are too short for so sharp a doom; but thy untimely death must pay for thy mother's debts, and her guiltless crime must be thy ghastly curse. And shalt thou, sweet babe, be committed to fortune, when thou art already spited by fortune? Shall the seas be thy harbour and the hard boat thy cradle? Shall thy tender mouth, instead of sweet kisses, be nipped with bitter storms? Shalt thou have the whistling winds for thy lullaby, and the salt sea foam instead of sweet milk? (20–21)

A passage like this, which in its closing lines moves us by an image pattern as relevant to Marina as to Perdita, shows that, in Greene's version of

euphuism, the logical balance within and between clauses and the allit-
erated antitheses do not exclude emotion. Much of Greene's rhetoric is
highly emotive; yet the total effect, as one reads the tale, is strangely
detached. There is, as I have already suggested, no doubt that the teller is
in control, nor that he sees the function of his language as being that of
constructing patterns, not of imitating the tempo of happenings or the
movement of mind in individual characters. Everything, we are told, is
done "with as much speed as might be" and the phrase "no rest" becomes
virtually a formula, but it is all *stated,* whereas in Shakespeare it passes
into the very tissue of language and action in the first half of the play.
Greene does not even pretend that he is giving the exact account of what
his characters said: repeatedly a speech is concluded with the comment
that the speaker uttered "these or such like words" or had "these or such
like doubts." Characterization gives way to formulaic constructions, aris-
ing from the topos, so that Bellaria and the Danish princess whom Egistus
wants his son to marry are identified in almost exactly the same words:

> . . . by birth royal, learned by education, fair by nature, by virtues
> famous, so that it was hard to judge whether her beauty, fortune or
> virtue won the greatest commendations. (2; cf. 41)

There is little description: the focus is on characters, rendered either in
oratio obliqua or in direct speech, but it is on characters as rhetorical
positions rather than people in particular circumstances. Their speeches
are either of inner debates, where the terms of a binary opposition are
scrutinized and weighed against each other, as in the deliberations of
Franion (Camillo):

> Egistus is a stranger to thee, and Pandosto thy sovereign: thou hast little
> cause to respect the one, and oughtest to have great care to obey the
> other; (9)

or they are laments, again—as in Bellaria's lines quoted above—generally
articulated in binary terms. A man possessed by jealousy does not have a
divided mind, and so Pandosto does not qualify for a soliloquy until
Bellaria and Garinter are dead and he can begin to lament (30–31). The
second and longer half of the tale, dealing mainly with Dorastus (Florizel)
and Fawnia (Perdita), starts more descriptively, but even the shepherd who
finds the baby exhibits (in oratio obliqua) a mind strictly divided between
joy and fear at his discovery. There is some attempt to give the shepherd
and his fabliau wife some "low" speech (36), but soon they are discussing
the problem of the Dorastus-and-Fawnia liaison in the antithetical idiom of
everyone else in the tale. Fawnia herself discourses on nature versus
nurture; and, as is not the case in *The Winter's Tale,* much is made of the

divided minds of both lovers. In Shakespeare, the love of the young people is a *fait accompli* by the beginning of act 4; in Greene's tale the interest lies in their gradual coming together despite all the reasons why they should not, and much is made of the rhetorical possibilities of Dorastus's guilty conscience. In all this speech, whether direct or indirect, the syntax remains the same—one, basically, of balancing opposites—and the vocabulary stays within a narrow frame of generalities: words that explain and categorize. The narrator holds his characters at arm's length, so that Pandosto himself—instead of being allowed to speak his perversions of truth directly—can have his jealousy summed up in a set of brackets:

> . . . remaining resolute in his determination (his fury so fired with rage as it could not be opposed with reason), he began with bitter taunts to take up his man, and to lay before him two baits, preferment and death. (8)

The strength of Greene's language is its quite formidable control; he gives us "a narrative owing its passion to detachment."[25] *Pandosto* is, in a sense, telling the story of its people a second time. Every performance of *The Winter's Tale* tells its story for the first time. And there's the rub.

It will be obvious that I have spent some time with the fabric of Greene's language in order to get to the point where Shakespeare definitely parts company with *Pandosto*. For all his use of Greene's tale and aspects of its language, he rejects its fundamental assumptions about language: that language validates by generalizing; that the truth about characters is stored somewhere outside them, in general experience; and that the task of language is therefore to measure out this truth in accurate words. What disturbs me, and brings my two aims together, is that if in the previous sentence we substitute "visual symbolism" for "language" and "emblems" for "words" we seem also to have the assumptions underlying some modern stagings of Shakespeare.

For, whatever else it does, Shakespeare's language renders, and his drama depends upon its rendering, the specificity of experience. This is never more clearly true than in what is perhaps the greatest crux in *The Winter's Tale:* the onset of Leontes's jealousy. Greene has it develop over a period of time and provides plausible motivation. Shakespeare dramatizes an explosion; and, if he has Greene's discussion of Pandosto in mind—"He then began to measure all their actions" (6)—the abstract "measure" becomes concrete and terrifyingly precise, taken on the body itself: "Inch-thick, knee-deep, o'er head and ears a fork'd one!" The Jacobean stage accepted such an explosion, whether this was because of the naturalism of Burbage's acting (he had, after all, practiced as Othello) or because of convention, or both. The twentieth century, as Bartholomeusz shows, has had difficulties with the psychological credibility of Leontes.

Both in 1969 and in 1976 those were largely solved by taking the responsibility off the language and placing it on stage setting, furniture, and
business. In his white nursery, Barrie Ingham as Leontes (1969) could
afford to show a "curious lack of intensity" and to toss off "Too hot, too
hot!" with "an almost casual air."[26] And in the Lapland milieu of 1976,
Ian McKellen's sudden and unpredictable jealousy seemed to more than
one critic "as natural as the entrance of a bear."[27] I don't want to decry
these two, in many ways impressive, productions nor to advocate an all-
out return to "bare stage" Shakespeare. I merely want to point out that, if
the audience's response to Leontes is controlled by external (here, visual)
means, then we run the risk of losing that closeness to his specific, self-
engendered agony which Shakespeare's language creates. And language is
Shakespeare's main dramatic tool in these early scenes where we watch
how the jealousy grows. Language, too, shows us the *why* contained in the
how: from inside the "affection" speech (1.2.138–46) we watch Leontes,
even as he speaks, enact the perilous imaginative leap from "nothing" to
"something," create the thing he imagines.[28] Of course this speech gener-
alizes, in that it tells us about the power of language to generate its own
meanings, but it does so *through* the particular human experience of
Leontes. As act 1 develops, there is an ever-widening gap between what
Leontes says and sees (sees because he says) and what we see. In 1969 this
was filled by a kind of dream sequence: Polixenes and Hermione, in a dim
blue light and with the rest of the court frozen into immobility, enacting
the sexual fantasies of Leontes. Effective as a visual projection of
Leontes's thoughts from a psychoanalyst's couch, this device again made
his language strangely impotent; whereas Shakespeare spends the next
two acts exploring its terrible, perverse potency. When, in the trial scene,
Hermione tells him:

> You speak a language that I understand not:
> My life stands in the level of your dreams,
>
> (3.2.77–78)

then those "dreams" signify to us, the audience, not a Freudian sub-
conscious but a specific, twisted "reality" which Leontes has been constructing in his speeches throughout these acts. The gap between his
reality and others' is the more tangible because it keeps being projected in
dialogue: not only with Hermione but with Camillo, with Antigonus, with
Paulina, and so on.

The dialogue with Camillo may seem to occupy a disproportionate
amount of time in 1.2: 155 lines, or exactly one-third of this momentous
scene. It could be because the corresponding episode is very fully developed in *Pandosto*. There, it gives the narrator a fine opportunity to
elaborate, first, "these and such like persuasions" whereby Franion tries

to argue Pandosto out of his murderous intent toward Egistus and, second, "these or such like words" in which Franion soliloquizes about his divided mind. Shakespeare, too, starts this interchange with self-conscious art, making Leontes accuse Camillo of being either "not honest," or "a coward," or "negligent," or "a fool" (242–49), and making Camillo reply to each of these accusations in an ingenious pattern:

> My gracious lord,
> I may be negligent, foolish, and fearful:
> In every one of these no man is free
> But that his negligence, his folly, fear,
> Among the infinite doings of the world,
> Sometime puts forth. In your affairs, my lord,
> If ever I were wilful-negligent,
> It was my folly; if industriously
> I played the fool, it was my negligence,
> Not weighing well the end; if ever fearful
> To do a thing where I the issue doubted,
> Whereof the execution did cry out
> Against the non-performance, 'twas a fear
> Which oft infects the wisest. These, my lord
> Are such allow'd infirmities that honesty
> Is never free of.
>
> (249–64)

I have quoted this speech at length because it seems to me to show Shakespeare using *and* subverting the rhetoric of *Pandosto,* all to his own particular end. The effect of Camillo's speech is not to clarify but to confuse: to suggest a blurring of qualities that in *Pandosto* are antithetically sharp. As "negligence," "folly," etc., fold into each other in the second half of the speech, Camillo shows Leontes's words to be pretty meaningless: his language, even before Leontes has uttered his accusation of Hermione, points to the gap that can, but need not, exist between word and thing. The whole of this passage was cut in both 1969 and 1976. So— no doubt to speed the scene—were many lines in the rest of this dialogue, where Leontes opens the gap by saying what Camillo ought to have "seen" and widens it by his "nothing" speech and his unanswerable "I say thou liest" (300).

If Shakespeare thus dramatizes by deconstructing Greene's language, he also deals with Leontes by what we might call a double dramatization. By 2.1, when it is natural for Leontes to insist that things *are* what he calls them, ("I have said / She's an adultress; I have said with whom": 2.1.87–88), it is also natural for him to rewrite what is happening into little plays, which are then given the status of actuality. His confrontation with Hermione in this scene largely takes the form of writing a script for the bystanders, including both dialogue and gestures:

> You, my lords,
> Look on her, mark her well; be but about
> To say 'She is a goodly lady' and
> The justice of your hearts will thereto add
> "Tis pity she's not honest—honourable.'
> . . . .
> . . . —these shrugs, these hum's and ha's
> When you have said she's goodly, come between,
> Ere you can say she's honest.
>
> (2.1.64–76)

The lines I left out, in the middle of the speech ("O, I am out," etc.) suggest how precarious is his control of himself; the speech as a whole enacts his epistemology. This is how he arrives at "truth." Only Hermione, the silent center and subject of this play-within-the-play, thinks of what the scene will look like in retrospect:

> How will this grieve you,
> When you shall come to clearer knowledge, that
> You thus have published me!
>
> (96–98)

Shakespeare's way with Leontes makes him wordy and word-conscious: his vilest abuse of Hermione, here, consists of going on about what he *won't* call her, lest he upset linguistic registers and decorum ("O thou thing! . . .": 82–87). It is then perhaps not surprising that both 1969 and 1976 cut those particular lines (although 1969 retained the thingifying of Hermione), nor that 1976 omitted all of lines 64–76, as quoted above.

I have written only of Leontes's language, but clearly there are examples all over the play of language that is specific and tangible, potentially a dangerous tool, but also—as in the case of Pauline—"as medicinal as true" (2.2.37). Its effect, as I suggested at the beginning of this essay, is to make romance both more real and more unreal—that is, marvelous—than it is in Shakespeare's source. Perhaps the best way to see this, in the end, is to look in the direction indicated by the lines of Hermione that I just quoted: at the tenses and moods of the play. The world of *Pandosto* is an indicative one, its geography defined by opposites and mapped out by rhetorical patterns. Its paradoxes effect emphasis and clarification. Its tense is on the whole the perfect, even when past, present, and future are spoken *about*. *The Winter's Tale* enacts man's, and woman's, experience of time; and its language helps to create a world where the resurrection of Hermione—the ultimate *coup de théatre* for those who came to see the play, knowing *Pandosto*—is possible. Time and its workings are in the language of the play.

Memory opens out the human perspective at the beginning, with the nostalgic glimpse of the "twinn'd lambs that did frisk i'th sun / And bleat the one at th'other," with the look back at Leontes's and Hermione's courtship, and with Leontes seeing himself, twenty-three years ago, in "the lines / Of my boy's face." Toward the end, 5.1 is most particularly a scene exploiting memory and exploring the subjunctive of what might have been. The language of Paulina, as scourge and minister, presses home the presence of the past. Calling, as always, a spade a spade, she refers to Hermione as "she you kill'd," provoking in Leontes a (presumably intended) reaction that points up the closeness of work and experience:

> She I kill'd! I did so; but thou strik'st me
> Sorely, to say I did. It is as bitter
> Upon thy tongue as in my thought.
>
> (5.1.17–19)

This closeness means, too, that Mamillius "dies again when talk'd of" (120). Both before and after the arrival of Perdita and Florizel—the links between past and future—there is much talk of what might have been. Language and stage image merge in bitter sweetness:

> I lost a couple that 'twixt heaven and earth
> Might thus have stood begetting wonder as
> You, gracious couple, do.
>
> (132–34)

Peculiarly interesting, because so rich in apparently contradictory tones, is a scene of might-be-if within the scene. That Hermione's ghost would appear to rebuke him, were he ever to marry again, is an idea first introduced by Leontes, in such a double dramatization as we have seen earlier in his language:

> No more such wives; therefore, no wife. One worse
> And better us'd, would make her sainted spirit
> Again possess her corpse, and on this stage,
> Where we offend her now, appear soul-vex'd,
> And begin 'Why to me'—.
>
> (56–60)

It is then elaborated on both by him and by Paulina, until they are virtually writing a mini-revenge play between them; and Paulina gets doubly worked up by imagining herself in the part of Hermione's ghost:

> Were I the ghost that walk'd, I'd bid you mark
> Her eye, and tell me for what dull part in't
> You chose her; then I'd shriek, that even your ears

Should rift to hear me; and the words that follow'd
Should be 'Remember mine.'

(63–67)

Memories of the suffering and death (real or assumed) witnessed in the
play mix with the bizarre wit of Donne's "The Apparition" to create a tone
that the early-seventeenth century might have responded to more easily
than a twentieth-century audience. In 1976 the entire passage, lines 54–67,
was cut; 1969 kept it but cut, as did 1976, a great many other lines of
reminiscence and reproach, notably the interchange between Paulina and
the Servant who reports Perdita as "the most peerless piece of earth."

In the final scene, the ravages of sixteen years are measured in the words
of Leontes's reaction to the statue:

But yet, Paulina,
Hermione was not so much wrinkled, nothing
So aged as this seems.

(5.3.27–29)

As neither of the two productions I have been discussing allowed its actors
to be visibly "aged," both omitted these lines. In 1969 a wrinkled Hermione would have been technically impossible as (not for the first time in
theatre history) Judi Dench doubled the parts of Hermione and Perdita. In
both, of course, the time theme was written out without words, in visual
symbolism. This also meant that the audience was deprived of most of the
words invoking the greatest might-have-been of all, as Leontes takes up
Paulina's comment on the "carver's excellence" in making Hermione "as
she liv'd now":

As now she might have done,
So much to my good comfort as it is
Now piercing to my soul. O, thus she stood,
Even with such life of majesty, warm life,
As now it coldly stands, when first I woo'd her!
I am asham'd: does not the stone rebuke me
For being more stone than it!

(32–38)

To lose Shakespeare's language here is to lose an interplay of simple words
with a grammar of moods and tenses that proves on our pulses the human
situation of loss and suffering, even as the paradox of the last two lines
(Leontes's being "more stone" than the statue) takes us forward to the
miraculous paradox of the stone's being alive: "O, she's warm!" It is a
moment of sheer human wonder, thrown free of any symbolism. Both
productions spoke wonderfully, through visual emblems, about the mean-

ing of Time; but Shakespeare spoke through words of a particular living experience. The directors communicated with the aesthetic sense of the audience, without the intermediaries of such experience—much as Greene pleased his readers by the rhetorical patterns of his romance, without involving them in firsthand experience.

The ultimate Shakespearean paradox achieved in *The Winter's Tale* is one of magic *and* realism, embodied (to me) in the way Leontes follows up his exclamation "O, she's warm":

> If this be magic, let it be an art
> Lawful as eating.
>
> (110–11)

We did not hear those lines in either 1969 or 1976. "The scene," wrote Bartholomeusz of the 1976 production, "was magical and not to be compared with anything so literal as eating."[29] But surely what Shakespeare created out of his source material was *both* the magic and the eating.

Notes

1. All Shakespeare quotations in this essay are from *Shakespeare. The Complete Works,* ed. Peter Alexander (London: Collins, 1951). A first version of this paper was given at the workshop on Shakespeare's use of his sources, arranged by the English Department of the University of Florence, as part of the Taormina Festival, in August 1985.

2. J. H. P. Pafford, ed., *The Winter's Tale* (London: Methuen, 1963), xxxi. Cf. Kenneth Muir, *Shakespeare's Sources* (London: Methuen, 1957), 1:247: "There are more verbal echoes from *Pandosto* than from any other novel used by Shakespeare as a source."

3. Printed, e.g., in Pafford, *Winter's Tale,* xxi–xxii.

4. *'The Winter's Tale' in Performance in England and America 1611–1976* (Cambridge: Cambridge University Press, 1962).

5. I am particularly indebted to Richard David, *Shakespeare in the Theatre* (Cambridge: Cambridge University Press, 1978), 222–27 for an illuminating discussion of the 1976 production; to the late Gareth Lloyd Evans, "Interpretation or Experience? Shakespeare at Stratford," *Shakespeare Survey* 23 (1970): 131–35; and Roger Warren, "Theory and Practice: Stratford 1976," *Shakespeare Survey* 30 (1977): 169–77; and to the late Robert Speaight's reviews of the two productions in *Shakespeare Quarterly* 21 (1970): 436–38 and 27 (1977): 188–89.

6. Cf. Gareth Lloyd Evans, "Interpretation or Experience?" 133–34: "The first scene is like a white-hued visual aid to the Freudian notion that in childhood lies the source of adult complex. Leontes . . . lives a Peter Pan inner life; his wife, friend and child are almost part of the nursery furniture. . . . Leontes' sudden jealousy is a terrible realization that relationship is a subtle thing—he cannot face it."

7. Cf. Harold Bloom, *the Anxiety of Influence* (New York: Oxford University Press, 1973).

8. "Theory and Practice: Stratford 1976," 173.

9. *'The Winter's Tale' in Performance*, 210.

10. Ibid., 209.

11. Stanley Wells and Gary Taylor, eds., *William Shakespeare. The Complete Works*, The Oxford Shakespeare (Oxford: Oxford University Press, 1986).

12. Best of all by Ernest Schanzer, "The Structural Pattern of *The Winter's Tale*," *The Review of English Literature* 5 (1964): 72–100; reprinted in Kenneth Muir, ed., *Shakspeare—'The Winter's Tale,'* Macmillan Casebook (London: Macmillan, 1968).

13. *The Faithful Shepherdess*, in J. St. Loe Strachey, ed., *Beaumont and Fletcher*, Mermaid (London, 1893), 2:321.

14. First published in 1588, *Pandosto* appeared in new editions in 1592, 1595, 1607, and fourteen times more before the end of the seventeenth century.

15. There *were* other sources: see Geoffrey Bullough, *Narrative and Dramatic Sources of Shakespeare*, vol. 8 (London: Routledge and Kegan Paul; New York: Columbia University Press, 1975). Thematically, the myths of Alcestis and of Persephone are significant. As always, of course, Shakespeare's own earlier plays are "sources": *Othello, Much Ado, All's Well, Pericles*, etc. But for narrative outline Shakespeare sticks unusually closely to *Pandosto*, with the following major exceptions: Greene motivates the Pandosto-Leontes figure more, letting his jealousy develop over some time; and he changes him less: he barely avoids incestuous rape and commits suicide in the end. Shakespeare invented Paulina and her function of scourge and minister; he invented Autolycus (although using material from Greene's coney-catching pamphlets); and he created the sheepshearing feast in 4.2. Above all, he "resurrected" Hermione, where Bellaria in the source is really dead, and so made it possible for Leontes to survive and for the play to end in multiple reunions.

16. In his British Academy Shakespeare lecture of 23 April 1986 Professor Georgi Melchiori interestingly expounded the idea that it is in the film industry, not the modern theatre, that we must find the contemporary analogues of Shakespeare's professional creativity.

17. See, e.g., S. L. Bethell, *The Winter's Tale: A Study* (London: Staples Press, 1947), and Howard Felperin, *Shakespearian Romance* (Princeton: Princeton University Press, 1972).

18. P. G. Thomas, ed., *Greene's Pandosto*, The Shakespeare Library (London: Chatto and Windus, 1907), 1. Page reference to this edition—chosen, because of its modernized spelling, in preference to that in Bullough, *Narrative and Dramatic Sources*, 156–99—will hereafter be given in the text.

19. See, e.g., the "familiar speeches," set out as a dialogue with speech headings, in which Pandosto attempts to seduce Fawnia and she resists.

20. Greene's "bonfires" (84) and Shakespeare's Second Gentleman's "Nothing but bonfires" (5.2.22) might be cited as an "echo" to support this.

21. That this is close to a proverbial saying—see Arden editor's note at 5.2.74–75—does not alter the argument.

22. Bartholomeusz, *'The Winter's Tale' in Performance*, 218.

23. See David, *Shakespeare in the Theatre*, 225–26.

24. Hermione, unlike Bellaria, does not soliloquize; the equivalent of this passage is her reference, in the trial scene, to how "my third comfort, / starr'd most unluckily, is from my breast— / The innocent milk in its most innocent mouth— / Hal'd out to murder" (3.2.96–99).

25. David Hughes, *The Pork Butcher* (Harmondsworth, Eng.: Penguin, 1984), 124.

26. Bartholomeusz, *'The Winter's Tale' in Performance,* 216–17.
27. Ibid., 223.
28. I have discussed this speech in "Shakespeare's Liars," *Proceedings of the British Academy* 69 (1983): 162–63.
29. Bartholomeusz, *'The Winter's Tale' in Performance,* 227.

The Nature of Speech in Shakespeare's Plays

JOHN RUSSELL BROWN

The two words "Shakespeare's plays" can signify many things. They may cause us to think of a single, fat, and familiar volume or of a row of uniform paperbacks, some more thumbed than others. There, in small space, is "the text," one of the most fabulous treasure houses of the past; there we can roam at will and appropriate whatever catches our fancies. We take speeches from this great hoard of words and reflect upon them, changing them according to our own individual thoughts and desires. Of course, we are troubled by problems of obscurity, authenticity, punctuation, and spelling, and by doubts about reference, definition, and interpretation. But "Shakespeare's plays," in this physical sense of type on the page, is a palpable, basic, and limited thing, a constant point of reference.

But in another sense "Shakespeare's plays" is much less manageable. The phrase can awaken a whole world of still-breeding thoughts: teeming theatrical images that have been introduced to our minds, selected not by ourselves but according to opportunity and chance. Shakespeare is not solely responsible for his plays in this sense. He has many collaborators who create in our day—and not in his—effects of their own by a variety of means: designers of set, costumes, sound, and light; carpenters, technicians, and stage managers; together with the actors who take his words upon themselves and the directors who control each evolving production. The plays in performance provide a multitude of interlocking sensations, all highly variable in origin, means, effect, and stability. "Shakespeare's plays," in this sprawling and spawning sense, cannot be defined or confined; they are shadows of the mind that resist our predatory grasp.

Between these two extremes of meaning, there is a great divide. On one side, it is proper to speak of the plays' language, vocabulary, images, gestures, style, syntax, dialogue, text. On the other side, other words can be added to our critical discourse: *delivery, action, play, performance, personification, perception, reception,* and *interplay,* together with *entertainment, celebration,* and *discovery. Interpretation* does not offer a crucial distinction between the two opposed meanings of "Shakespeare's plays," because the text and its theatrical enactment are equally hospitable to many different readings; both await our differing attempts at decoding. Nor does *speech* or *dialogue, discourse* or *speech-act,* with reference to words allocated to particular characters in a certain sequence, take us decisively away from the comparatively secure world of the printed word. Only *Speech* as the act of speaking and a part of performance provides the crucial distinction. Speech, in this sense, identifies an element of Shakespeare's plays that is close to the text and yet also releases a seemingly unfettered theatrical life.

Speech originates from words on a page, but it also introduces the individual performer, idiosyncratic, specific, and always changing. Speech involves us as members of an audience and not as independent readers. Of course, speech does not account for all that happens in a theatrical event, but it is such a crucial element, dividing and yet connecting a text and its performance, that we should think as clearly as we can about its nature. Such inquiry might help us to respond more fully and perhaps more suitably to the plays as they lie inert and ready for our reading on the printed page.

There is no need to call for more study of Shakespeare's speeches in a textual sense. The words spoken by individual characters have been studied with great finesse, especially in recent decades. We have become increasingly interested in what words *do*. We can now understand how rhetoricians in Shakespeare's day manipulated the minds of their auditors by varying their methods of exposition, the structure of their speeches, and choice of words, figures of speech, and modes of address. We have learned how Renaissance poets were aware of subtle influences of meter, rhyme, assonance, and all the musical effectiveness of sound, how silence can be given meaning over against the spoken word, how text can suggest subtext, how words mask and disguise thoughts, how questions may be answered by avoidance of direct response. We have studied, too, how speeches in Shakespeare's plays imply gestures and actions that add visual effects to the auditory operation of words. We have begun to understand how meaning is never fully present in any utterance but depends also on what is *not* said, on the difference from other possible words and sets of words. We look beyond an editor's annotation that offers a single definition or paraphrase and would like to know what words Shakespeare did *not* select. We recognize that a subversive use of ordinary means can effect huge changes of understanding; and so familiar words have become as interesting as those "hard" words which Shakespeare forged for the very first time or borrowed from obscure sources. Personal pronouns—*us* and *them,* and, particularly, *she* and *he*—auxiliary verbs, exclamations, the most routine modes of address and reference, now seem to leap forward for our attention and signal innovative thoughts.

Words swim in our minds, assemble together, and break apart. They change as we study them; they float and sink and get carried downstream into other regions. Words are stimulating and elusive, mocking and bewildering. We realize now that we shall never pin down the effect of Shakespeare's text in our minds or in those of other readers and audiences.

This new awareness is changing our view of Shakespeare's plays while older methods of study continue to grapple with the words in print. Verbal and visual images, ambiguities and associative subtleties, repetitions, variations, and other devices to refine and extend meaning; semantics, syntactics, pronounciation, and morphology: all are being considered and reconsidered. In calling attention to the nature of speech in Shakespeare's plays, I may well seem to be redundant, because so much investigation is in hand at present that few people can keep up-to-date with all that is being discovered.

But speech is an individual human activity as well as a collection of printed signs to be listed, described, and decoded. Speech is physiological and therefore as complex as a living organism, and in each manifestation it is therefore unrepeatable. Even when an actor has prepared for speech with the utmost care and efficiency, he or she will respond in a highly instinctive, unconscious manner to the exigencies of each moment in each new performance. Speech in theatrical terms is part of a continuous activity in space and time, within the speaker and without; and every single sound has special qualities not shared by any other.

For example, it is not enough to disentangle by temperate study the signs encoded in the words "To be or not to be. . . ." What that speech communicates in performance depends a great deal on the set of mind and body in the actor who speaks it. To whom does he speak? In what direction or at what distance? Is it to himself, or to a real or an imagined audience, or to a mixture of all three? Where does he breathe in the course of uttering all those words? What quality of sound is natural to his voice, and how is this altered by his speaking within this particular dramatic context? How loudly or quietly does he begin and continue and conclude? What is his pulse rate, how steady his tempo, how insistent or hesitant his inflections? Beyond all this, what happens within the actor as he attempts to present Prince Hamlet at this point in the play? How the actor has fared in the performance before this moment will influence very strongly—and sometimes in unexpected ways—the game that he now plays with the text, with his fellow actors, and with his audience.

(A crude indication of what is involved physiologically in the performance of such a speech can be obtained by memorizing it and then speaking it loud and clear for at least one auditor some thirty feet away. Four or five attempts to make the speech work and communicate will demonstrate an actor's need to gather and control the expenditure of energy, to choose moments for emphasis, to maintain an intelligible phrasing of the words, to follow through from one moment to another, to make the speech his own. Such speech is a challenge, and the chance of winning or losing in that game is part of the excitement and meaning of the play.)

All attempts to evaluate the nature of speech in Shakespeare's plays that do not take into account the actor's contribution to the exigencies and pleasures of performance are grounded solely in textual matters and confined to the page. Studies with titles such as *Littérature et Spectacle, The Semiotics of Theatre and Drama,* or *Reading the Signs* promise to engage with this problem. But they exact a large price by insisting on specialized jargon, parenthetical references, and exhaustive enumeration, and then these scholarly works deliver very little to our purpose. Keir Elam's latest study of Shakespeare's *Discourse* (1984) speaks of the "presence of the voice" without considering the actor responsible for it.[1] (The phrase "presence of the voice" seems somewhat ridiculous to me because it is the actor who has "presence" and not a disembodied "voice.") Professor Elam considers "the body," but only as a "sign-maker," not as something made of flesh and blood; he is content to list textual references to bodies and physical gestures and bypasses without comment the living, breathing, feeling person who is doing the speaking or making the gesture. "Speech production" is here a convenient heading for listing such textual devices for referring to an actor's art and craft as reading a letter. Similarly "units of deictic orientation," discussed in a recent study by Alessandro Serpiere, are defined by the text alone and stand well clear of the ambiguity, excitement, and pleasure of performance.[2] The gestural resources and conventions—the participation frameworks and embedded quotations—that enable Erving Goffman to describe "forms of talk" show that dialogue is like a game with various possible moves but one that seems to be played without physical commitment.[3] All these scholars consider the speaker as a disembodied functionary, rather than as an individual human being who is alive in thought and action and involved in processes of change and chance.

The result of this new research is an old-fashioned rhetorical enumeration, tricked out in a quantity of curious categories. It is scholastic not theatrical, concerned with text and not with play. So Professor Elam writes in the concluding section of his latest book:

> There is quite a distinct kind of dramatic 'dispersion' of the proverb in its citation form (the codified wording, that is, in which it is normally quoted and collected): the paraphrase containing no specific lexical clues to its own proverbial status. What is retained, rendering the transformed saying recognizable, is no longer the key word but the *kernel proposition.* And the audience's cognitive or re-cognitive task is not so much a 'filling-in' as a 'translating back.' The effect is still,

however, that of a defamiliarizing estrangement of the codified proposition as such. . . .[4]

The numerous quotation marks and parentheses and the italicization in this passage, together with its curious syntax and punctuation, show how ingeniously this new rhetorical theorizing has been applied to some few words given by Shakespeare to Orsino in the text of *Twelfth Night*. But the effort of mind needed to follow such exposition does little to further our understanding of the speech in performance. The concern here is limited to the content and organization of some words upon the page.

Any inquiry into the nature of speech in Shakespeare's plays must also consider what happens when actors assume the personages of the drama, perform their actions and speak their words. We must try to follow as this activity calls upon an individual's resources and involves him or her in a passionate or fantastic game. We should observe how a company of actors are taken out of their ordinary selves in exploration, contest, and discovery. We must notice, too, how actors are able to satisfy and amaze an audience, who will in return influence the way in which the game is played.

When we go to the theatre, we know that Macbeth will die, but neither we nor the actor can know exactly *how* he will die. We know that the pipers will "strike up" at the end of a comedy, but not how far that music will seem to resolve outstanding issues, change the behavior of the dancers, or influence the way in which we perceive the concluding action.

Performance is a complicated phenomenon and hard to study seriously. It is very tempting to conclude that performance is so out of our control that we should be content either to study the text on a page or else to enjoy, without interruption, whatever performances may please us. But I want to argue that speech, that element of performance which is most closely entwined with the smallest details of the text, does hold some clues that can be followed and help us to a greater understanding of the plays.

*   *   *

Shakespearean critics and students should observe actors at work and learn about the nature of acting. They have suffered by being confined to university departments of English where plays are never seen in performance by skilled and practiced actors.

I do not think that the variety of acting styles in evidence today or the difficulty of knowing how Elizabethan actors practiced their art should stand in the way of such inquiry. Nor should an actor's reliance on instinctive reactions cause a critic to undervalue his or her contribution to performance. A company of experienced actors in rehearsals for a Shakespeare play will show an observer how they discover each day new qualities inherent in the text and respond to demands that they had not recognized hitherto. The play seems always to move ahead of the actors' understanding, exerting its own influence more and more as the words become realized or substantiated in performance. Such an impression of progress toward a distant target could be merely an illusion, a product of the actors' need to trust the material on which they are working, but when theatre people speak of Shakespeare's directing them through his text, as they frequently do, they are scarcely aware of using a metaphor; this seems to be no less than the literal truth. As John Barton says in his *Playing Shakespeare:*

> if you want to do [Shakespeare] justice, you have to look for and follow the clues he offers. If an actor does that then he'll find that Shakespeare himself starts to direct him.[5]

When all rehearsals are done, on the first night when the whole play is performed before an audience, good actors go further and give every appearance of growing in power and subtlety, as if summoned by what unfolds before them. How does this happen? How can actors encourage it to happen? What can we learn about Shakespeare's plays from the actors' attempt to give life to the words?

Barton's book, based on a number of television programs showing the rehearsal methods of the Royal Shakespeare Company actors, is a rare attempt to describe how actors work on a text. It reveals some of the questions actors ask as they explore a play and provides some examples of how willfulness or playfulness may carry them toward sufficient confidence to stand up and perform upon a stage. It could serve as an introduction to a study of the nature of speech in Shakespeare's plays. One of its great virtues is that it raises as many questions as it seems to solve for those who had taken part in the studio rehearsals.

John Barton shows how actors can "listen" to versification and to Shakespeare's choice and arrangement of words, and how this leads on to further problems: what words should be stressed? when should there be a pause? how should a speech or phrase be inflected? Barton encourages his actors to find what he calls the "verbal energy" for a sustained passage in *Love's Labour's Lost,* because without this supercharge it would be "hard to follow and difficult to listen to."[6] He asks each actor to "serve up the key words for the others to play off them"—as if the play were a game of tennis. They must be sure to "play with words, to give the audience the right information," and to "relish" the sounds of resonance and onomatopoeia for the same purpose.[7] Actors must not "fight shy" of rich and vivid language, even if the effort to respond leaves them, at first, breathless and bewildered. They must make the unusually demanding sounds and yet be "real": "it's a question of balance" between these two demands, as he admonishes repeatedly.

Barton's book shows actors being stretched and excited by the sheer energy needed to make these speeches their own and at the same time being exhorted to use their discretion and judgment in order to maintain close and watchful attention to small details of the text as it surges into dramatic life—and sometimes resists their hold. An army of students could find pretexts for their essays in the short compass of this very practical book.

But an exploration of "the nature of speech in Shakespeare's plays" can be taken further than this. Barton's repeated injunctions to "find the language and make his listeners feel the words"[8] are too incidental, too piecemeal, to cope with whole sentences. He pays little attention to syntax and the shape of thought. His actors can sound precious, unreal, and overheated, because they are not taught to seek out the main verb of every sentence and to organize all its words around this central activity of mind. Speech should be more than interesting and effectively colored; it should develop from the motive force or action that has formed the sentence as a whole and in a particular order. The only way to make utterance convincing is to balance its parts and find an appropriate rhythm from the needs and forces within the character in the dramatic situation as it develops throughout the play. "Relishing" words and "feeling" the language can become an almost mindless mastication.

In the television series on which his book is based, Barton was content to leave problems of character to the actor's instincts, but it is noticeable how often the actors pull him back to consider why certain words are spoken in a particular context by a particular person. Occasionally, Barton helps to make a speech sound more forceful by calling for some generalized emotional charge—as when he encourages the speaker of the Chorus in *Henry V* to be more "excited" within himself and then rewards the new rendering with "I thought the first half of that was great"[9]—but too often, in my opinion, he deals with speakers and not with characters or persons in a drama. He seems content with an actor's intellectual understanding and does not lead forward from this into the expression of a total and individual involvement in the play. He asks actors to "make the images more concrete," not to look for ways to make the words necessary to their characters in performance at the moment of utterance.

Barton takes time off from the plays to set actors working on Shakespeare's sonnets where he can avoid problems of interplay between speakers and their response to the drama's developing action. This also avoids questions about the nature of a character's involvement in words with the idiosyncrasy of a particular physical human being. But his exercises on the sonnets, with their regular form of fourteen rhymed lines, does permit him to develop the actor's ability to shape a whole speech, a task that is often missing in his other rehearsal sessions.

The Royal Shakespeare actors have to project Shakespeare's words out into the far reaches of the Stratford Theatre or the broad expanse of the Barbican Theatre in London, and this has led them, in my opinion, to simplify and exaggerate. It is important to realize that actors trained in other than the classical repertory, those used to the close scrutiny of the camera and inspired by its ability to direct attention to small signs of unspoken thoughts and sensations, can also find appropriate ways of acting Shakespeare, and they may well be more able to create characters that live intensely on the stage. I have seen a film actor, unused to Shakespeare's plays, seek to make the movements of Polonius's mind, as expressed in his convoluted prose, a part of a complete personification. The words came very slowly at first, but so did the amazing complexity of a man who was father of Ophelia and Laertes and also the chief counselor of the King. The shape and rhythms of speech governed the inner workings of the actor and his physical activity; there was no contradiction between what was heard and what was seen and sensed. The result was a character made wholly visible, palpable, true, and arresting. Polonius's speech stopped the rehearsal once the actor had achieved the connection between text and being; so strong an impression of reality had been created that the other actors in the scene were not ready to respond.

Reading the signs in a text is not enough; we need to cross over the dividing line and ask how these words can be spoken and how they can best become part of an image of fully lived experience. Experimentally, in rehearsal with trained actors, we can learn more and become skilled at reading the multitude of clues that lie implicit within it and which actors thrive upon. It is from the text that the whole play springs to life so that our study of performance will in turn lead to a fuller understanding and, perhaps, a revaluation of the most familiar plays.

* * *

Three brief examples will serve to indicate some of the possibilities that a study of speech may open up. The first is from *Othello:*

> Strumpet, I come.
> Forth of my heart those charms, thine eyes, are blotted;
> Thy bed, lust-stain'd, shall with lust's blood be spotted.
> (5.1.34–36)[10]

The rhythms, syntax, and vocabulary of this soliloquy are so difficult that most directors have pity on their actor and cut it from the production script. The words are in starkest contrast to the Moor's previous utterance, which was still under control for Lodovico's sake. And the tone of his next words changes yet more surprisingly, as he is rapt in wonder and contemplates "the cause" that draws him toward murder and suicide. I have seen Paul Scofield in the pauses of rehearsals moving around and flexing his body, as he spoke these words to himself, seeking the bodily changes that could draw forth and give credibility to their emphatic, lurid, and crudely vindictive qualities, and to the syntax which piles up epithets within each line and moves from present, to past, and to future without transitional phrase. By watching the actor I realized that here the whole person of Othello passes through a dark and violent experience: it comes upon him and the audience with a sudden shock and will radically alter the way in which he approaches the final scene, when his repetitions are not violently charged and when delicacy, tenderness, and far-reaching images have repossessed his mind and made his body hesitate and remain poised above his sleeping wife.

Any one speech tends to influence others. Consider Claudius's words to Laertes, in the middle of their plotting the assassination of Hamlet:

> There lives within the very flame of love
> A kind of wick or snuff that will abate it;
> And nothing is at a like goodness still;
> For goodness, growing to a pleurisy,
> Dies in his own too much. That we would do,
> We should do when we would; for this 'would' changes,
> And hath abatements and delays as many
> As there are tongues, are hands, are accidents;
> And then this 'should' is like a spendthrift's sigh
> That hurts by easing. But to the quick of th'ulcer:
> Hamlet comes back; what would you undertake. . . .
>
> (4.7.114–24)

The first ten lines of this passage insist that the breathing, rhythms, pitch, and inflections of the actor playing Claudius must all change. It seems in performance as if the thought of Gertrude has drawn Claudius off target, taking possession of his mind without his volition. He had spoken of the Queen at the beginning of the scene but despatched her from his thoughts easily enough; now, however, the structure of his thought is drawn out, the weight of sound lightens, and a new field of imagery is introduced (the same flame image that was to haunt the mind of Othello). Yet Claudius does not mention the Queen directly; and soon his thought quickens once more, as he knows he has to act alone, regardless of his pain, in order to lance the ulcer that he *can* cope with and which Leartes can recognize easily. Response to these changing demands of the text is more than a technical feat employed for the instant: the actor will make this speech credible only by preparing for it long before, by establishing a particular relationship to Gertrude in silence as well as words. This incidental passage is then capable of an impression of instinctive, private thought and of fugitive, delicate, and yet strong feeling. Claudius is forced to torture himself. We can see this in his breathing as he speaks, in the movement and changes of his eyes as he alters the object of his attention, in the relaxation and tension of his body, and in his nervous impulses as his thoughts change and seek to hide irrepressible feelings. He is suffering already and doomed; Hamlet's final actions only complete for Claudius what has started earlier in the play.

Verbal clues to crises in performance may be very brief and easily passed over until explored in the rehearsal room. I remember Sir John Gielgud preparing to play Prospero at the National Theatre in London and seeking the deep assurance and inner suffering required to make "Tis new to thee" and "In this last tempest" (*The Tempest*, 5.1.184 and 153) register fittingly in their context, using their precise phrasing. As his long role drew toward an end in imperfect reconciliations, Shakespeare's text could bear the great weight of feeling required by the dramatic context only after the actor had discovered, with difficulty, the appropriate means for himself, a delivery that was most delicate and softly spoken and yet reached to the back of the theatre because of the authority, poise, and timing used. Indeed the effect was richer than this, because Gielgud's Prospero seemed also to share with the audience a consciousness of the inadequacy of what was actually spoken; he was playing a part for the sake of those who knew less than he did, and he seemed to take some consoling—or some briefly diverting—pleasure in doing so. These short speeches were so immaculately phrased that the magician and rightful ruler was like a dramatist completing a play, rather than speaking his mind; and yet, at the same time, the father suffered in private and felt a quickening joy.

* * *

One objection to the kind of study I am recommending is that modern actors are not those Elizabethan and Jacobean actors for whom Shakespeare wrote his plays and that they bring to rehearsals many prejudices and skills which Shakespeare could not have imagined and lack others that he took for granted. But the same argument can be leveled against any reading of the plays. No one person can reconstruct a historically accurate response, even if we could know what that might be.

Of course, any encounter with the text will be flawed and could benefit from a greater understanding of the variety of life and history of thought. But the reading that takes place in a rehearsal room has one great advantage over that of a literary student. Whatever an actor discovers must always be realized in terms of performance, and that includes a great many features of lived experience; it cannot survive as some new argument set forth in words alone. Perhaps Elizabethan actors were cruder or more eloquent, or more formalized and less lifelike, than their modern counterparts, but every actor who steps onto a stage has to bring a whole self into play and must relate what is spoken to what is there, palpably, before the audience. No actor can cheat for very long; incomplete performances, or those which have some elements at odds with others, will be recognized for what they are by audiences and by fellow actors. We need have little doubt that modern actors are responding to qualities inherent in Shakespeare's text; if they did not, they would find acting in his plays a troublesome labor and not a great pleasure.

Another objection to my argument is that rehearsals do not have comparable authority with great performances by the most famous actors from the past. We are told to study the stage history of plays to discover the undoubted nature of their theatrical life. But this is to interpose a further historical distortion between ourselves and the text. Accounts of eighteenth-century actors or even of those two or three decades before the present must all be interpreted in light of the production styles of those days and the idiosyncrasies of the star performers. Moreover the earlier performances are no longer there for us to encounter as best we may; all we can do is to read newspaper accounts that were written to make interesting copy rather than to describe performances accurately or comprehensively. We can take special note of what appealed to the crowd as well as to the more judicious critics, but that tells us only about the broader effects and, sometimes, about topical and passing enthusiasms. We can read whatever an actor or biographer has deemed fit to publish about aims and achievements, but very often these books and articles were written by way of apology or self-advertisement. Promptbooks are firmer ground for the student, but stage managers have always been concerned to record the traffic of the stage rather than the nature of performance; their reasons for noting anything were related to the smooth functioning of a complicated operation, not to the interests of an audience or future students.

The study of theatre history is useful as a corrective and stimulus. Anyone can be blind to some opportunities inherent in a text, and suggestions from the past can alert our attention. But the growing number of books that record the fortunes of plays in the theatre cannot replace the more basic and exploratory work which may be undertaken every time a play is rehearsed by skilled and experienced actors and brought to the pitch of subsequent performance. Every student of Shakespeare, of whatever experience, learning, or talents, needs access to this laboratory and to the testing ground of performance, which is also a place of entertainment. Here is where "speech" as I have defined it earlier will bridge the divide between text and theatrical understanding.

Notes

1. Keir Elam, *Shakespeare's Universe of Discourse: Language-Games in the Comedies* (Cambridge: Cambridge University Press, 1984).

2. Alessandro Serpieri, "Reading the Signs: Towards a Semiotics of Shakespearean Drama," trans. Keir Elam, in *Alternative Shakespeares,* ed. John Drakakis (London: Methuen, 1985), 119–143.

3. Erving Goffman, *Forms of Talk* (Oxford: Basil Blackwell, 1981).

4. Elam, *Shakespeare's Universe of Discourse,* 280.

5. John Barton, *Playing Shakespeare* (London: Methuen, 1984), 168.

6. Ibid., 73.

7. Ibid., 52.

8. Ibid., 86–87.

9. Ibid., 50–51.

10. All Shakespeare quotations are from *Shakespeare. The Complete Works,* ed. Peter Alexander (London: Collins, 1951).

Shakespeare and Beckett

What the Words Know

HOMER SWANDER

Beckett's or Pinter's, Shakespeare's or Marston's "play": what is it? *Catastrophe* and *The Tempest* only play out, in an open use of the medium, what is true of every "play": the script is not the play. A poem is a poem, a novel is a novel, a play is a play; but a play is not a set of words on a collection of pages. Which performance of *Catastrophe* is Beckett's play? Is Alan Schneider's deeply loyal production Beckett's play? Beckett's stage directions tell us about the female Assistant: "White coverall. Bare head. Pencil on ear. Age and physique unimportant." But give us, instead (as Schneider did with Beckett's ultimate approval), a tight black skirt, split provocatively; lush hair, piled luxuriously; pencil in hair; high heels (for looks *and* sound). And cast the beautiful Leigh Taylor-Young, whose legs are unforgettable and who lights the director's cigar so sensuously that it is hard to believe, afterward, you haven't seen the sexual act performed. Then put all of this to work in the context of the woman's apparent compassion for the Protagonist and her apparent loathing of the Director; and the powerful theatrical signs, created by Schneider and Taylor-Young, constitute a contribution of major significance to what is called "Beckett's play." By contemplating and honoring that simple, obvious fact, we learn a good deal about the difference between plays and novels. For critics and scholars, for audiences or readers, a play is a moving target, a novel is (comparatively) a sitting duck.

But the victory of the literary establishment in territory that belongs, by right and in essence, to the theatre has been so devastatingly complete and lengthy that we find ourselves, in the eighth decade of the twentieth century, without so much as a disciplined vocabulary widely enough shared to enable us adequately to communicate with one another as we try to understand and discuss the work of the playwrights who interest or inspire us. Anyone who doubts the validity of my pessimism should spend a few moments wondering why modern theoreticians of drama, however sophisticated, are unable to assume that even the most basic distinctions between literature and drama can be taken for granted; or should compare

60

any of the useful definitions of drama (by, say, Beckerman in *Dynamics of Drama,* Langer in *Feeling and Form,* or Styan in *Drama, Stage and Audience*)[1] with the actual use and comprehension of the word in discussions of Sophocles, Shakespeare, Ibsen, Pinter, or Beckett over the last thirty years—even in the work of the so-called radicals: the postmodernists, historicists, Marxists, feminists, semioticians, or deconstructors.

Of all living playwrights, the one who can most help us to understand the fundamental nature of scripts and the primary meaning of "wright"— to free us from the notion that scripts are a form of literature and to launch us into a discipline worthy of the name—is Samuel Beckett; of all dead playwrights, Shakespeare. The following description of Beckett at work, written by the French actor Pierre Chabert out of personal observation, would, if applied to Shakespeare, more satisfactorily account for his scripts and the known facts of his professional life than almost anything ever written specifically about him.

> Beckett is already the director long before he takes charge of the rehearsals and works with the actors. . . . The direction is always written into his texts in the most literal way, showing itself in a theatrical language where the word is never dissociated from the place where it is spoken or from the concrete language of the stage, where the word is never conceived outside the framework of the accompanying gesture, the movement, place, the physical stance and the bodily posture.
>
> In this way we can understand the stillness of the physical bodies and the apparent extension of the Beckettian stage, consisting of a rigorous mastery of theatrical space, where the word in its relationship to the gesture, the phrase to the movement, the language to the body, the writing to the direction, are all thought out and explored to their extreme limits. The result is a staging full of constraints, that must be read and performed like a musical score in terms of sound and vision, textually and spatially. The staging emerges from a change of status between the word and the stage space . . . and consists of the act of translation, of illustration, and of derivation of which Artaud speaks.
>
> Beckett, author and director, is of course the same person. In becoming his own director, he is simply taking up again the act of writing, prolonging it, sharpening it, making it come to life in spite of all the hazards, resistances—the limitations—of the interpretation. His theatrical poetry, already so much a part of the text, is now given to us in its most naked form.[2]

The radical nature of Beckett's commitment to the entirety of the theatrical process—from mental image and first word through to the staged form—reveals in a flash the radically nonliterary nature of drama. The insights in the quoted paragraphs could perhaps only have been achieved by an unusually perceptive actor who has been directed in a major Beckettian role (in this case, Krapp) by Beckett himself. One can amuse and educate oneself by imagining a similar kind of testimony from the pen of Richard Burbage. Chabert's words develop precisely, with no such intention, the most important implications of Hamlet's advice to the players. Hamlet is in fact an extreme example. His purpose, one would think, is entirely political and domestic, his mind entirely devoted to revenge. Yet when, like Beckett, he *scripts* "a speech of some dozen or sixteen lines" (2.2.535), he can no more than Beckett let it go at that: "Speak the speech, I pray you, as I pronounced it to you . . .," and "do not saw the air too much with your hand, thus, but use all gently. . . . Leave thy damnable faces and begin" (3.2.1–45 and 247).[3] For Hamlet, as for Beckett—and for Shakespeare—the word on the page is only one step in a necessary and seamless theatrical process.

Chabert goes far beyond, indeed explodes, the shaky and misleading consensus on which the Shakespearean academy is these days congratulating itself—a consensus based on the extraordinary discovery (widely accepted only in the last decade) that Shakespeare was a "man of the Theatre." The man would, I suppose, be relieved to hear that we have, however superficially, embraced the obvious. But Beckett alive and working in our time; Beckett challenging us with words devised for novels, stories, poems, *and* scripts; Beckett conceiving scripts for stage, radio, film, and television; Beckett collaborating with actors, advising directors, directing his own plays, and writing scripts with specific actors in mind; Beckett intricately and knowingly involved in the process begun by words that come alive only in voices, bodies, costumes, properties, spaces, and live audiences; Beckett doing in his time and in his own way essentially what Shakespeare did in his—it is this phenomenon that takes us beyond the obvious into its implications and consequences. If, that is, we pay attention.

Chabert has paid attention, and nearly every phrase beckons us toward a revolution in the criticism, scholarship, teaching, and staging of drama. How much do we really know about the nature of language in which "the word is never dissociated from the place where it is spoken or from the concrete language of the stage, where the word is never conceived outside the framework of the accompanying gesture, the movement, place, the physical stance and the bodily posture"? How much, that is, do we know about *scripted* words, words that are not at home on a page, words that exist only in a state of search (searching for bodies, spaces, audiences), words that *know* they are not literature? Can we reasonably claim to possess a shared, developed, academically or theatrically respectable discipline that is as rooted in all the energies and possibilities of words as is literature but that is wholly independent of and untainted by literary investigative procedures and literary modes of thought? Where are the hundreds of critics, scholars, and directors, and the thousands of teachers, who are sufficiently educated, trained, and experienced in the fundamentally different languages of literature *and* theatre that they can carry us into the century of disciplined research and dialogue for which we can at least now see the need?

Peter Brook has given us the most radical and challenging statement of our ignorance:

> What is living theatre? We have no answer today. Whatever we know, is not it. Whatever we have seen, is not it. Whatever is labelled theatre, isn't. Whatever is defined as theatre, misses the point. Whatever has been handed down to us, has been cheapened out of recognition. Whoever claims to know what theatre was or could be, doesn't. We are now before a long period of perpetual revolution, in which we must search, attempt to build, pull down and search again.[4]

Brook was of course speaking primarily to and about the practitioners of theatre—actors, directors, designers. I am, I suppose, speaking primarily to and about Shakespeareans who work in the academy and, for the most part, in literature departments, people who habitually think of themselves as critics, scholars, and teachers of literature. But to say so is only, in another significant way, to state the problem. In the New Discipline, although nowhere else, these two communities are one.

The careers of both Shakespeare and Beckett are the models that insist upon such a union. As Chabert describes the absolute unity of Beckett's creative process, he is returning us to the primary meaning of the word "playWRIGHT": not a writer but a maker of plays. And he is beckoning us toward a discipline in which the burden of knowledge will be severe, including—as it must—all that is demanded in the study or practice of literature *and* in the study or practice of theatre. When Shakespeare writes a sonnet, he is—like Beckett in the novels—a writer. When Shakespeare scripts a sonnet for *Romeo and Juliet,* he is the wright described by Chabert. Such wrights are rare but no more rare than greatness.

Although wrights create scripts, they are not scriptwriters. Although they shape their own plays, literally, in the theatre, they are not directors. Our traditional language and ways of thinking imply a division that does not exist. We say that writers should not direct their own work. Perfectly true—for writers. But wrights will necessarily do all of the work that defines them, from the act of writing to the act of telling an actor how to speak or move. The latter act is in fact only part of the former—"prolonging it, sharpening it," as Chabert says. The power that wrights must assume over actors as well as over words—both being the materials with which they work—is exactly the power that, in *Catastrophe,* Beckett places in a political context and reveals as (even in its own terms) potentially dangerous: both words and actors must be, for the wright, raw material; but actors are human beings. Which doesn't mean that Beckett feels less responsible to language than to people.

Our traditional professional language leads to additional difficulty. I have, for example, been using the word "script" as if I believed we were all agreed upon its meaning and significance. A common word, possessed of a clear and useful denotational meaning, it nevertheless almost never appears in the active vocabulary of scholars and teachers of Shakespeare—for a very good reason: its use, at least its thoughtful use, pushes one toward what, in the literary world, is perceived as heresy. With one blow, it cuts all literary moorings and plunges us into an exploration of "meaning" that has nothing whatever to do with literature but everything to do with *The Tempest* and *Catastrophe, Hamlet* and *Happy Days*.

A Shakespearean or Beckettian script presents language not as meaning but as a set of signals, one of the signals of course being the sense of the words. Although the words may "make sense," their presence is not—as we are traditionally used to believing of words—equivalent to the presence of meaning. Genuinely scripted language is not equivalent to meaning, is not reducible or expandable to meaning. Taken as any "meaning" whatever—traditional or postmodern—it will always mislead. Its energy desires and flows toward meaning; but such a process differs entirely from an attempt to present on the page or in the reader's mind a set of words that contain or project a meaning (even a meaning defined merely as "experience"). Unlike literary energy, the energy of a script drives toward an aesthetic being, a formal and authentic life, beyond itself: a highly precarious life in the bodies of actors moving in an agreed-upon space as an invitation to spectators to become an audience.

Ontologically, that is, in the world of art an authentic script has not achieved—and cannot achieve—an authentic state of "being." It is not, by itself, a work of art. In this, it is like the stone in which a sculptor senses rich possibilities. In spite of the fact that the stone is a natural and the script an artificial object, we are in each case faced with all of the ontological differences between "potential" and "being." Shakespeare's contemporary John Marston puts it exactly when he regrets that "scenes invented merely to be spoken should be enforcively published to be read." He apologizes for "the unhandsome shape" that his script of *The Malcontent* presents to the reader and hopes for pardon because of the "pleasure it . . . afforded . . . when it was presented with the soul of lively action."[5] The key word here is "soul." We must break ourselves of the unfortunate and nearly universal habit of seeing performance as the embodiment of a script. The script is an "unhandsome *shape*," itself a body only. As a body, it can, against its nature, be *"enforcively"* published for readers; but its soul, its only authentic life, is the "lively action" of the stage. As a body, it desires and expects to be united with its soul; as a body (not a corpse), its energy drives toward the union of soul and body that constitutes "being"; and that union is not the kind that takes place in the quiet study of a literary critic or scholar or—even—in the head of a director seeking a "concept."

Chabert's imagery, in its own precision, similarly instructs us and is, if anything, more radical, more clarifying and disciplining than Marston's. Chabert sees the creative process—from conception to script to production under Beckett's own guiding mind—not as an embodiment, or as some audiovisual illustration, of the words, but as a move toward nakedness: purity, essence, in Marston's terms, "soul." If the poetry of a text is theatrical—if the text is in fact a script—the poetry will appear "in its most naked form" not in the pages of a book but on the stage. How different this is from the literary view in which the seclusion of the study is seen as protecting scholars and critics from the distracting clutter and noise of the theatre, from the unstable elements of performance, and allowing them the time that is needed to find the most intricate patterns and deepest meanings—or "readings"—of a play. Chabert's imagery requires us to see the move from text to performance not as a process in which words gather around them costumes and bodies and properties (designs and concepts)—a dressing-up process, an accumulation, an embodying—but as the austere, continuing, *narrowing* search of the creator for the essential expression, the utterly naked poetry of word *and* action. In this radically different view, the distracting clutter and noise—and the misleading, nonfunctional time frame—are found not in the theatre but on the printed page and in the study. The naked poetry of drama—Shakespeare's or Beckett's—is available *only* in the theatre.

Everything we know about Shakespeare suggests that what mattered to him most was not the words and the reader but the performance and the audience. He might, like Athol Fugard, have said, "I have always regarded the completed text as being only a half-way stage to my ultimate objective—the living performance and its particular definition of space and silence."[6] Even more insistent than Fugard, Shakespeare—once *Othello* or *The Tempest* had achieved its own stage definitions—did not pause to publish the "half-way stage." What then do we—as actors, directors, scholars, and teachers—do with his halfway stages, now that, by many other hands, they have long been published? What do we do with words that were initially conceived and arranged to function only through performance? How do we enter into, get inside, a set of words that from first to last, in *one continuous living process*, exists only for that ultimate moment when—physically, noisily, in front of and with an audience—they play their role in defining space and silence?

Literature does not, through the control of sound and movement, define space or silence. A novel is in no analogous sense a halfway stage. And

Langer is only saying the obvious: "drama is not made of words as a piece of literature is. . . ." Nor is drama "literature embellished with concurrent appeals to the sense of sight. . . ."[7] Even *Hamlet* is not words, words, words. It is not a collection of words longing to be interpreted or waiting to be embodied. Its only legitimate "being" is something else entirely: "poetry in the mode of action."[8] Everything in a script is a signal for actors. *Everything,* even those things conventionally thought of as literary: diction, syntax, imagery, meter, rhyme, punctuation, rhythm, lineation, scenic structure, and juxtaposition. Shakespeare was an actor writing for actors. He wrote a script only to make a play.

To do as most directors do—to read, interpret, find a concept, create a design, and enter the rehearsal room seeking to embody the concept—is as alien, as violating, as "literary" as anything that the literary critics and scholars do to the scripts. To search, each time, for the signals that lead to the playwright's naked theatrical poetry, for his "particular definition of space and silence," is an entirely different enterprise, a different discipline, involving the only theory and practice capable of leading us further and further into as-yet-undiscovered Shakespearean country. Prevailing practice, in decade after decade, is as new as the latest fad, and just as deep. Fashioning productions by presenting currently popular images—Caliban as black victim or rebel, Hamm and Clov in a graffitied New York subway—only deflects us, in each new decade, to what is currently, stylishly taken to be profound. This gives us only the surface of ourselves, in time, instead of the inner surfaces of Shakespeare's or Beckett's lasting probe: a probe the specific theatricality of which is borne in and through the words, and that can be discovered only by means of the deepest comprehension of a totally theatrical language.

That the playwright's words are not intended for readers, are not literary in purpose or function, in no way decreases their importance and can in no way provide comfort for those actors and directors who, appalling in their numbers and influence, wish for whatever reasons to escape the discipline of the script. Quite the reverse. The words retain their primacy—the staging is initially *in* them, as Chabert says—and the nature of their function as they join with all the other tools of the wright is far more complex than that of words which remain comfortably on a page.

The consequences, for the Shakespearean academy, of such a point of view are incalculable. If Marston, Hamlet, and Chabert are right, then an entire professional establishment is mired in falsehood: false assumptions and false procedures protected by agreements about professional qualifications that decade after decade prolong the commitment of valuable critical, scholarly, and pedagogical energies to tasks rendered illegitimate by the basic confusion in which, throughout an academy ostensibly dedicated to the truth, drama parades as literature. When a literary critic or scholar picks up a script, he or she at once becomes an amateur, a dilettante. Those qualified by education, experience, judgment, and taste professionally to explore and illuminate literature—Shakespeare's poems and Beckett's novels—are not thereby professionally qualified to explore and illuminate words the sole purpose of which is to initiate and participate in an awesomely complex creative process the nature of which is fundamentally unlike literature.

In our time, it is Samuel Beckett whose work most vividly gives the lie to the lazy habits of thought that allow Shakespeare to remain unlocated in the theatre and the academy. Like Shakespeare, Samuel Beckett investigates and analyzes the genres and the media in which he works; and as in Shakespeare, the investigative analysis itself becomes an integral force in creating, with each new work, the new form that will initiate and, with the help of the audience, define the dramatic experience. Shakespeare's explorations on the frontiers of genre and of his medium—his exploitation and employment of them as distinguished from a conventional fidelity—is probably most obvious in such "problem comedies" as *Troilus and Cressida* and *All's Well That Ends Well* or in the comical tragedy of "Pyramus and Thisbe" and other plays-within-plays; but in fact such explorations are one of the most persistent elements of his work, stretching from, say, *Love's Labour's Lost* through *Twelfth Night* to *Pericles* and *The Tempest*. Beckett's inclusion of the genre or the medium of any given dramatic work as part of its specific strategy *and* subject matter started as early as *Eleutheria* (perhaps even with *The Kid*) and has continued unabated into, for example, *Quad I* and *Quad II*. His own comments also reveal that his thinking about a new work is likely to be at least as deeply involved with the nature and possibilities of the medium as with any other category of idea or subject matter: "Never thought about Radio play technique but in the dead of t'other night got a nice gruesome idea full of cartwheels and dragging feet and puffing and panting"—an idea, a line of thought, a sequence of increasingly audible images that became his first play for radio, *All That Fall*.[9]

Shakespeare and Beckett seem equally unwilling to leave any element of their chosen medium unscrutinized, and occasionally their resultant strategies are surprisingly similar. For example, the strategies of *The Tempest* and *Catastrophe* similarly insist that the form of the work remain radically open until, *at each performance,* the audience acts; and the nature of the act, varying from night to night in the apparently conventional moment for applause, will for both plays, each time, newly define the form and create the meaning of the event. Each playwright, using the medium of live drama to its limit, forces the audience to close— not simply to applaud—the play and in that act of participation to act out its own state of awareness: at the last moment, the audience must reveal, for one another and for the actors, the degree of its own humanity in exactly the terms devised by the playwright for the characters in the rest of the play. Thus the spectators become—always to the degree that they have composed themselves into an audience—a character: but one whose response has not been rehearsed and thus cannot be wholly predictable. The revelation, that is—and thus the play—will differ from performance to performance depending upon the nature and success of the audience.

Each playwright has, in other words, taken as a specific strategy and subject matter the incessant struggle for form, for order, that unavoidably characterizes live drama—the struggle in which the chaos of life rages against the presumption of art, against its hubristic attempt to achieve artistic order in a medium composed of living human beings instead of relatively stable paint, wood, stone, or words. That no two performances of any play can ever be exactly the same has, in these two plays, become precisely the final point of interest, excitement, and revelation. And both scripts therefore provide an extreme example of words that know they do not belong to the page, are in no functional sense literature.

In *The Tempest,* the revelation is instigated by the scripted Prospero and by the actor playing Prospero. Near the beginning of the fifth act (the last scene of the play), Ariel leads Prospero to make a choice that defines him, very specifically, as human. He has all of his enemies wholly within his power and has already begun the revenge for which he has so long waited when Ariel says:

> . . . your charm so strongly works 'em
> That if you now beheld them, your affections
> Would become tender.
> *Prospero.*   Dost thou thinke so, Spirit?
> *Ariel.* Mine would, Sir, were I humane.
> *Prospero.*   And mine shall.
> Hast thou (which art but aire) a touch, a feeling
> Of their afflictions, and shall not my selfe,
> One of their kinde, that rellish all as sharpely,
> Passion as they, be kindlier mov'd then thou art?
> Thogh with their high wrongs I am strook to th'quick,
> Yet, with my nobler reason, gainst my furie
> Doe I take part: the rarer Action is
> In vertue, then in vengeance: they, being penitent,
> The sole drift of my purpose doth extend
> Not a frowne further: Goe, release them Ariel,
> My Charmes Ile breake, their sences Ile restore,
> And they shall be themselves.

(5.1.17–32).[10]

This speech of Prospero's allows us to understand the last action of the play. The final speech (misleadingly but not inaccurately called "Epi-logue," as if the play were over, which, in a sense, it is) comes from three characters with a single voice and body: Prospero, an actor playing Prospero, and the man who is the actor. That is, the actual, flesh-and-blood, twentieth-century actor suddenly finds that he is simultaneously playing three roles: the character named Prospero; an actor, not entirely identical to himself, who is playing that character; and himself. Prospero wants to be forgiven so he can leave the island and go home, across the sea, to Naples; the actor wants to be released so he can leave the stage, satisfied, and go to his dressing room; the man wants to leave the theatre and go home, across town, to friends or family:

> Now my Charmes are all ore-throwne,
> And what strength I have's mine owne.
> Which is most faint: now 'tis true
> I must be heere confinde by you,
> Or sent to Naples, Let me not
> Since I have my Dukedome got,
> And pardon'd the deceiver, dwell
> In this bare Island, by your Spell,
> But release me from my bands
> With the helpe of your good hands:
> Gentle breath of yours, my Sailes
> Must fill, or else my project failes,
> Which was to please: Now I want
> Spirits to enforce: Art to inchant,
> And my ending is despaire,
> Unlesse I be reliev'd by praier
> Which pierces so, that it assaults
> Mercy it selfe, and frees all faults.
>   As you from crimes would pardon'd be
>   Let your Indulgence set me free.
>   (Hinman Folio, 37)

At this point—after the final line of the play—the audience is granted total power to confine him (them) by remaining silent or to "release" them (him) with the prayerlike clapping and the "gentle breath" of prayerlike cheers that are so profoundly begged. In answer to the final appeal, the audience will or will not, through the quality of its "praier," *assault* "Mercy it selfe" and set Prospero, the actor, and the man free. And the individual members of an applauding-praying audience will or will not recognize that in the precise religious terms of the last six lines, they are being asked to understand that the freedom for which they are praying is, ultimately, the freedom of souls—eternal freedom from the consequences of sin—and that they are being asked to believe that, out of an awareness of their own need for pardon, they possess the power not only to reach God but through God's mercy to free the souls of Prospero, the actor, and the man.

The actor finds that he is—and is playing—those who cannot leave the island-stage or be pardoned for their "crimes" unless freed by the audience. It is his responsibility to help the spectators, through the intelligence and passion of his playing, to understand the new and specific meaning of the conventional act that they are so used, in the theatre, to performing. If the actor convinces us that, in his "despaire," he cannot leave the stage unless our applause is transformed through understanding and compassion, then Shakespeare (with the actor's help) has structured the play so as to bring each spectator, now fully a member of the audience, to the same defining choice to which Ariel has earlier brought Prospero. To choose to applaud—to pray, that is, for the complex being before us—is to choose, like Prospero, to be human. The last action of the play, except for the exit of the actor, is performed by a character named Audience. But the choice Audience makes, although participating in the formal aesthetic pretence of the occasion, may also—in the life of any individual spectator—be real. And, with an educative irony, to choose at this point and in this way to be human will have special force and its own meaning if the performance itself was wretched—did not, that is, "deserve" applause. Shakespeare has once again, if we have understood and cooperated, entangled us in form.

When a recent production of *The Tempest,* in which Patrick Stewart of the Royal Shakespeare Company played Prospero, embraced this entangling form with an unusually searching commitment, Stewart found that the play ended differently at each of the three performances and that his own relationship with the audience was impossible to predict and nearly impossible to control.[11] While Prospero gives the audience an ultimate salvational power, to save not only lives but souls, the actor must try to maintain control. He must hold the audience and let the words of the epilogue instruct them, attempting to break through their routine, powerfully habitual preparedness for conventional applause. Such applause is so much a part of what audiences simply expect to do that to reeducate them in one short speech is a daunting task. Yet when the actor releases them at the scripted moment—the moment at which the wright no longer supplies him with words, thus depriving him of the "Art to inchant"—he must hope that they are prepared both to understand and to believe.

For Stewart, this fully scripted problem became not only his last but his most challenging. Through the clearly signaled insistence of Shakespeare, he found himself thrust directly into the essential problem of form itself; and in this instance a form that—utterly faithful to the theatre, rejecting absolutely any alliance with literature—creates an uncertainty and a range of possibilities that can legitimately be resolved only in the particular Dionysian dynamics of each performance.

This production, under the direction of John Bouchard, took the Folio's

"Exeunt omnes" at face value, expecting the audience to applaud when left with an empty stage and a play that was obviously over. But the first-night audience, apparently too knowledgeable about *The Tempest,* refused to be misled: Prospero-Stewart was forced to return to a silent house. Then, two-thirds of the way through the epilogue, one man suddenly responded: he had heard the earnest request for applause, and he complied. Stewart stopped him before it spread; and as only one person had erred, the rest of us could either learn from the error or simply feel superior. I suspect that the general applause did not represent a very great rise in consciousness.

The second-night audience applauded—as they were "supposed" to do—at the general *"Exeunt,"* and Prospero-Stewart turned (just before he was entirely off) to stop it and to work us toward the kind of applause he had come to want. But this audience, having been instructed against their first error, had become cautious: there was a long silence. It was at last broken by one of its members who, deeply moved, quite deliberately took the lead, and the general applause seemed actually to arise, at least in part, out of thought.

On the third and last night, the *"Exeunt"* again generated the conventional applause from which Prospero-Stewart could work to educate the house. But his pleading was now so powerful that at the words "Which was to please" everyone burst—*"erupted,"* as he felt it—into an applause which went on and on. He met it with a hard, stony stare and at last more or less bludgeoned them into silence. Raw and angry, he deliberately shouted the last lines, demanding that the audience hear his deep need and admit their own. When he finished, there was no applause, only a silence so profound and so long that he thought he might indeed be there on that stage forever. It was, he says, a dreadful, painful experience. When at last someone broke the silence, and others followed, he let them know, with a very strong and emotional gesture, that at last they had it right: he was free, and they had freed him. But even then there was no way to know how many of them had, in their act, *assaulted* "Mercy it selfe," freeing "all faults."

Both Bouchard and Stewart came to understand—with a clarity that separates them radically from the dozens of other directors and Prosperos whose work I have experienced over a period of forty years—that in the script of *The Tempest,* Shakespeare has accepted absolutely the *living* struggle for form which separates theatre or drama from literature and has scripted that struggle as the final event of each performance. In each of his performances, Stewart made perfectly clear—in the urgency of his pleading and in his unique expression of gratitude for the freedom mercy had achieved—that without us he could not leave the stage and that only an applause understood as prayer would free him. He made it impossible for us to miss the surprising fact that without us the play could not end, could not achieve its wished-for form. But how many of us, each night, fully understood that ours was the *rare action,* the act of *noble reason* that, empowering divine mercy, defines us as human? In a theatrical form in which the last actor is deeply entangled but unrehearsed such a question necessarily remains unanswered.

At the end of *Catastrophe,* Beckett, too, entangles us, although his means are different. The moment, the action, and the issue are the same as in *The Tempest:* what will we do—and what will we "mean"—when we arrive at the conventional moment for applause? As in *The Tempest,* the play does not end until we have acted. The moment for that nearly automatic theatrical courtesy to which we are accustomed suddenly demands, in *Catastrophe,* both understanding and a moral decision; but Beckett, more than Shakespeare, opens a range of choices, leaving the burden of the decision more completely to us. Even after experiencing the play four times, I am not quite sure what I shall do the next time.[12] Nor am I quite sure what, if anything, I *ought* to do. The complexity, that is, is true to the complexity of life. Those reviewers who speak of the "relative lightness" of the play have, I think, remained aloof from its power by failing to accept its burden.

Castastrophe is "about" a Director who is and is not like Beckett himself. The work, as when Beckett directs, is entirely his: for this Director, there is no playwright lurking, dead or alive, in the background; there are no textual restraints from another artistic source. Although he must deal with the suggestions of an Assistant, he is in artistic terms the sole creator and in practical terms the final authority. His power in the theatre appears to be total. And the Director's play—entirely in the figure of a single actor, the Protagonist—is precisely like a play by Beckett: *"P midstage standing on a black block 18" high. Black wide-brimmed hat. Black dressing gown to ankles. Barefoot. Head bowed. Hands in pockets."*[13] Like the actors in *Play, Not I, That Time,* and *Rockaby,* the Protagonist is molded to the shape desired by a Director-playwright who knows exactly what he wants and has the power to get it. It is deeply disturbing that he is served submissively, in every conceivable way (in visual implication, even sexually), by a female assistant who loathes him so much that when he leaves and she sits in his chair, she immediately *"springs* to her feet . . . takes out a rag, wipes *vigorously* back and seat of chair, [and] *discards* rag. . . ." I have italicized the three words in order to suggest the powerful revulsion revealed in Taylor-Young's movements.

Unlike Beckett, the Director also functions in a political sphere. He is on his way, he says, to a caucus. Both the dedication of the play to Vaclav Havel and the Director's fur coat and toque suggest that the political activity is the kind to which Havel himself would have to submit in order openly to pursue his art. It is clear, too, that on this stage all art, unlike Beckett's or Havel's, will serve the state: "Where do you think we are? In Patagonia?"

The play is political, then, but is more than that. As the Director has two lives, one in art and one in politics, the play takes place in two territories: on Beckett's own stage, where his power is total—and where he is famous for using it totally (even moving arms, legs, heads as if the actors were puppets)—and on a political ground where total power is precisely the issue, having corrupted the stage. One of the great beauties of the play is that Beckett cannot be critical—even of a totalitarian regime—without being self-critical and can criticize a political system for creating catastrophes from human beings only if he reminds us that politics is thereby imitating life itself. For Beckett, human agony is always deeper than politics.

From its opening lines—as perhaps I should already have said—the play occupies a third territory: it explicitly appropriates for its purposes the auditorium, the "stalls," of the theatre in which it is being performed. The Director and his Assistant are arranging—costuming, positioning, coloring, lighting—the Protagonist, who "submits, inert," even when his fists are forcibly unclenched and head pushed down. This activity of rehearsal proceeds, of course, for the effect upon the people who, when the show opens, will be seated in the stalls:

D: Why the plinth?
A: To let the stalls see his feet.

And a little past midway, the Director exits to "go and see how it looks from the house." For the rest of the play he speaks as if from the house ("off")—"I'm sitting in the front row of the stalls and can't see the toes" (we may look to see if he is really there), and the Assistant looks out at us as she replies and follows orders. In no very unusual way (see Pirandello), we are made to feel that we are not present, that the seats we are sitting in are empty. At the same time, we are silently taking part: from where we are sitting, we note that we can or cannot "see the toes." The more the play draws us in, the more it insists that we are not there. I found myself feeling like a ghost, an involved ghost, present to myself but defined as absent: thus, invisible. Perhaps a little like May in *Footfalls*, who, according to Beckett, "is not quite there."

We are invited to watch while the director of a play, using the everyday language and strategies of theatre, deliberately fashions, for artistic-political purposes, a human catastrophe: "Good. There's our catastrophe. In the bag. Once more and I'm off." Under the fashioning mind of the Director and the fashioning hands of the Assistant, the entirely silent, submissive figure of the Protagonist rapidly changes, as a visual sign, from the character in a play by Beckett to the tyrannized, docile occupant of any of those camps or hospitals, so-called, that haunt the twentieth-century consciousness. The script says "old gray pajamas"; the theatrical sign says "camp uniform": we have seen the pajamalike garb in a thousand ugly pictures. And here in the comfortable theatre we watch an explicitly theatrical transformation—from Sufferer to Victim—accomplished in the theatre, by the theatre, for the theatre. The figure is a real actor named David Warrilow. The figure is an "actor" in the "Director's" company (but then why is he so quiet?). The figure is an "actor" cooperatively playing a role in a Beckett-like play. The figure is, increasingly, a victim—*the* Victim, not an actor at all, the Victim as Protagonist. Part of what may frighten us is that the very theatre we treasure grants power which can destroy; and if the theatre, then every institution of human making. And each of us, like Beckett, will perhaps look at himself or herself: merely to pursue our own creative work—directing or teaching, for example—may be to cooperate with the executioner who makes victims of us all.

In fashioning the catastrophe, the last step is proper lighting, the details of which are crucial, in a structure defined by the script:

D: Black out stage.
L: What?
(A *transmits in technical terms. Fadeout of general light. Light on* P *alone.* A *in shadow.*)
D: Just the head.
L: What?
(A *transmits in technical terms. Fadeout of light on* P's *body. Light on head alone. Long pause.*)
D: Lovely.
(*Pause.*)
A (*timidly*): What if he were to . . . were to . . . raise his head . . . an instant . . . show his face . . . just an instant?
D: For God's sake! What next? Raise his head! Where do you think we are? In Patagonia? Raise his head! For God's sake! (*Pause.*) Good. There's our catastrophe. In the bag. Once more and I'm off.
A (*to* L): Once more and he's off.
(*Fadeup of light on* P's *body. Pause. Fadeup of general light.*)
D: Stop! (*Pause.*) Now . . . let'em have it. (*Fadeout of general light. Pause. Fadeout of light on body. Light on head alone. Long pause.*) Terrific! He'll have them on their feet. I can hear it from here.

Through two long pauses, we watch the catastrophe that has, to the Director's delight, narrowed to a grotesquely lit man's head forced down in total defeat. And then, oddly, we hear the applause of that imagined first-night audience; and the play moves to its close:

> (*Pause. Distant storm of applause. P raises his head, fixes the audience. The applause falters, dies.*
> *Long pause.*
> *Fadeout of light on face.*)

Beckett thus presents the rebellion—actor against Director, victim against the state—but only to complicate it with the ambiguous character of the audience. That the Protagonist can kill the distant applause by staring at *us* creates a troubling identity: is something in *me* applauding the catastrophe? With his look, he fills the stalls, at this moment, with the applauding audience that until now was "distant" (more in time than space), and at the same instant we are no longer absent, no longer ghosts: he fills the empty seats with us and *fixes* us there. He "fixes" them, and he fixes us. What he says to them, he says to me: what is it? One reviewer saw "mute misery"; another, "abject supplication"; and a third, a "horrifying death mask that makes the complacent audience shudder."[14] But according to the second of these reviewers—Mel Gussow—Beckett himself "carefully corrected" him, explaining that the Protagonist "is meant to cow onlookers into submission through the intensity of his gaze and of his stoicism." David Warrilow, as he fixes the audience, is thinking, "Fuck you."[15]

The distant audience is this audience. This audience gets the stare that the distant audience deserves. Does this audience deserve it, too? The distant audience *is* cowed, *does* submit. Should this audience—should we—allow ourselves to be cowed, to submit, to be fucked? If we do, need the submission be of the same quality, the same meaning as the other? Through that last "Long pause," what are we thinking and feeling? And when the face at last fades away, do we applaud? *Can* we applaud? Or should we submit and go? Cowed? Or merely quiet? If we applaud, what does the action mean? If we are silent, what does the silence mean? And have we—out of a group of spectators—become an audience, a community aware of itself, possessed of a coherent response?

The answers must be earned in the theatre, each time. The play exists only there, each time. One time (not the first), I applauded—thoughtlessly caught up, I believe, in the "storm" of applause around me. Three other times—when the "storm" seemed no less, everyone seemed to be clapping—I was unable to do so. I don't think my refusal was wholly deliberate: something in Warrilow's face silenced me. Cowed me? Fucked me? I am told that one night in New York an audience composed mostly of blacks stood and cheered. They were, as the Director says, on their feet. *I can hear it from here!* Do I want to hear it? And what did it "mean"? Certainly, their action that night became part of the reality that Beckett's play explores. *Catastrophe* was for that night a play it may never be again, and that audience permanently expanded the possibilities raised by a script which, taking all the risks of the medium, gives its last action to the unpredictable character, the unrehearsed actor: Audience.

In my own experience, I find that the longer I live with those four performances, the more I want to create a lasting response of some complexity to the complex demands of the play—some unique way of despising the Director, a man who devotes his own creativity to using and crushing the spirit of others; some unique way of loathing the ambiguous mixture of complicity and distaste revealed in the Assistant, whose reluctant but complete submission to orders leads to the catastrophe; some unique way of honoring the Protagonist's ultimate, triumphant refusal to be, for anyone, a catastrophe of the human spirit. As with *The Tempest,* the last action begins in the theatre but may follow one forever.

I take it that even in a popular medium like theatre, knowledge and experience serve all serious art. The more that individual spectators know, through study and experience, about the conventions of genre, the nature of the media, and a wide variety of already-existing formal strategies, the more readily and fully will any given group of spectators be enabled to compose itself into an audience: into, that is, the appropriate receiving-responding element of and community for the carefully initiated experience a script envisions. But a radical blurring of the fundamental differences between drama and literature so dominates most critical, scholarly, pedagogical, and even theatrical activities that precision and legitimacy in the study or experience of Shakespearean drama are rare. When, toward the end of the nineteenth century, an educational system increasingly unable to insist on Greek and Latin therefore needed English literary classics, Shakespeare was the most obvious and only unanimous choice. At the time, no one of any significance was so crudely devisive as to point out that scripts are not, in any legitimate sense, literary works at all. Thus our greatest theatre artist, an artist extraordinarily sensitive to genre and medium, has been compelled to walk through the twentieth century disguised, frequently even in the theatre itself, as a novelist or a poet. And we have yet fully to face the unpleasant, frustrating fact that while we possess his scripts, we have forever lost his plays: a fact as disorienting, in the world of professional Shakespeareans, as was the loss of Ptolemaic stability in the world at large.

Given the institutional size and structure, the pedagogical procedures, and the publishing demands of the modern academy, there is no way that Beckett and other modern playwrights could entirely have escaped the devastation consequent upon the capture of Shakespeare by the literary establishment. Shakespeare and the Shakespeare Industry are so powerful and so central to our culture that their history is everyone's history, and to perceive Shakespeare as literature is to perceive drama as literature. A clear, working grasp of the function of genre and medium in the hands of a great artist—a shared understanding of theoretical distinctions and practical consequences—so far eludes us that those who in their teaching use recorded, filmed, or televised versions of Shakespeare normally do so in the belief that such versions legitimately derive from, embody, reveal, or illuminate the words of the scripts. These teachers seem wholly unaware that the poetry—the "naked form"—of a theatrical script can appear only in the theatre and is no more evident on film or tape than on a page. A profession dominated by such confusion, a profession that is failing to perceive and to teach the fundamental distortions imposed upon a set of words by any medium for which the words were not intended is a profession ill prepared to understand—or to prepare others to understand—master explorers of the media like Shakespeare and Beckett. And there is no way out of the confusion until we accurately locate the *playwright* and the *script*.

But I conclude by allowing myself to dream of that golden day when the latest young applicant to teach the plays of Beckett or of Shakespeare arrives at some English department somewhere and—for a first and defining question—is asked, "How many plays have you seen—or directed or performed in—in the last month?" Would we hire someone to teach Shakespeare's sonnets who didn't read poems? someone to teach Beckett's novels who didn't read novels? Professional qualifications must be instructed by the nature of the subject matter. It is finally that simple and that demanding. If such a demand is ever widely accepted, the golden day will in fact arrive: Shakespearean scholarship and Shakespearean pedagogy will be the twin legitimate sources of imaginative and intellectual vitality not only in Shakespearean theatre but, by inevitable influence and extension, in the theatres of Marston, Beckett, Pinter, and Fugard.

Notes

1. Bernard Beckerman (New York: Knopf, 1970); Suzanne Langer (New York: Scribners, 1953); John Styan (London: Cambridge University Press, 1975).

2. "Beckett as Director," *Gambit* 7, no. 28 (1968): 41.

3. Quotations from *Hamlet,* New Arden edition, ed. Harold Jenkins (London: Methuen, 1982).

4. *US,* Playscript 9, (London: Calder and Boyars, 1968), 9.

5. Revels Edition, ed. George K. Hunter (London: Methuen, 1975), 5–6.

6. *Statements,* "Introduction" (Oxford: Oxford University Press, 1974).

7. Langer, *Feeling and Form,* 314, 321.

8. Ibid., 322.

9. Letter to Nancy Cunard, 4 July 1956, quoted in *No Symbols Where None Intended,* ed. Carlton Lake, Catalogue to the Beckett collection, Humanities Research Center, University of Texas at Austin (1984), 93.

10. First Folio, ed. Charlton Hinman (New York: Norton, 1968), 34. Line numbering from the New Arden edition of *The Tempest,* ed. Frank Kermode (Cambridge: Harvard University Press, 1958).

11. An Oberlin Theatre Institute production, it included, in addition to Stewart, American professional actors and Oberlin faculty and students. Unfortunately, the circumstances of the splendid experiment limited performances to three.

12. Directed by Alan Schneider, with David Warrilow (Protagonist), Alan Epstein (Director), Leigh Taylor-Young (Assistant), Mark Taper Forum, Los Angeles, 15–18 March 1984.

13. *Collected Shorter Plays* (London: Faber, 1984), 295–301. *"P"* in the stage directions is Protagonist, *"D"* is Director, *"A"* is Assistant, *"L"* is Luke.

14. Dan Sullivan, *Los Angeles Times,* 16 March 1984, part 6, p. 16; Mel Gussow, *New York Times,* 31 July 1983, sec. H, p. 3; Jack Viertel, *Los Angeles Herald-Examiner,* 16 March 1984, sec. D, p. 21.

15. Mentioned in conversation with the author of this essay.

Subtext in Shakespeare

MARVIN ROSENBERG

One major contribution of performance criticism has been to make scholarship aware of a theatrical insight into the deep layers of Shakespearean character, specifically, subtext: the felt life that so often underlies—and sometimes resists or contradicts—the conscious objectives of the men and women in great drama (and in life).

Freud was not the first, but was probably the most beguiling, instructor in reading life's subtexts. He made us supersensitive to obscure signals of veiled motivation behind the most ordinary of daily activities: an eye blink, a hand twitch, a sign, a word slip. Are we all playing roles and never sure if we are following our true scripts? If nothing we say or do is accidental, if all overt behavior is a mask for forbidden erotic or hostile impulses, what are we really? Lately, Freud's guides to our inner mechanisms have been supplemented by the social scientists who study role playing and by professors of body language who explore our unguarded mannerisms that can betray our secret self.

Which brings us back to Shakespeare and the drama: he knew all along. He knew, better than Hamlet, that the action must be suited, not only to the word, but also to the life burrowing under the word. We are the more ready to recognize this because a theatre contemporary of Freud's, similarly concerned with the covert springs of our behavior, developed the concept of subtext to direct actors toward the deepest impulses of dramatic character and action. This was, of course, Stanislavsky, the distinguished Russian actor and director. Devoted to the language of drama, he yet experienced what great theatre artists have always known: that the actors

> have to have recourse to a character's inner vision, thought, inner action. Words are part of the external embodiment of an inner essence of the role.[1]

There is some resistance in the British theatre to the so-called Stanislavsky method that has, in America, institutionalized for many actors, sometimes with an excess of self-indulgence, Stanislavsky's theories. But all of the many British actors I have spoken to have recognized that the actor, whether or not in concert with a director, must make interpretative choices—and the choices will ultimately depend on what Stanislavsky called the "inner vision" of the background, impulses, and ideas that motivate character.

Superficial comedies and shallow drama do not much challenge the actor's deeper penetration; they play on a level of interaction uncomplicated by the contradictions in human nature. Great drama deals largely with the distances between overt behavior and masked motivation, where the mystery of the self is explored to the very outer edge of its perceived world, and where some light is thrown into the vast darkness beyond. The vehicle of this exploration is the textual and subtextual whole conveyed by what the actor says and does—or does not say, not do. It may well be an axiom that the greater the drama, the more profound the subtextual element. And we may declare even more confidently that the master of subtext, in all its forms, was Shakespeare.

The simplest form of the instrument that he enjoyed was in the lighter comedies, where subtext can be a shared joke. The speaker, the listener to the speaker, and we the audience all have fun with it. One delightful early example comes in *Two Gentlemen of Verona*.[2] Lucetta has brought a letter to her mistress, Julia, from Proteus. Julia would dearly love to read the letter. She knows it. Lucetta knows it. We know it. Julia can't admit it. In so transparent a model as this, the character's pretext is a guarantee of subtext. Julia, to preserve her self-image of maidenly modesty, must pretend that she does not want the letter.

> Dare you presume to harbour wanton lines?
> . . . .
> There, take the paper: see it be returned,
> Or else return no more unto my sight.
>   (1.2.42; 1.2.46–47)

Lucetta leaves. Instantly Julia is full of regret. She describes subtext.

> And yet I would I had o'erlooked the letter:
> . . . .
> What fool is she that *knows* I am a *maid*
> And would not *force* the letter to my view!
> Since maids, in modesty, say "no" to that
> Which they would have the profferer construe "ay."
>   (1.2.50; 1.2.53–56; emphasis added)

Finally Julia yields and calls,

> Lucetta.

Lucetta, who has been waiting at the door for just this recall, pops in.

What would your ladyship? (1.2.66)

[Uh . . . uh . . . uh . . . uh . . .]—we seem to hear Julia fumbling for a pretext?—

Is it near dinner-time? (1.2.68)

Lucetta knows that time is wasting, drops the letter, and picks it up. Julia waits for it to be handed to her. Lucetta holds it.

> *Julia.*   [Uh] What is't that you
>   Took up so gingerly?
> *Lucetta.*   Nothing.
> *Julia.*   Why did'st thou stoop then?
> *Lucetta.* To take a paper up that I let fall.
> *Julia.* And is that paper nothing?
> *Lucetta.*   Nothing concerning me.
> *Julia.* Then let it lie . . . [Uh] . . . for those that it concerns.
>
> (1.2.68–73)

The tantalizing Lucetta holds on, and finally Julia, after failing to wheedle the letter from her, has to seize it. So we see her, in the theatre, wrenched between text and subtext, forcing herself to tear to scraps the letter she loves.

> [Stares down at it. Gestures Lucetta away without looking at her]
>   Here is a coil of protestation.
>   Go, get you gone, and let the papers lie.
>   You would be fingering them, to anger me.
>
> (1.2.96–98)

Lucetta hears between the lines.

>   . . . she would be best pleas'd
>   To be so angered with another letter.
>
> (1.2.99–100)

Nay, says Julia, after Lucetta leaves,

Would I were so ang'red with the same . . . (1.2.101)

and she kneels to rescue the dear scraps she has scattered: subtext in action.

In those comedies where mistaken identity dominates, subtext in both action and speech is common. *Twelfth Night* includes a good deal of double talk, as for instance when Viola-Caesario must resist Olivia's overtures of love—themselves at first subtextual—when we begin to see, without being told, that Olivia is succumbing. Shakespeare himself almost invents the words for the subtext here, as he takes care to stipulate that "text" may be formal, even rehearsed speech. Olivia asks Viola-Caesario, "Now sir, what is your text?" (1.5.219–220) and, as if looking beyond the words "Where lies your text?" (1.5.223). Then, when Viola seeks to see her face, "You are now out of your text" (1.5.232). Her own decorous text, meanwhile, is being betrayed by her subtext, expressed in visual imagery: as Viola later describes it:

> She made good view of me, indeed so much,
> That methought her eyes had lost her tongue,
> For she did speak in starts, distractedly. . . .
>
> (2.2.19–21)

Often, as here, we must search for clues to Shakespearean character in lines that come much later than the earlier scenes for which they are relevant. Shakespeare did not bother to write down these stage directions for his actors, since he could tell them what to do.

In the deeper comedies characters mistake their own identities as well as others'. The audience sometimes is in on the joke, as are some of the other characters in the cast. So Beatrice and Benedick prick each other with the kind of stabs that we recognize as an archetypal prelude to romantic consummation: we know long before the two lovers do how they regard each other; we recognize their taunts as masked declarations of love.

As comedy gets darker and moves toward the uncertainties of tragedy, the mystery of character deepens, and the subtext is subtler, more open to variable interpretation. Sometimes there are only slight clues, in the language and stipulated action, of the subterranean currents of behavior. There is, for instance, a surprising flash of self-exposure in Cressida that lights up, for a moment, an inwardness deeper than her expressed uncertainties over her relationships with men. It is when she first meets Troilus, and they discover their mutual love—Cressida suddenly feels the need to withdraw, to be alone. This girl, so mixed of guile and grace, of love and latitude, puzzled by her own motivations, and sensing the divisions in herself, says:

For this time will I take my leave, my lord. (3.2.139)

Troilus is astonished: all has gone so well.

Troilus. Your leave, sweet Cressid!
. . . .
  What offends you, lady?
Cressida. Sir, mine own company.
Troilus. You cannot shun yourself.
Cressida. Let me go and try.

(3.2.140, 144–47)

For the actor and the reader inhabiting Cressida's felt life, here is a clue to the shadows molding her native coquetry and those which will be forced upon her.

We search for similar cues to subtext in some of the momentary hints of character depth in the histories. In *Richard III,* we would wonder more at the seemingly conscienceless aggression of the vicious Richard and see his nightmare at the end as an unexpected aberration, if it were not for Anne's revelation, deep in the play, in act 4, scene 1. Anne says, sadly,

> For never yet one hour in his bed
> Did I enjoy the golden dew of sleep,
> But with his timorous dreams was still awak'd.

(4.1.82–84)

Here is the subtextual worm in Richard that we are to sense eating away at this apparently iron-fleshed man in his most triumphant moments.

There may be no words at all in crucial, ambiguous crises to cue us to the subtext of a pivotal action; we can only then relate it to the whole flow of the characterization and extrapolate the essential action. Think of that last scene in *Measure for Measure* (5.1.). The Duke calls Isabella a wretch and a liar before the people of Vienna and orders her, at line 12, to be taken to prison. She asks that Friar Lodowick be sent for; and for three hundred and more lines she is silent, except for three brief interruptions. Even after the Duke is revealed, he still makes her believe that her brother has been executed and asks her to make it her comfort that Claudio was happy in his death.

  I do, my Lord, (5.1.399)

she says. The only other time she speaks in this final scene is when Mariana begs her to plead for Angelo's life. She accedes (5.1.443–54).

So we come to the final bit. The Duke unmuffles Claudio, and without any apology for tricking Isabella, he asks for her hand. There is no textual response from her. The Duke turns to a final acerbic dialogue with Lucio, then again proposes to Isabella. Again no answer—except by subtextual gesture.

The conventional interpretation posits a happy ending: Isabella, speechless at the honor offered, nods, and the Duke carries her off. If she does accept, hers will be one of three imminent marriages: Lucio's with his whore, Mariana's with the man who betrayed her, and Isabella's with the man who had played those jokes on her. So unsavory does this seem that one critical gambit to explain Isabella's assumed acceptance has been that Shakespeare meant a mockery of the conventional happy ending to comedy.

What is the subtext? If character is to influence action—as in Shakespeare it so powerfully does—Isabella's decision will be extrapolated from what she has been. Does she feel so honored by the proposal that she forgets her novitiate as a nun, the Duke's deceptions practiced on her, his shaming her before the populace, and the agony of believing her brother dead? If the Duke's offer is at all attractive to her, then almost certainly at least some subtextual indecision will be felt between her own experience of the Duke and the chance to be his duchess—this at least would project the kind of complexity her character's careful development through four and a half acts deserves. In a paper to a Stratford meeting about a dozen years ago, imagining myself the male actor playing the role for Shakespeare, I could not see my Isabella, once so ready to enter a convent, so passionate in my convictions, so scarred by the deceptions and public humiliations visited on me by the Duke, happily accepting his offer. I did not see my playwright asking for that turnabout in character. I suppose another actor's Isabella might marry the Duke just to punish him; but mine would only stand there and be left alone as the crowd followed him out to his castle. What might remain ambiguous is whether I intended to resume a secular or a religious life. This nonacceptance interpretation has subsequently surfaced in a number of stagings, including some at Stratford. To mixed approval and blame.

At least *Measure for Measure* provides us with substantial, continuous character development leading up to a final, crucial interpretative choice. Elsewhere—I am thinking of *The Winter's Tale*—Shakespeare gives us almost no preparation for a pivotal character crisis. Leontes's first words hold no hint of the inner turbulence that must suddenly break into the open. Only a quick, compressed subtext can begin to orient us to his sudden storm. Are there any felt traces of residual jealousy? Sibling rivalry? Pervasive insecurity? Delayed maturity? Much depends on the genius of the actor to convey, as much by sheer subjective feeling as by subtle signals of voice and gesture, the springs of his fury. We grasp at the partial answers he provides—they can only be partial—to the old questions: How could he have done a thing like that? What possessed him to do it?

The mysteries of the self largely reveal and resolve themselves in the romances and happier comedies. If characters like Prospero and Malvolio are not entirely redigested into society, their very names give us some promise that they will at least endure in their name-assigned roles.

It is in the great tragedies that Shakespeare plucks most deeply at our mysteries and points further to the unplumbed depths left for us to explore. Into each of the major tragic characters is compressed an encompassing multiplicity of qualities and roles that shift and transform fluidly the character's interactions with others and with the inner self. I have used the metaphor "polyphony" to suggest changing emphases in the dynamic as one or more of the many character tones dominates and then recedes. The ground notes continue in counterpoint as the personae experience their best and worst, in youth and age, in peace and war, in private and public, in passion and reason, in sanity and madness. Shakespeare, who could say the most that could be said of this dynamic in words, was yet theatre artist enough to say much of what was most meaningful in it in silences, in gestures, in resonances of the verse and prose realized in accompanying physical imagery. Tragic experience is largely inward, and the inwardness is substantially a matter of subtext—of the buried life of which language and action are symbols.

In *Othello,* Iago corrupts Othello with evidently sincere manifestations of deep friendship. To Othello, Iago's pretenses spring from a loyal subtext, while we know it is a false one. We know something more: that behind Iago's conscious manipulation of his mask, a deeper subtext than he himself can comprehend drives him to his violences. He searches himself for his mystery, speculates on his motive:

I know not if't be true. . . . (1.3.388)

The relentless pressure from within to mangle all about him—rivals, gulls, superiors, men, women—twists him so much that, he says, it is like a poisonous mineral: it gnaws his innards. He seeks for reasons to take out on others the pain in his gut and casts about for motivation, while confessing,

I know not if't be true. . . .

Behind his secret plans for wrecking other lives, his passionate, convulsive subtext burdens him as much as he would burden others. We are never to know the deepmost sources of Iago's destructive—and self-destructive—energy; but we feel the heat of it.

Othello is more transparent. Iago, telling us privately how wicked he is, makes us sense the deeper evil; Othello, by informing all who hear of his goodness—

> my parts, my title, and my perfect soul
> Shall manifest me rightly
>
> (1.2.31–32)

—as much as assures us of a susceptibility to doom. We have learned to recognize the vulnerability of hubris. The seeds of Othello's insecurity are ultimately opaque; but in his seesaw between his dream of Desdemona's purity and the Iago-enforced illusion of her degradation, we get glimpses of the ricochet between the man and the beast that Shakespeare finds in all his heroes.

We experience one of the important manifestations of subtext from what has passed, in some of the tragedies, between consecutive appearances of a major character. *Macbeth,* short as it is, has gaps during which startling changes must have taken place in the two leading roles. The subtextual bridging of the gaps that must be achieved by the actor helps the spectator—and the imagining reader—to extrapolate the unobserved development. The actor Macready was noted for this, as one observer pointed out:

> Who does not feel, in reading Shakespeare, that the unwritten part of the character is a vastly larger part than the written? That there exist between the speeches vast intervals of passion? . . . It is this unwritten portion of the character which Mr. Macready gives us. His acting fills up these chasms, and is the complement of the worded part; he not merely tells us what Macbeth thought when he spoke, but shows us all he felt before he spoke.[3]

Shakespeare confronts Macbeth and his Lady with stage props, real or imagined, to intensify subtextual emotional conflicts on and off stage; and as in all the tragedies, the effects of their experiences may be understood from what the characters become by the end of the play.

Macbeth has stolen into Duncan's chamber with murder on his mind. The actor, until he returns, imaginatively endures the violence of the killing—Macready, offstage, stabbed fiercely at a stage wall—and then must stumble back, a different figure, conveying a shock from his unseen ordeal that will mark him for the rest of the play. Lady Macbeth's last scene, the sleepwalk, is stained with images of blood that explicitly trace back through a series of suppressed emotional traumas not revealed in her text. When Macbeth, after he has killed Duncan, refuses to take the bloody daggers back to the murder chamber, she takes them, in words that betray no uncertainty:

> Infirm of purpose!
> Give me the daggers. . . .
>
> (2.2.49–50)

She goes with them to gild the faces of the grooms with blood; and when she returns again, her words give no sign of the scare that she will later nurse while asleep. Verbally she seems only full of scorn for Macbeth's dismay:

> My hands are of your color; but I shame
> To wear a heart so white. . . .
>
> (2.2.61–62)

The words are iron-hard; but what of the subtext under them that will surface in the sleepwalk? Actresses, while showing their fiercest faces to Macbeth, have yet betrayed, subtextually, the felt horror of the moment when their fingers first closed on the bloody handles of those daggers; and they have returned from the chamber speaking the brave words about the color of their hands but unable to hide subtextually the effect of seeing how much blood the old man had in him. The sleepwalk becomes full of resonances of the earlier, masked wounds.

Subtext always flourishes when internal division in a character impels such anxiety that the very identity of the self is called into question. Lear is a primary example. Confused in his roles, he suffers a continuous turmoil of contending impulses: toward love and hate, toward power and dependence, toward reason and madness. Bewildered at finding himself divorced from his royal image of himself, he pretends to deny an identity that in fact will soon escape to lunacy:

> This is not Lear. Does Lear walk thus? Speak thus?
> . . . .
> Who is it that can tell me who I am?
>
> (1.4.226, 230)

Not Lear; and he only earns glimpses of the thing itself very late in the play. Lear's career turns on a critical moment that depends on subtext for its meaning. The first scene: Goneril and Regan have told Lear how much they love him. Cordelia's turn. *What can you say to draw / A third more opulent than your sisters?* (1.1.85–86; emphasis added). Nothing. And again, nothing. And, pressed for a tender word, she cannot utter one; instead she offers him love according to her bond, no more nor less. We know, from her later behavior, that she truly loves her father, but something prevents her from openly expressing warmth, even from calling him "father" except when he is asleep. Why cannot she—or will not she—speak her love now? Various interpretations have been offered; what concerns me here is how she can convey, subtextually, her deep love masked in the decision to instruct him in his folly, or to shame her sisters, or to make him feel foolish, or simply to sulk—or possibly all of these, perhaps more. It is one of the most difficult challenges for an actress to undertake.

Later Edgar faces a similar challenge when he meets his cruelly blinded father, who begs, as Lear did, for a gentle acknowledgment from his wronged child. Edgar also, we come to know, is the "good" son: he, like Cordelia, does, briefly, rescue his father; but when blind Gloster cries,

> . . . O dear son Edgar,
> Might I but live to see thee in my touch . . .
> I'ld say I had eyes again,
>
> (4.1.21–22, 24)

like Cordelia, Edgar withholds the benison of love. Until—*O fault!* he will say—it is too late. What complex of feelings must nerve the subtext as he denies his father comfort: love, resentment, pity, the impulse to punish, inexplicable inhibitions—all coated in his pretext of curing his father of despair—which of course he does not? Not words, but face, body, and voice must convey his mix of motives.

The ultimate mystery of the self in drama is, of course, encased in Hamlet. Consequently, his play is most dependent on subtext. We know from his surfaces only flittingly what he might be, and while his soliloquies reveal more of him, they also deepen his mystery. His reality is filtered through so many of the purposes and cross-purposes of the human under pressure, shocked by traumatic circumstances in his immediate family and in his society, impelled mysteriously to an act of violence not congenial to his nature, surrounded by people hostile, disloyal, predatory. To protect himself, he plays roles, and roles within roles, and while moving among them he tries to locate himself. He asks the questions we ask of our own subtexts: How can I behave like this . . .? What can I be thinking of . . .? What has possessed me . . .?

Every solitary introspection, every relation with others, resonates with the clustering, polyphonic pressures on and within him. And these must be conveyed largely subtextually. So A. C. Bradley, no great enthusiast for the theatre, turned to it for the meanings of Hamlet's ambiguous treatment of Ophelia in the nunnery scene that baffled the learned scholar's analysis. There are so many questions: does Hamlet indeed love Ophelia, or not? Is he playing primarily to the eavesdroppers behind the arras, or to her? Does he urge her to a nunnery out of caring, or anger? Is he pretending madness, or partly experiencing it? Does he abhor all women, or grieve for their frailty? Is he lost in a dark mood? Only subtext, Bradley seems to be saying, could begin to tell us.

If we could see a contemporary representation of *Hamlet* (in Shakespeare's time) our doubts would probably disappear. The actor, instructed by the author, would make it clear to us by looks, tones, gestures, and byplay, how far Hamlet's feigned harshness to Ophelia was mingled with real bitterness, and again how far his melancholy had deadened his love.[4]

Not only Hamlet moves through the play with unspoken secrets. Claudius twice reveals in words the inner divisions that Shakespeare surely intended to be subtextual undertones throughout. Ophelia, like Lady Macbeth, moves from normality toward an irrationality full of echoes of the past. Here, too, actresses have differed on when the murmur of unease would first sound under the social mask, and how subtextually it would grow before the madness came. When does her objective become madness, when suicide?

Gertrude, too, betrays flashes of inwardness that insist on subtextual effect. Shallow as she is sometimes said to be, she yet discovers startling sensitivities. There was a striking hint of this in the *Hamlet* at Stratford in 1980, directed by John Barton. In the closet scene, Hamlet—Michael Pennington—was berating his mother—Barbara Leigh-Hunt—for her attachment to Claudius, that king of shreds and patches. Suddenly Gertrude stiffened, as if an inner antenna was vibrating to some uncanny signal. Her eyes widened in terror. As the ghost appeared, and began to speak, she clasped her hands over her ears, her terror increasing. Hamlet tried to make her admit that she heard or saw the ghost, but she denied it with increasing hysteria until he finally forced her face around to where it stood—whereupon she fainted. Her faint covered Hamlet's lines for the ghost's exit. When she recovered, she continued to insist, textually, that the appearance was the coinage of Hamlet's brain—but with such intensity as to suggest her desperate fear of admitting awareness. She was playing against her lines; but later she found warranty for her subtextual experience when, in the next scene, she said to Claudius, with a shudder,

What have I seen tonight! (4.1.5)

There were shivers in the audience, too. And disapproval among some spectators. Was this an insight into Shakespeare's meanings? Did it point to a subtext, an objective, for the Queen throughout the play? Might the mother share with the son a capacity to vibrate to the supernatural? Or was this an excessive extrapolation, a route to the wrong text?

So actors help scholars explore the deep rifts of gold in Shakespeare's characters—the subtexts. It means taking risks: but so do all enterprises of great pitch and moment.

* * *

I am at present collecting manifestations of subtext in *Hamlet:* any moments of stage business by actors that reveal the motivations of the main characters, any gestures that illuminate Shakespeare's characterization. I will be grateful if any colleagues remembering instances of this kind will let me know of them.

Notes

1. Constantin Stanislavsky, *An Actor's Handbook,* trans. Elizabeth Reynolds Hapgood (New York: Theatre Arts Books, 1963), 136–37. See also his *Building a Character,* trans. Elizabeth Reynolds Hapgood (New York: Theatre Arts Books, 1949); and *Creating a Role,* trans. Elizabeth Reynolds Hapgood (New York: Theatre Arts Books, 1961) for related aspects of this approach.

2. Line reference of quotations from Shakespeare's plays are to *The Riverside Shakespeare,* ed. G. Blakemore Evans (Boston: Houghton Mifflin, 1974).

3. Marvin Rosenberg, *The Masks of Macbeth* (Berkeley: The University of California Press, 1973), 61.

4. A. C. Bradley, *Shakespearean Tragedy* (London: Macmillan, 1956), 131.

Performer and Role in Marlowe and Shakespeare

MICHAEL GOLDMAN

Attempts to compare Marlowe's characters with Shakespeare's have usually focused on theme and language and assumed that where ideas and imagery coincide—when Aaron talks like Barabas, say, or the Guise like Richard III—the theatrical effects achieved will be very similar or stand in some simple relation, like parody. In drama, however, characterization is not just something to be performed; it *is* performance. In the theatre, characterization is felt, not as a static array of qualities, a set of attributes, but as a process continually flowing between the person on stage and the objects and persons around him, including the audience in the theatre. It will be deeply affected by our sense of the relation between the actor and the role he is playing or between the character the actor plays and *his* role in the world of the play. In this essay, I want to sketch—very broadly and provisionally—some contrasts in the kinds of performance Marlowe and Shakespeare seem to imagine for their major characters.

My comments are, inevitably, general. They are attempts to open up some areas of difference that strike me as suggestive, but I am aware that such descriptions tend to oversimplify and that the most valuable analysis must look much more closely than I will be able to do here at the structure of individual plays and at their integration of many elements, rather than the few I single out. I should point out, too, that the distinctions I shall be making among Marlowe, Shakespeare, and other dramatists are not absolute but ones of emphasis. So the observations that follow are in several ways only parts of a picture, and I hope they will be accepted in that spirit.

A comparison of performance modes is particularly helpful in understanding Marlowe, because he has suffered from our very natural assumption that his histrionic methods are similar to Shakespeare's. We can begin to get a sense of how different they actually are by focusing on the way Marlowe's major parts generate what a modern director would call subtext—the felt presence of something added by the actor both to and through the text. The term "subtext" originates with Stanislavsky, of course, but subtextual life, performance life, has always been a necessary part of theatrical writing, indeed perhaps its defining component.

Let me start by making a connection between a fairly well-recognized point about Marlowe's heroes and its subtextual embodiment. Standard Stanislavskian analysis breaks up roles into objectives and superobjectives. Thus a superobjective for Mrs. Alving in *Ghosts* might be, in Francis Fergusson's phrase from *The Idea of a Theater,* "To control the Alving inheritance for my own purposes," while nested within it might be objectives like "To jolly Pastor Manders around" or "To explain to Oswald what his father was like." Although Elizabethan parts cannot fairly be reduced to motivational terms, still there are many such motivational subtexts in Elizabethan drama. In *Hamlet,* objectives like "To make the Ghost speak to me" or "To make amends to Laertes" nest within a superobjective like Fergusson's "To identify and root out the source of the disease in Denmark." Now, in Shakespeare as in Ibsen, the superobjective tends moment by moment to coalesce into its local objectives, which often quite make us forget the superobjective at the local instant. But for the Marlovian hero, it seems more accurate to talk of a *magical* objective rather than a superobjective, a larger project that overshadows the local objective, indeed tends to blot it from sight, as the general thirst for supremacy magically beckons to Tamburlaine and entirely overshadows any particular conquest or crown. This is simply the histrionic correlative of a peculiarly Marlovian version of desire that has often been commented on. Here we need merely note the subtextual difference it makes and how its presence as subtext allows us to feel the hero pulling tremendous energy into himself by invoking the magical objective.

Closely related to this is another general characteristic of Marlowe's dramaturgy, which has received less attention. Where many Elizabethan heroes seem driven by an urge to self-presentation, self-conscious dramatization of their characters for an audience, either on stage or in the theatre, Marlowe's heroes are appropriately described as driven to what might be called self-conjuration. Richard III, for example, may seem Marlovian in his hyperbolic self-definition, but with him we have the sense of a very definite character, speaking from well inside himself, who enjoys displaying his personality to the audience. Tamburlaine, by contrast, while he also enjoys playing before audiences, seems far more inclined to discover and assemble the elements of self-definition, to attempt to produce himself at each instant, to call himself into being. When he refers to himself—frequently by name—and to objects and people around him, he sounds like an actor trying to make the notion of Tamburlaine "happen" in the theatre:

> Lie here, ye weeds that I disdain to wear!
> This complete armor and this curtle-axe
> Are adjuncts more beseeming Tamburlaine.
>
> (*2 Tamburlaine,* 1.2.41–43)[1]

or

> Think you I weigh this treasure more than you?
> Zenocrate, lovelier than the love of Jove,
> Brighter than is the silver Rhodope,
> Fairer than whitest snow on Scythian hills,
> Thy person is worth more to Tamburlaine
> Than the possession of the Persian crown.
>
> (84–91)

Here the name "Tamburlaine," the heaps of treasure on stage, Zenocrate, her name, and the geographical images are all annexed in gestures of self-manifestation. The thrust of the speech is not *let me tell you something about myself,* but *watch me make "Tamburlaine" appear.*

Let me suggest another way of looking at this process of self-conjuration. All acting roles have a quality we may call iconic—they give the impression of a fixed or masklike definition. We feel we are watching a figure that, although animated, is yet a type or effigy. It's through the interplay between the iconic and the animate, between mask and face, that drama is able to deploy some of the uncanniness associated with acting itself. So we may think of the actor's task as both projecting an icon and filling it with life. Now, Marlowe seems frequently to work by asking that his actor first give us an icon and then animate it in a way which revises it or breaks it open by a kind of fanatic energy. Thus Barabas is first the greedy Jewish merchant absorbed in fingering his coins:

> So that of thus much that return was made
> And of the third part of the Persian ships . . .
>
> (1.1.1–2)

and then, suddenly gripped by his magical objective, he breaks open the tight iconic silhouette:

> Fie, what a trouble 'tis to count this trash!
> . . . .
> Give me the merchants of the Indian mines
> That trade in metal of the purest mold.
>
> (7, 19–20)

and so on to "Infinite riches in a little room." We are made sharply aware of the actor both activating an icon and altering it.

It helps to keep in mind the distinction between self-presentation and self-conjuration when we read, for example, the first speech of the Guise in *The Massacre at Paris.* This passage is easy to underrate if we see it as a kind of mediocre version of self-presentation along the lines of *Richard III*

or the iconic definition of Machiavelli in *The Jew of Malta,* whose prologue is, indeed, an example of self-presentation. But in the *Massacre,* the
Guise begins with Faustus-like self-address and moves to some Tambur-
lainean annexation:

> Now, Guise, begins those deep-engendered thoughts
> To burst abroad those never-dying flames
> Which cannot be extinguished but by blood.
>
> (2.34–36)

Now, it's true that in parts of his speech, the Guise does proceed in the
vein of a Richard or Machiavelli:

> Set me to scale the high pyramides
> And thereon set the diadem of France
> I'll either rend it with my nails to naught
> Or mount the top with my aspiring wings,
>
> (43–46)

although here we may note a characteristic instability with respect to the
objective—he seems equally ready to grasp the crown or render it
"naught." And even at this moment there is a tendency to dwell on details
that suggest a turn inward into the actor's equipment in an attempt to
conjure a self into being:

> For this I wake, when others think I sleep,
>
> . . . .
> For this, this head, this heart, this hand, and sword
> Contrives, imagines, and fully executes
> Matters of import aimed at by many,
> Yet understood by none.
>
> (48, 52–55)

The half lines scattered through the speech seem to accent this turn into
the self, which breaks not only the mode of self-presentation but the icon
of the Machiavel, as we watch an actor summoning up the very attributes
that he hopes will constitute his part:

> Give me a look that, when I bend the brows,
> Pale death may walk in furrows of my face,
> A hand that with a grasp may gripe the world,
> An ear to hear what my detractors say,
> A royal seat, a scepter, and a crown,
> That those which do behold, they may become
> As men that stand and gaze against the sun.
>
> (102–8)

The Marlovian actor needs a quality of what I've elsewhere called
abandon, a readiness to open himself headlong to his character's desires,

the unlocking of his mind and body to what has ravished him. Historically, any such impression of abandon would have been reinforced by the particular use Marlowe makes of what his contemporaries would have seen as the transgressive aspect of acting itself. Transgressive role playing is, of course, common in some degree to all Elizabethan drama including Shakespeare, but Marlowe foregrounds it. He draws our attention to it (1) because the process of self-conjuration is so conspicuously *actorly* and (2) because in Marlowe it is also disturbingly transgressive at the level of theme.

In a sense, the Marlovian hero is presented as an actor looking for his great role, restlessly testing and discarding gestures, stances, props, tones of voice and by these means boldly and ceaselessly attempting to make himself appear. "Lie there, ye weeds that I disdain to wear," says Tamburlaine. And Dr. Faustus from the first is rushing through the attributes of several careers, summoning them up only to discard them. In his first scene, Gaveston rehearses rapidly the different styles available to the role of favorite, dropping them until he is performing all the roles in a play-(within his mind) within-the-play—Dian played by a naked boy, Actaeon gazing at the scene, and the hounds tearing Actaeon apart—thus pulling into one speech, and into one passage of playing, the whole career of the drama to follow.

This process heightens or makes more necessary the sense of abandon in performance. That is, Marlovian performance requires that the actor constantly *try on* his gestures of self-creation, and make them work in the context of trying them on, rather than hiding behind them. It might be noted for contrast that Shakespearean heroes often begin their plays by refusing this type of revelation, either by rejecting a role that is offered to them—particularly a role which offers an entry into the play's action—or by insisting on a role that muffles them up. We think of Viola taking on a disguise to bide her time, of Hal dropping his loose behavior only long enough to tell us he isn't ready to drop it yet and will continue to smother up his beauty from the world, of Hamlet in his inky cloak holding his tongue, holding back from the engagement the Ghost will force upon him, rejecting even the inky cloak as a mere role, like all roles unreal. Like Hamlet, many of Shakespeare's tragic heroes seem to have an initial suspicion of theatre. Like Macbeth, they resist being dressed in borrowed robes. Later, of course, they discover they cannot avoid being implicated in theatrical modes. But the Marlovian hero from the very start embraces theatricality in a doubly emphatic way. He seems to want to abandon the role in which we discover him—to expand it, question it, push it this way and that, in order to find and manifest his real role.

When I try to put these observations together and think of what they may imply for Marlovian heroic performance style in general, the impression I get is of a subtle version of the alienation effect, a kind of passionate presenting of the materials of performance simultaneously with the content of performance. The passion is in the abandon—and again it is a double kind of abandon. There is abandon on the level of character: the opening of the actor to the desires and experience of Tamburlaine or Faustus; but of at least equal power and risk must be the actor's abandon on the level of performance, the stress on nakedly conjuring a role into life. With a gesture that is hypnotic but also a gesture, the actor offers to the audience the icon he is creating. The icon is tempting and terrifying, and the actor fully enters into its allure. But he is also tensely aware of his accomplishment as he conjures the icon into place, aware that it only exists, moment by moment, by virtue of such conjuring—and he must project and use this awareness as a means of capturing us.

> And see, my lord, a sight of strange import,
> Emperors and kings lie breathless at my feet.
> The Turk and his great empress, as it seems,
> Left to themselves while we were at the fight,
> Have desperately dispatched their slavish lives;
> With them Arabia too hath left his life;
> All sights of power to grace my victory.
> And such are objects fit for Tamburlaine,
> Wherein, as in a mirror, may be seen
> His honor that consists in shedding blood
> When men presume to manage arms with him.
>   (1 Tamburlaine, 5.2.405–15)

Here the actor works on us and on himself—on one level by entering into the mind of a conqueror who can draw a flooding sense of pleasure and power from the sight of his dead victims, but also by showing us Tamburlaine creating his identity through conjuring with these bodies, literally seeing his honor in them as in a mirror. This type of self-projection, familiar in the role, makes us aware of the actor sustaining his oversize part by a series of theatrical gestures. Our heightened awareness of the actor's process, although it may alienate us from the character of Tamburlaine in the sense that it makes us aware of Tamburlaine as a produced illusion—relatively more aware than we are in the case, say, of Richard III or Hamlet—does not diminish our involvement with Tamburlaine as Marlowe conceives him, because the actor's process, if it masters the text, gives us Tamburlaine as precisely this annexation of attributes into an assertion of self. This is the self that can so define itself, that can harness the mighty line.

A similar effect can be felt in "How I am glutted with conceit of this!" where Faustus, as so often, seems to be urging his own identity into existence by describing his experience of his own desire. And when we talk of Faustus's identity, we are aware of a role created by augmenting and sloughing off other roles. This is not Johannes Faustus, the old scholar of Wittenberg. Rather, this is what Johannes Faustus became or tried to become, the archetypal pursuer of forbidden knowledge. The actor gives us Faustus's abandonment to the appeal of magic by opening up to us the gesture by which, at this moment, the character is created. And indeed Faustus continues after this line in a speech that breathlessly seems to try on a series of gestures, possible versions of the role of magician, seems in a Brechtian sense to "quote" them as a way of making real the new identity he is rushing to possess:

> Shall I make spirits fetch me what I please,
> Resolve me of all ambiguities,
> Perform what desperate enterprise I will?
> I'll have them fly to India for gold,
> Ransack the ocean for orient pearl,
> And search all corners of the new-found world
> For pleasant fruits and princely delicates.
> I'll have them read me strange philosophy
> And tell the secrets of all foreign kings;
> I'll have them wall all Germany with brass. . . .
>
> (1.1.80–89)

Comparison with Shakespeare will help highlight the features of Marlovian performance we have been examining. Let me cite three examples.

1. Richard's great speech in *3 Henry VI,* where he suddenly emerges as a new Shakespearean creation, exhibits many Marlovian qualities, notably a quick survey of roles or gestures in the mode of Faustus. But where Faustus seems always to be trying on possibilities he hopes will prove satisfying or substantial, Richard is confidently relishing a capacity he knows he has. His survey issues from a self-possessed center of consciousness:

> Why, I can smile, and murder whiles I smile,
> And cry, "Content" to that which grieves my heart,
> And wet my cheeks with artificial tears,
> And frame my face to all occasions.
> I'll drown more sailors than the mermaid shall;
> I'll slay more gazers than the basilisk;
> I'll play the orator as well as Nestor. . . .
>
> (3.2.182–88)[2]

Richard is not conjuring up a series of attributes or gestures to fill a void. He is enjoying the sensation of his capabilities.

2. Aaron and Barabas are frequently compared, and of course they have two speeches that famously sound alike:

Aaron. Even now I curse the day—and yet, I think
Few come within the compass of my curse—
Wherein I did not some notorious ill:
As kill a man or else devise his death,
Ravish a maid or plot the way to do it,
Accuse some innocent and forswear myself,
Set deadly enmity between two friends,
Make poor men's cattle break their necks;

. . . .
Oft have I digged up dead men from their graves
And set them upright at their dear friends' door,

. . . .
And nothing grieves me heartily indeed,
But that I cannot do ten thousand more.
                    (*Titus Andronicus,* 5.1.125–32, 135–36, 143–44)

Barabas. As for myself, I walk abroad 'a nights
And kill sick people groaning under walls.
Sometimes I go about and poison wells.

. . . .
Being young, I studied physic and began
To practice first upon the Italian;
There I enriched the priests with burials
And always kept the sexton's arms in ure
With digging graves and ringing dead men's knells.

. . . .
But mark how I am blest for plaguing them:
I have as much coin as will buy the town.
                    (*Jew of Malta,* 2.3.171–73, 178–82, 196–97)

But even at this moment of closest approximation, the two characters are very different in their dominant mode of self-performance. Aaron describes his wicked career to taunt Lucius, while Barabas invokes a similar past to make himself present to Ithamore, to heap up a character as he has heaped up coin and jewels at the play's beginning. Indeed, he makes it clear earlier in the scene that his aim is to teach Ithamore a role he wants him to play. Aaron stands inside the figure he presents to the world, using it to torment his enemy, while Barabas seems, as so often, to be standing beside himself, showing Ithamore how the great Jew-of-Malta puppet works. At the end of his life, Barabas, like Aaron, will curse his enemies with his dying words, but these too are at least as much an attempt to conjure up a reality the speaker calls "Barabas" as to gall his tormentors:

        Then, Barabas, breathe forth thy latest fate,
        And in the fury of thy torments strive
        To end thy life with resolution.

Know, governor, 'twas I that slew thy son.
I framed the challenge that did make them meet.
Know, Calymath, I aimed thy overthrow,
And had I but escaped this strategem,
I would have brought confusion on you all,
Damned Christians, dogs, and Turkish infidels!
But now begins the extremity of heat
To pinch me with intolerable pangs.
Die, life! Fly, soul! Tongue, curse thy fill, and die!

(5.5.78–89)

Of course, part of Barabas's drive here is to cause pain, and part is simply to express his own physical anguish. But there is also a slightly distanced or anxious relation to his own presence, a need to realize both his villainy and his pain by spectacular performance.

3. My last example is a moment when Shakespeare actually uses a Marlovian performance mode. When York returns from Ireland to claim the throne in *2 Henry VI,* he enters with a short speech whose Marlovian imagery has been noted by many commentators:

From Ireland thus comes York to claim his right,
And pluck the crown from feeble Henry's head.
Ring, bells, aloud; burn, bonfires, clear and bright,
To entertain great England's lawful king.
Ah, sancta majestas! Who would not buy thee dear?
Let them obey that knows not how to rule;
This hand was made to handle nought but gold.
I cannot give due action to my words,
Except a sword or scepter balance it:
A scepter shall it have, have I a soul,
On which I'll toss the fleur-de-luce of France.

(5.1.1–11)

What is most interesting here is that York does not sound like his old self, even though he is pursuing his most frequently stated ambition and is as arrogant as ever. There is a new, strident, forced quality—as of a man trying to assure himself that he *can* play the role of king. York is not dissembling now, but he seems to insist too much that he is royal and to support his claim by an inventory of gestures and postures. It is significant that Shakespeare introduces this self-conjuring style at the moment when York makes his intentions public. He becomes Marlovian when he transgresses.

Up to this point, I've treated Shakespeare largely as a kind of normative contrast to Marlowe's histrionic methods. And it's true that where Marlowe tends toward a version of the alienation effect, Shakespeare follows

the more familiar pattern of an "Aristotelian" subtext. Certainly there is at
least as much emotional identification between actor and role in Shakespeare as in any of his contemporaries. But although such broad cate-
gorizations are useful, they obscure the fact that subtextual processes vary
significantly from playwright to playwright and even from role to role, a
point of potential importance for dramatic scholarship. Let me proceed,
then, to suggest some distinctive features of the actor-role relation in
Shakespeare.

By comparison with Marlowe, the relation in Shakespeare is felt more
typically as a gap between *character* and role. Such gaps are of course
common in drama—for instance in situations calling for deceit or disguise—but in Shakespeare the relation can be much subtler. Its quality is
manifest in characters like Hal and Richard III, who are actors conscious
of the roles they wish or are compelled to play. What is most Shakespearean here and in many other parts in the canon is a kind of contemplation of the role from within, the creation of a space of awareness
even in the midst of engagement.

This distance is no guarantee of self-knowledge or self-possession. Lear,
for example, has it, though he but slenderly knows himself. He is always
aware of performing, sanely or madly, as king or father or weak old man.
Hamlet, even in moments of immense agitation, is aware both of his
passion and of the show he makes as a player of his passion. Inside
Macbeth there is someone who keeps raptly examining the fact that
Macbeth is an imaginer of murder, a desirer of murder, a murderer. It
bewilders him; he can never adjust to it—but we are aware both of the man
with the murderous imagination and of an inner presence watching this
imagination wash over Macbeth's mind.

Thus Shakespeare's major characters seem frequently to be imagined as
presences separate from, though deeply inside, their roles, and both role
and presence enter into the dynamic of performance. Marlowe's characters are typically imagined as roles built up out of nothing that have to be
maintained or renewed at every instant by the efforts of the actor.

In the course of Shakespeare's development, there is an increasingly
complex sense of how the iconic is embedded in the world of play. It
becomes something seen by the other characters, of which the character
who is speaking is aware in a way that is separate from his or her iconic
presentation. It is part of the speaker's relation to the other characters and
not simply part of the relation between the character and the theatre
audience.

A corollary of this, especially after 1600, is the complexity of relation
Shakespeare's speeches often exhibit to their multiple audiences, both
onstage and off. It is as if the presence within the role were turning around

inside it, glancing through it at the different figures that surround it. The effect may be felt in the liveliness of a speech like Antony's

> Let Rome in Tiber melt, and the wide arch
> Of the ranged empire fall! Here is my space,
> Kingdoms are clay: our dungy earth alike
> Feeds beast as man. The nobleness of life
> Is to do thus; when such a mutual pair
> And such a twain can do't, in which I bind,
> On pain of punishment, the world to weet
> We stand up peerless.

(1.1.33–40)

The suppleness and vigor of these lines, the sense they convey of strength, alertness, even brilliance, as well as self-indulgence, flows in large measure from the way their language is taking on a variety of audiences—the Egyptian court, the Roman messengers, Roman "public opinion," Antony's own men, Cleopatra both as a lover to be wooed and a disputant to be parried, and history itself, of which we in the theatre audience are tentatively casting ourselves as representatives. There is a different ring for each of these audiences in "When such a mutual pair / And such a twain can do't," and the merely literary ambiguities of *binding the world on pain of punishment* are as nothing to the vibrations set up in performance by the different layers of address implicit in this language. In a single phrase, Antony can both make fun of his role as world commander and use his detached ease within that role to command it still.

With these features of Shakespearean characterization, we reach a convenient place to end our discussion, for they begin to draw us away from the comparison with Marlowe. From this point on, it would likely prove more valuable to follow separately each playwright's treatment of the performer-role-audience relation. It might be helpful, for example, to trace how Shakespeare develops a style of civic utterance whereby we hear the character not only performing publicly but drawing on a private self to achieve that performance; within his public voice, we hear a personal voice carefully tuned to public cadences. (Titus and the King of Navarre don't have it; Theseus and Henry IV do.) And in Marlowe's case, once the similarities among his great roles have been noticed, it becomes more important to explore the differences. Each of his major characters, for example, possesses a distinctive style of self-conjuration, and it would seem worthwhile to go on to discriminate among them without further reference to Shakespeare.

At least one practical theatrical conclusion, however, can be drawn from our comparison as it stands. Marlowe will not be done justice by any method of acting that relies purely on the Shakespearean tradition. He is not to be understood simply as a dramatist with a narrower range than Shakespeare or one who died before he could develop his great competitor's mature ability. He was the master of a substantially different performance style, and if we do not find a way to realize this style *in* performance, what we are playing will not be Marlowe.

Notes

1. Line references to quotations from Marlowe's plays are to *The Complete Plays of Christopher Marlowe,* ed. Irving Ribner (New York: The Odyssey Press, 1963).

2. Line references to quotations from Shakespeare's plays are to *The Complete Signet Classic Shakespeare,* ed. Sylvan Barnet (New York: Harcourt Brace Jovanovich, 1972).

Egeus and the Implications of Silence

PHILIP C. McGUIRE

One way to glimpse what the future might hold for performance-centered criticism of Shakespeare's plays is to ponder the challenges posed by a silence that occurs in act 4, scene 1 of *A Midsummer Night's Dream,* soon after Duke Theseus and his hunting party find the four young lovers asleep on the forest ground following their baffling experiences of the night before. Lysander, "Half sleep, half waking" (4.1.146),[1] begins to explain that he and Hermia were fleeing "the peril of the Athenian law" (152) that sentences Hermia to death or to a life of perpetual chastity if she persists in refusing to marry the man her father has chosen to be her husband. Egeus, Hermia's father, interrupts, fiercely calling upon Theseus to apply the law most rigorously: "Enough, enough, my lord! you have enough. / I beg the law, the law, upon his head" (153–54).

During act 1, Theseus had warned Hermia that "the law of Athens" was something "Which by no means we may extenuate" (1.1.119–20). Now, however, after hearing Demetrius, Egeus's choice to be Hermia's husband, explain that his love for Hermia has "Melted" (4.1.165) away, Theseus proceeds to set aside the very law upholding an Athenian father's right to "dispose" (1.1.42) of his daughter that he had earlier declared himself powerless to "extenuate." Theseus declares,

> Egeus, I will overbear your will,
> For in the temple, by and by, with us,
> These couples shall eternally be knit. . . .
>
> (4.1.178–80)

What is Egeus's response to Theseus's decision to disregard not only his will but also Athenian law? In both the Quarto of 1600 and the Folio of 1623—the two texts of *A Midsummer Night's Dream* surviving from Shakespeare's time that are considered independently authoritative[2]—Egeus says nothing. The agreement between Quarto and Folio gives us as much certainty as we can get that Egeus's silence is an authentic feature of *A Midsummer Night's Dream,* but probing that silence in an effort to determine its specific meaning(s) and effect(s) brings us face-to-face with bedeviling uncertainties.

Evidence from Shakespeare's era prevents us from assuming that Egeus's silence is in and of itself definitive evidence that he withholds assent to a wedding that Theseus will no longer allow him to prevent. The marriage ritual set down in the 1559 *Book of Common Prayer*—like many of the rituals observed these days—specified functions for the bride's father that he is to carry out in silence. After bringing his daughter to the altar, the father "stands by in mute testimony that there are no impediments to the marriage."[3] A logical response to the question "Who giveth this woman to be married to this man?" is for the bride's father to say "I do," but the response the ritual calls for him to make is nonverbal; he is to relinquish his daughter without speaking. However, since what happens in act 4 is not a marriage ceremony, we cannot take evidence of the kind provided by the 1559 *Book of Common Prayer* as certain proof that Egeus's silence establishes his consent.

Recent productions of *A Midsummer Night's Dream* demonstrate the range of alternative meanings and effects that can emerge from Egeus's silence. In Richard Cottrell's 1980 production for the Bristol Old Vic Company, Egeus said nothing after hearing Theseus "overbear" his will, but before exiting with Theseus, Hippolyta, and their attendants, Egeus embraced Hermia. In an act that suggested the traditional wedding ceremony, Egeus then relinquished his paternal authority by placing his daughter's hand in Lysander's. With that action he gave Hermia to the man whom he had earlier denounced before Theseus for having "filched my daughter's heart, / Turned her obedience (which is due to me) / To stubborn harshness" (1.1.36–38). The Egeus of that production was a father who had come to accept without reservation the combination of ducal authority and erotic attraction that was soon to make his daughter Lysander's wife.

Elijah Moshinsky's 1981 production for the BBC-TV/New York Life series "The Shakespeare Plays" enacted alternatives that are different but equally consistent with the silence that the Quarto and the Folio assign to Egeus. After hearing Theseus's words authorizing her marriage to Lysander, Hermia moved to her father and they embraced. The reconciliation implicit in those gestures took on an added dimension when, before exiting, Egeus kissed his daughter's hand. In the opening scene, Theseus had warned Hermia "To fit your fancies to your father's will" (1.1.118). By kissing Hermia's hand, the Egeus of Moshinsky's production conveyed that he would now "fit" *his* will not only to the duke's authority but also to his daughter's "fancies."

In Celia Brannerman's 1980 production for the New Shakespeare Company at the Open Air Theatre in Regent's Park, London, Egeus, in his silence, submitted obediently but without any enthusiasm to Theseus's dictate. Egeus did not move to embrace Hermia after hearing Theseus declare, "Egeus, I will overbear your will." He did allow Hippolyta to take his hand in a comforting gesture that also implied that he would remain a valued member of Athenian court. Egeus exited with Theseus and Hippolyta, but there was no reconciliation between father and daughter, and Hermia's father did not acknowledge her husband-to-be.

The most acclaimed of recent productions of *A Midsummer Night's Dream*—Peter Brook's for the Royal Shakespeare Company in the early 1970s—enacted possibilities radically different from those already described.[4] When Theseus finished announcing ". . . by and by, with us, / These couples shall eternally be knit," Egeus stepped from where he had been standing between Theseus and Hippolyta and strode toward the exit downstage right. He paused briefly, even expectantly, as he heard Theseus begin to speak again—"And, for the morning now is something overworn" (181). Once it was clear, however, that Theseus was simply announcing the cancellation of the hunting, Egeus continued to make his departure. Before Theseus could call, "Away, with us to Athens" (183), Egeus was gone, leaving through an exit different from the one used moments later, first by Theseus and Hippolyta and then by the four lovers as they returned "to Athens." In the specific context established by that production, Theseus's words "Three and three, / We'll hold a feast in great solemnity" (183–84) registered the fact that "Three and three" did not include Egeus. The exit that Egeus made in Brook's production established that he was withdrawing from Athenian society.

The standard tactic for discriminating among alternatives such as those acted out in the four productions I have cited, for deciding which is "right" and which "wrong," which honors Shakespeare's intentions and which violates them, is to scrutinize the words of the play for evidence of what Shakespeare himself intended. When we look to those words, however, we find that neither the Folio nor the Quarto gives information of the caliber we need. Because each gives Egeus nothing to say, there are no words of his to scrutinize. The stage directions in the Quarto and the Folio are also of limited utility. They give no precise sense of how the silent Egeus makes his exit, and they help to drive home how little the words others speak reveal about Egeus's response to Theseus's decision authorizing Hermia's marriage to Lysander.

The Folio specifically requires that Egeus enter in act 4, scene 1 with Theseus: *"Enter Theseus, Egeus, Hippolita and all his traine."*[5] The stage direction for the exit to be made after Theseus overrules Egeus is less precise: *"Exit Duke and Lords."* There is, perhaps significantly, no specific mention of Egeus. Egeus could be one of those *"Lords"* who exit with Theseus—as happened in Elijah Moshinsky's 1981 production for BBC-TV. In such a case, Egeus remains a member of Athenian society, whether or not he accepts Hermia's marriage to Lysander.

However, nothing in the Folio *requires* that Egeus departs with Theseus. By first specifically including Egeus among those who enter with Theseus and by then not specifically listing him as one of those who leave with Theseus, the Folio allows for the possibility—enacted in Brook's production—that Theseus makes an exit separate from Theseus and those who go with him. Such an exit—which the Folio permits but does not mandate—would establish that Egeus's response to Theseus's exercise of ducal authority is to withdraw from Athens. Earlier Lysander and Hermia had fled from Athens in order to escape the punishments proscribed by "the sharp Athenian law" (1.1.162). The law they fled is the law that Egeus invokes when he calls for "the law, the law" upon Lysander's head, and it is that law that, overbearing Egeus's will, Theseus sets aside. The Athens to which Hermia and Lysander return is an Athens that will officially accept and validate their marriage: "In the temple, by and by, with us," Theseus says, "These couples shall eternally be knit." It is also the Athens from which Egeus could choose to withdraw. If he does, then Egeus in his silence is, like Malvolio and Jacques, a man who excludes himself from a renewed social order in which he is welcome to participate. We might even see in such an Egeus a forerunner of those tragic fathers, Lear and Brabantio, who cannot bring themselves to accept a daughter's will.

The corresponding stage directions in the Quarto are, if anything, open to even more diverse possibilities. The Quarto reads: "*Enter* Theseus *and all his traine*"— a phrasing that does not single out Egeus and Hippolyta as the Folio does. The Quarto provides no stage directions for the exit beyond what is implicit in Theseus's final words in the scene:

> Away, with us, to *Athens*. Three and three,
> Weele holde a feast, in great solemnitie. Come *Hyppolita*.

As stage directions, Theseus's words were inconclusive. "Away, with us, to *Athens*," for example, may be words of reassurance to Egeus—an effort to include him that Egeus may either accept or refuse. The words could also be an order from the Duke to Egeus, a command that he may or may not obey. In the opening scene, after what might be called Hermia's trial, Egeus leaves with Theseus, emphasizing his allegiance by declaring, "With duty and desire we follow you" (1.1.127). His words on that occasion resonate against the silence with which Hippolyta responds to Theseus's words calling for her to depart with him, "Come, my Hippolyta" (1.1.122). Hippolyta again says nothing when in act 4 Theseus says, "Come *Hyppolita*." This time, however, Egeus is silent too. He may wordlessly obey or he may wordlessly disobey the words that Theseus may direct to him: "Away, with us, to *Athens*." However, those words need not be addressed specifically to Egeus. Spoken to Hermia after Egeus has departed in anger, they could be Theseus's effort to ease whatever anguish Hermia feels at the departure of her embittered father: "Away, with US, to *Athens.*"[6] Thus, like the Folio, the Quarto allows the possibility that Egeus exits with Theseus and his *"traine"* but does not require it. Also, like the Folio, the Quarto does not require that Egeus exit apart from them either.

If we seek to clarify the meanings and effect of Egeus's silence by looking at the wedding festivities of act 5, we find differences between the Quarto and the Folio that compound our difficulties.[7] The Folio begins act 5 with a direction that specifies the presence of Egeus: *"Enter Theseus, Hippolita, Egeus and his Lords."* The corresponding stage direction in the Quarto, however, reads *"Enter* Theseus, Hyppolita, *and* Philostrate." There is no specific mention of Egeus as there is in the Folio, and there is no term equivalent to the *"Lords"* of the Folio that can be taken to include Egeus. In the Quarto Philostrate is the only person present to overhear the conversation between Theseus and Hippolyta, while the Folio requires that at least several be present, one of whom must be Egeus. Thus, the Folio, in contrast to the Quarto, establishes a situation in which Egeus stands by without speaking as he and others hear the Duke, who has overruled his will and Athenian law in order to permit Hermia's marriage, explain that he "never may beleeve" the lovers' account of what transpired during their night in the woods. Egeus must come to terms with a marriage that is one of the consequences of "Fairy toyes" in which Theseus himself does not believe.

Egeus's absence from festivities celebrating three weddings, one of which is his daughter's, is certainly compatible with interpreting Egeus's silence after Theseus overrules him as a refusal to accept Hermia's marriage to Lysander. The Quarto, then, justifies a production like Brook's in which Egeus, embittered at having Theseus "overbear" his will, ignores his daughter and withdraws from Athens rather than accept Hermia's marriage to Lysander. A father absent from his daughter's nuptial festivities would be another of those elements in *A Midsummer Night's Dream* that call attention to the darker, destructive possibilities inherent in the dynamics of sexual attraction and the processes of familial and communal renewal that the wedding revels and the play itself celebrate.[8]

Egeus's absence from the wedding festivities poses what I should like to call a dramaturgical problem: what means does Shakespeare provide to give that absence theatrical impact, to make it register on those watching a performance? One way to appreciate the problem is to try to remember whether Egeus was absent from the wedding festivities in the last performance of *A Midsummer Night's Dream* you saw. Shakespeare faced the same problem in act 5 of *The Merchant of Venice,* and there he insured that Shylock's absence would be an element of the audience's experience by having characters refer to Shylock. Lorenzo tells Jessica that the moonlit night they are enjoying together at Belmont reminds him of the night in Venice when she left her father to run away with him:

> In such a night
> Did Jessica steal from the wealthy Jew,
> And with an unthrift love did run from Venice
> As far as Belmont.
>
> (5.1.15–18)[9]

Antonio refers explicitly to his bond with Shylock when he offers to guarantee Basanio's fidelity to Portia by entering into another bond on his behalf:

> I once did lend my body for his wealth,
> Which but for him that had your husband's ring
> Had quite miscarried. I dare be bound again,
> My soul upon the forfeit, that your lord
> Will never more break faith advisedly.
>
> (249–53)

After Portia and Nerissa reveal the parts they played at Shylock's trial, Nerissa explains to Lorenzo and Jessica how the sentence imposed on Shylock benefits them:

> There do I give to you and Jessica
> From the rich Jew, a special deed of gift,
> After his death, of all he dies possessed of.
>
> (291–93)

There are no equivalently direct references to the absent Egeus in act 5 of the Quarto version of *A Midsummer Night's Dream*. Twice, however, what characters say could refer to Egeus. Early in act 5, Theseus asks, "Where is our usual manager / Of mirth?" The possibility that Egeus is the *usual* manager of mirth cannot be ruled out conclusively, but even if Theseus's question does refer to the absent Egeus, a reference so oblique is unlikely to register with much force on a theatre audience. A second possible reference to the absent father comes after the end of the play-within-the-play, when Snug, stepping out of his role as Lion, explains why Wall is not one of those "left to bury the dead": "No, I assure you," he tells Demetrius and others in the Athenian audience, "the wall is downe that parted their fathers." Again, however, if this is a reference to Egeus, it is indirect and of questionable theatrical impact.

Words, however, are not the only means at a dramatist's disposal.

Doubling Egeus with another character is a tactic available to Shakespeare that could use the visual dimension of drama in order to draw attention to Egeus's absence.[10] Doubling Egeus and Philostrate, for example, would create a theatrical situation in which seeing Philostrate, whom Theseus calls upon in the Quarto to provide the wedding entertainment, could also make the audience conscious that Egeus has absented himself from the nuptial merriment. Brook's production of *A Midsummer Night's Dream* doubled Egeus and Peter Quince. The presence during act 5 of the novice director who struggles to bring theatrical order out of the impulses and imaginings of the rude mechanicals was a visual reminder of the absent father who had tried to make his daughter's fancy and sexual energies fit his will. I might also point out that the visual parallels generated by doubling Egeus would enhance the theatrical effectiveness of what are otherwise no more than possible, very indirect verbal references to him in the Quarto.

The Folio—in contrast to the Quarto—not only calls for Egeus to be present during act 5 but also provides a means for directing attention to him by giving him words to speak that the Quarto assigns to Philostrate. Clearly, by mandating the presence of Egeus during the wedding festivities, the Folio rules out the possibility that Egeus's response when Theseus overrides his will is to withdraw *permanently* from Athens. Even if the silent Egeus stalks off alone when he exits in act 4, he must, according to the Folio, be present in act 5. The presence of Egeus increases the possiblity—more difficult to envision if, as the Quarto permits, he is absent—that he is fully reconciled to the marriage of Hermia and Lysander. The Folio has Egeus provide the list of "sports" from which Theseus selects the nuptial entertainment. In the Folio, it is Egeus, not Philostrate, who explains how the play of Pyramus and Thisby can be "merry" and "tragicall" as well as "tedious" and "briefe." As part of that explanation, Egeus confesses that watching the play in rehearsal "made mine eyes water: / But more merrie teares, the passion of loud laughter / Never shed."

Although the Folio certainly allows for full reconciliation between father and daughter, it does not mandate it. The first words that Egeus speaks are in response to the ducal command "Call *Egeus*." Egeus answers, "Heere mighty *Theseus*," and by stressing "mighty," the actor playing Egeus can make his reply a telling reference to the power Theseus exercises, power capable of overriding both a father's will and the law upholding that father's right to exercise his will. Even Egeus's account of how his eyes watered is less conclusive than it first appears. The phrase "more merrie teares" can be spoken so that it implies that Hermia's father has also shed other, less merry tears. Note, too, that while "more" can serve as an adverb of comparison, it can equally well function as an adjective meaning "additional." When it does, the sentence of which it is a part says that Egeus has not shed any merry tears since the rehearsal.

For me the most persuasive evidence for the possibility that Egeus's presence at the wedding festivities can signify nothing more than dutiful obedience to his duke is the fact that all the words he speaks are addressed to "mighty Theseus." He never speaks to Hermia or Lysander, and neither of them ever speaks to him.[11] Thus, Egeus's acts of speaking during act 5 also establish a silence that he maintains toward his daughter and her new husband and that they maintain toward him.

An especially important set of differences between Quarto and Folio turns on how the list of possible entertainments is presented. In the Folio Theseus asks Egeus what entertainments are available, while the Quarto has him ask Philostrate. In the Quarto Philostrate provides a "briefe" from which Thesus proceeds to read out the titles of the various sports, interspersing comments on each. The Folio changes what the Quarto presents as a single speech given by Theseus into a dialogue involving Lysander and Theseus. Lysander reads out the titles, and Theseus responds to each. What needs emphasis is that Egeus himself never carries out Theseus's charge that he "SAY, what abridgement have you for the evening" (my emphasis). That charge is the first of a series of questions Theseus asks: "What maske? What musicke? How shall we beguile / The lazie time, if not with some delight?" The questions can be asked very rapidly, but if Theseus pauses after each question, waiting for an answer that does not come before asking the next, the lines can emphasize that when Egeus does at last speak, he does not "Say" what the entertainments are. Instead, he says, "There is a breefe how many sports are rife [sic]: / Make choice of which your Highnesse will see first."

By having Lysander be the one who then reads out what is in the brief, the Folio establishes a situation in which Hermia's new husband speaks what her father was called upon to say. Although it is clear that Lysander reads from the brief to which Egeus refers, it is not clear how that document gets into Lysander's hands, and it is equally unclear what significance emerges from the fact that Lysander rather than Egeus says what the "sports" are. Does Egeus himself hand the brief to Lysander and by that action both acknowledge and (literally) give his voice to Lysander? Does giving the brief to Lysander indicate that Egeus is declining to read it himself—a reluctance to speak that could echo his silence after Theseus overbears his will? Instead of giving the brief to Lysander, Egeus might place it on a table—"THERE is a briefe . . ." (my emphasis)—and Lysander could then step forward and read it. Another possibility is that Lysander snatches the brief from Egeus before he has a chance to read it, in effect taking Egeus's voice and his place as he has taken his daughter.

Perhaps Egeus hands the brief—deferentially? defiantly?—to Theseus, who then passes it to Lysander. Such a sequence could establish a harmony between father and son-in-law centered on the figure of the duke. Alternatively, however, the same set of actions could convey that Theseus's response to an Egeus unwilling or unable to bring himself to "Say" what entertainment is available is to confer new status upon Lysander by giving him the opportunity to "Say" what Egeus will not.

By requiring the presence in act 5 of an Egeus who speaks, the Folio rules out the possibility that Egeus withdraws permanently from Athens rather than be present for a wedding he does not want, but the Folio leaves us unable to determine whether Egeus is present at his daughter's wedding festivities as a rejoicing father or as a dutiful courtier. Thus, neither the Folio nor the Quarto provides information that allows us to decide how Shakespeare wanted Egeus to respond to Theseus's decision authorizing Hermia's marriage to Lysander and to the marriage itself once it is performed. Even if we could convince ourselves that we had divined Shakespeare's intentions, the differences between the Quarto and the Folio suggest that those intentions did not remain fixed and constant but were fluid and changing. The Folio may be a revision of the Quarto, but if it is, the revising process was not one that worked toward clearer definition and greater specificity of intention. The aim of any revision that may have occurred seems to have been to give Egeus's response to Hermia's wedding—whatever that response is—greater theatrical effectiveness by requiring that, after his silence in act 4, he be present and speak during act 5.[12]

The differences in how the Quarto and the Folio present Egeus in act 5 are radically incompatible. There is no way to halve those differences nor to mediate them away by conflating the two texts. Egeus cannot be absent as well as present. The dialogue between Theseus and Hippolyta cannot be a relatively private conversation that only Philostrate is present to overhear and a public exchange that takes place in the presence of Egeus and the "Lords." Nevertheless, recent editors—among them Madeleine Doran,[13] David Bevington,[14] G. Blakemore Evans,[15] Stanley Wells,[16] and R. A. Foakes[17]—have concurred in providing a stage direction at the beginning of act 5 that follows the Quarto in requiring the pesence of Philostrate and follows the Folio in specifying the presence of others identified as lords and attendants. As a result of such conflation, the beginning of act 5 available to the vast majority of scholars, students, and theatre artists is significantly different from the two beginnings with the best claim to being Shakespeare's—the one in the Quarto and the one in the Folio.[18]

We can, of course, deal with the problems posed by Egeus's silence and the differences between the Quarto and the Folio by dismissing them as trivial. Egeus is a minor character, such a line of thinking would run, and his response to the wedding that Theseus declares will take place is a peripheral matter of no major significance. The inadequacy of such reasoning comes into focus if we think of *A Midsummer Night's Dream* in terms of the three phases that the anthropologist Arnold van Gennep has identified as the components of all rites of passage: separation, transition, and reincorporation.[19] Lysander and Hermia enter the woods as part of a conscious decision to separate themselves from Athens, and once in the woods they, as well as Helena and Demetrius, undergo experiences that ultimately permit the four young lovers to pair off as male and female: each "Jill" ends up with a "Jack." Theseus then makes possible the reincorporation of Lysander and Hermia into an Athens they had fled when he overrules Egeus and sanctions their marriage. The postnuptial festivities of act 5, which is set in Athens, make that reincorporation manifest, but the precise nature of that reincorporation varies according to how Egeus responds to his daughter's marriage.

If Egeus's silence and (in the Quarto) his absence from the wedding signifies his permanent withdrawal from Athens, *A Midsummer Night's Dream* is a play in which marriage and the movement toward it occasion an irreparable break between father and daughter. The family composed of father and daughter fragments as the more inclusive social unit of the city accepts and validates the formation of a new family through marriage. Reincorporation coincides with Egeus's withdrawal. Athens loses a citizen in the process of acquiring a new couple with the potential to bring forth offspring who will be part of the next generation of Athenians. Renewal of the city becomes possible through a process of change that exacts a lasting cost.

The reincorporation that occurs in *A Midsummer Night's Dream* is radically different, however, if Egeus and Hermia are reconciled and he wholeheartedly accepts her marriage. In such a case, the family unit into which Hermia was born survives her entry into the marital family that she and Lysander form. The social unit of the family—in both its natal and its marital embodiments—and the social unit of the city emerge from the process of renewal intact and regenerated.

Should Egeus do no more than obediently submit to Theseus's authority, a third variety of reincorporation takes place. The continuing estrangement of father and daughter testifies to the shattering of the natal family, but the city itself remains capable of including both the embittered but dutiful father and the marital family her marriage to Lysander brings into existence. Egeus loses Hermia, and Hermia loses Egeus, but Athens loses no one. The city itself benefits as the result of a process that sees one family break apart as a new family that will help to ensure the city's future comes into being.

We are accustomed to thinking of Shakespeare's plays as works that he himself completed in all important details, and we routinely expect—if we do not demand—that those who study, teach, edit, and (especially) perform his plays will honor Shakespeare's intentions as codified in the words he wrote. Once we accept the importance to Egeus, however, the limits of the concepts of completeness and intentionality become inescapable. The very words mandating that Egeus respond to Theseus's decision to "overbear" his will and (in the Folio) to the fact of Hermia's marriage do not give us information adequate to determine what Shakespeare wanted those responses to be, yet those responses are essential components of the play's vision. In this instance, the notion of fidelity to Shakespeare's intentions does not suffice, and as we try to come to terms with the consequences of that insufficiency, one of our first priorities must be to rethink, to reenvision the relationship between Shakespeare and those who perform what we reflexively call *his* plays. Perhaps because of Shakespeare's own dramaturgical design, perhaps because of the accidents of textual transmission, the Quarto and the Folio present circumstances requiring that those who perform *A Midsummer Night's Dream* be responsible for determining what Egeus's responses are. The only way to know with anything approaching precision what those responses are is to know how the play has been performed, to take into account what actors actually do or have done. The responses enacted will vary—I would even say must and should vary—from performance to performance, production to production. Each time specific alternatives from among the panoply of available responses are enacted, *A Midsummer Night's Dream* achieves a particular state of completion, an actual coherence of vision, that it does not have in either its Quarto or its Folio manifestation. Those who perform the play endow it with essential, necessary details that Shakespeare's words require but do not themselves furnish. In so doing, theatre artists do more than serve as agents obediently implementing Shakespeare's intentions. They act as virtual cocreators with him, bringing to completion a process that he initiated. As they do, *A Midsummer Night's Dream* becomes their play as well as his and challenges all who study what we (misleadingly) call "Shakespeare's" plays to come to terms with their character as works that come into being through a process that is collaborative, collective, and communal in nature.

Notes

1. The modern edition of *A Midsummer Night's Dream* from which I quote is Madeleine Doran's in William Shakespeare, *The Complete Works,* The Pelican Text revised, gen. ed. Alfred Harbage (New York: Viking Press, 1977).

2. A second quarto of *A Midsummer Night's Dream* was printed in 1619 with the false date of 1600 on the title page. Since it was based on the first, it has no independent authority.

3. Lynda E. Boose, "The Father and the Bride in Shakespeare," *PMLA* 97 (1982): 326. In this impressive essay, Boose observes, "Hence in *A Midsummer Night's Dream,* a play centered on marriage, the intransigent father Egeus, supported by the king-father figure Theseus, poses a threat that must be converted to a blessing to ensure the comic solution" (327). I am less certain than she is that the conversion she says must happen actually takes place.

4. See *Peter Brook's Production of William Shakespeare's "A Midsummer Night's Dream" for the Royal Shakespeare Company: The Complete and Authorized Acting Edition,* ed. Glen Loney (Chicago: Dramatic Publishing Company, 1974), 67b.

5. Quotations from the Folio follow *The Norton Facsimile: The First Folio of Shakespeare,* ed. Charlton Hinman (New York: Norton; London: Paul Hamlyn, 1968). Quotations from the Quarto of 1600 follow *Shakespeare's Plays in Quarto: A Facsimile Edition of Copies Primarily from the Henry E. Huntington Library,* ed. Michael J. B. Allen and Kenneth Muir (Berkeley and Los Angeles: University of California Press, 1981).

6. Rather than italicize words that I emphasize, I have resorted to capitalizing all letters in them. This enables me to preserve the italicization present in the Folio. It should be noted, however, that we cannot be sure that in Shakespeare's time italicization was an indication of emphasis.

7. I am deeply indebted to Barbara Hodgdon. Her essay "Gaining a Father: The Role of Egeus in the Quarto and Folio," *Review of English Studies,* n.s. 37 (1986): 534–42, has enriched my understanding of Egeus's role in act 5 of the Folio.

8. Those elements include Titania's account of how the changeling boy's mother died giving birth to him (2.1.135–37), the deaths of the lovers Pyramus and Thisby in the play-within-the-play, and Oberon's closing incantation against birth defects:

> So shall all the couples three
> Ever true in loving be;
> And the blots of Nature's hand
> Shall not in their issue stand.
> Never mole, harelip, nor scar,
> Nor mark prodigious, such as are
> Despisèd in nativity
> Shall upon their children be.
>
> (5.1.396–403)

9. Quotations follow Brent Stirling's edition of *The Merchant of Venice* in William Shakespeare, *The Complete Works,* Pelican Text revised.

10. For a discussion of doubling in various plays by Shakespeare, including *A Midsummer Night's Dream,* see Stephen Booth's "Speculations on Doubling in Shakespeare's Plays," in *Shakespeare: The Theatrical Dimension,* ed. Philip C. McGuire and David A. Samuelson (New York: AMS Press, 1979), 103–31. An expanded version of that essay was published as appendix 2 in Booth's book, *"King Lear," "Macbeth," Indefinition, and Tragedy* (New Haven: Yale University Press, 1983), 129–55.

11. In fact, Hermia, like Helena, says nothing at all during act 5. In both the Quarto and the Folio we have a situation in which two brides remain silent throughout festivities celebrating their weddings. Their silence is all the more intriguing when set against their insistence on speaking at other moments in the play. In act 1, for example, Hermia first asks Theseus's pardon, then "made bold"

by "I know not" "what power," goes on "In such a presence here to plead my thoughts" (1.1.59, 61). The silence of Hermia and Helena accentuates the fact that Hippolyta, who remained silent during Hermia's trial in act 1, is the only bride who speaks during the festivities. For a discussion of Hippolyta's silence in act 1, see chapter 1, "Hippolyta's Silence and the Poet's Pen," in my *Speechless Dialect: Shakespeare's Open Silences* (Berkeley and Los Angeles: University of California Press, 1985), 1–18.

12. In "Gaining a Father," Barbara Hodgdon points out that by requiring Egeus's presence the Folio raises the issue of when and how he makes his exit. She comments on several possibilities, and the point I should like to emphasize is that his final exit, whenever and however it occurs, is made in silence and is therefore open to various, even conflicting alternatives.

13. P. 169: *"Enter Theseus, Hippolyta, and Philostrate [with Lords and Attendants]."*

14. *The Complete Works of Shakespeare,* ed. Hardin Craig and David Bevington, rev. ed. (Glenview, Illinois; Brighton, England: Scott, Foresman and Company, 1973), 201: *"Enter* THESEUS, HIPPOLYTA, *and* PHILOSTRATE, [Lords, *and* Attendants]."

15. *The Riverside Shakespeare* (Boston: Houghton Mifflin, 1974), 241: *"Enter* THESEUS, HIPPOLYTA, *and* PHILOSTRATE, [Lords, *and* Attendants]."

16. New Penguin edition (Harmondsworth, Middlesex: Penguin Books, 1967), 107: *"Enter Theseus, Hippolyta, Philostrate, Lords, and Attendants."*

17. The New Cambridge Shakespeare (Cambridge: Cambridge University Press, 1984), 115: *"Enter* THESEUS, HIPPOLYTA, PHILOSTRATE, *Lords and Attendants."*

18. The New Oxford Shakespeare (William Shakespeare, *The Complete Works,* gen. ed. Stanley Wells and Gary Taylor [Oxford: Clarendon Press, 1986], 371), comes close to following the Folio: *"Enter Theseus, Hippolyta, [Egeus], and attendant lords."*

19. Boose, "Father and the Bride," 325. Another way of establishing the importance of Egeus is to link him with the issue of authority; see Leonard Tennenhouse, "Strategies of State and Political Plays: *A Midsummer Night's Dream, Henry IV, Henry V, Henry VIII,"* in *Political Shakespeare: New essays in cultural materialism* (Ithaca and London: Cornell University Press, 1985), 109–28.

Asides, Soliloquies, and Offstage Speech in *Hamlet*

Implications for Staging

MAURICE CHARNEY

The frozen, stream-of-consciousness soliloquies and asides in Eugene O'Neill's *Strange Interlude* (1928), conceived in the Elizabethan and Freudian mode, which always seemed such a stumbling block to performance, were beautifully integrated into the play in Keith Hack's recent revival in London (1984) and New York (1985). The principal characters, especially those played by Edward Petherbridge and Glenda Jackson, made no obvious distinction between public speech and private reflection, and the soliloquies and asides were spoken in the same voice as ordinary dialogue and made continuous with it, so that there was no way for the characters to hide, as O'Neill said, "behind the sounds called words." Keith Hack's production went against O'Neill's symbolic division between the inner and outer play, public and private speech, yet he managed to make the Elizabethan conventions believable and fluid, whereas in O'Neill's conception they are heavy, static, rhetorical, and moralistic.[1]

This continuity between the conventional speech of soliloquy and aside and ordinary dialogue throws light retrospectively on Shakespearean and Elizabethan practice. In order to be effective dramatically, soliloquy and aside cannot be either interruptive or segregated from the rest of the play. There can be no special soliloquy and aside voice that highlights these conventional utterances, nor do most soliloquies and asides provide a window into the souls of the characters. Critics have misguidedly used the soliloquies and asides of *Hamlet* to psychologize the play and to transform it from an exciting revenge action into a novel of inner revelation. There is a tendency to overstate the function of soliloquies and asides as if that were the core of the real, private play of consciousness while the external, public play swirled meaninglessly around us. Francis Berry has reminded us in *The Shakespeare Inset*[2] how much nondialogue there is in a typical play by Shakespeare, so that soliloquy and aside are not the only devices interrupting the dialogic flow. Shakespearean drama is posited on narrative and other discontinuities, and it is structured as a montage of significant pieces of action that serve as a synecdoche for an action that may be fully imagined but is never presented in its entirety.

If we consider soliloquies and asides in their dramatic context, they are usually well integrated into the action. I would like to look at some of the implications for staging of asides, soliloquies, and offstage speech in *Hamlet* in order to see how they function as a response to the stage situation. One example of the "privatization" of *Hamlet,* or the attempt to convert the public play into a psychological, inner drama of conscience, is the excessive number of asides claimed for the play. Most modern editions print Hamlet's first words, "A little more than kin, and less than kind!" (1.2.65),[3] as an aside, following Theobald's second edition of 1740, but these are clearly intended as bitter, ironic, punning, public speech. The isolated Hamlet, still in mourning, is attacking the gaudy cheerfulness of Claudius's court. If his words were an aside, the satirical outrage would definitely be muted.

In the Play Scene, Hamlet's sardonic comment, "That's wormwood" (3.2.187) to the Player Queen's protestation, "In second husband let me be accurst! / None wed the second but who killed the first" (185–86), is hardly an aside, despite all the editors who have followed Capell (1768). Like "A little more than kin, and less than kind," "That's wormwood" is an interruptive, public comment on the play like those of the onstage audiences to "Pyramus and Thisby" in *A Midsummer Night's Dream* and the play of the Nine Worthies in *Love's Labor's Lost*. Hamlet plays the all-knowing wise guy in this scene. His antic disposition, which no one fully believes in anymore, gives him license to make wisecracks and to act the part of what we would call a kibitzer. "That's wormwood" is spoken not to relieve the prince's private tensions but to taunt the audience and to express publicly his superiority to the tedious old "Mousetrap" play.

The most important asides in *Hamlet* are those that express guilty conscience: the King's, the Queen's, and Laertes's. These "solo" asides (in the terminology of Bernard Beckerman[4]) all function like brief soliloquies, but their purpose is so compact and so deliberate that they seem excessively expository. In other words, they serve the needs of the play at the expense of the immediate context of the character speaking and the development of the dramatic action. The most blatant in this regard is the aside of Claudius just before Hamlet's "To be, or not to be" soliloquy. Both Claudius and Polonius will be, in the King's words, "lawful espials" for Hamlet's soliloquy, and the King's aside answers Polonius's crass remarks to Ophelia as she is set up as a decoy for Hamlet:

> Read on this book,
> That show of such an exercise may color
> Your loneliness. We are oft to blame in this,

> 'Tis too much proved, that with devotion's visage
> And pious action we do sugar o'er
> The devil himself.

(3.1.44–49)

Ophelia and her prayer book echo the emblematic representation of Richard, duke of Gloucester, according to Buckingham's instructions: "And look you get a prayer book in your hand / And stand between two churchmen" (*Richard III,* 3.7.46–47). It is the essence of hypocrisy.

The King's aside continues the moral platitudes and pat style of Polonius's speech:

> O, 'tis too true.
> How smart a lash that speech doth give my conscience!
> The harlot's cheek, beautied with plast'ring art,
> Is not more ugly to the thing that helps it
> Than is my deed to my most painted word.
> O heavy burden!

(3.1.49–54)

This anticipates Claudius's soliloquy in the Prayer Scene ("O, my offense is rank" 3.3.36–72), and it is the first confirmation of his guilt for the audience. It corroborates the Ghost's narration in act 1, scene 5. We can understand why this aside would be important, structurally, as a context for Hamlet's "To be, or not to be" soliloquy, yet the aside itself is painfully obvious. It is inserted into the play in a schematic form that would be more appropriate for Polonius than for the King. It is not until the Prayer Scene (3.3) that we come to understand the King's confessional but not fully repentant frame of mind.

The King's aside does its expository work at the expense of dramatic vividness and full characterization. The Queen's couplet aside in 4.5 is similarly frigid and didactic:

> To my sick soul (as sin's true nature is)
> Each toy seems prologue to some great amiss;
> So full of artless jealousy is guilt
> It spills itself in fearing to be spilt.

(4.5.17–20)

The Queen, who had at first refused to speak with the mad Ophelia, is finally persuaded by Horatio and a nameless Gentleman to "Let her come in" (4.5.16). Gertrude's expresson of guilt recalls the Closet Scene (3.4), but the brevity and epigrammatic form of the couplets tend to work against the characterization of Gertrude, who sounds more like the Player Queen of "The Mousetrap" than the grieving and heartsick mother and recent widow of the Closet Scene. The jingle of "So full of artless jealousy is guilt

/ It spills itself in fearing to be spilt" echoes the formulaic sentiments of the Player Queen: "Both here and hence pursue me lasting strife, / If, once a widow, ever I be wife!" (3.2.236). The aside is unworthy of Gertrude at this point; we had expected something more acute and more revealing.

It is curious that the most important asides in *Hamlet* are so thoroughly didactic, as if they served a moral function different from dialogue. In the final scene of the play, the strenuous effort to rehabilitate Laertes and to reconcile him with Hamlet is partly accomplished by Laertes's aside: "And yet it is almost against my conscience" (5.2.297). In the immediate context, the Queen has already drunk from the poisoned chalice prepared for Hamlet, and the King registers his stoic shock in a factual aside: "It is the poisoned cup; it is too late" (293). Laertes is now determined to score in the fencing match by fair means or foul—"My lord, I'll hit him now"— but the King is not convinced: "I do not think't" (296). It is at this point, before the foul play that will kill Hamlet is unleashed, that Laertes expresses his moral regret: "And yet it is almost against my conscience."

How typical of Laertes is the sentimental, moral equivocation in "*almost* against my conscience," as if there were some way to excuse or palliate his dirty deed. This reservation recalls Laertes's cagey answer to Hamlet's openhearted desire for forgiveness. Laertes stands "aloof" in his "terms of honor" until "some elder masters of known honor" will provide a "precedent of peace" to keep his "name ungored" (247–51). The legalism of these bogus formulas is still touched on in "almost." Laertes's aside is not fully frank and candid, and it seems peculiarly unrelated to the dramatic context. It is, in essence, a moral declaration rather than a thought or feeling that impinges on the immediate action. The asides of Laertes, Gertrude, and Claudius may be grouped together by their artificiality, their deliberateness, and their attempt to make large moral points that are not necessarily those of the dramatic context.

The more conventional asides of *Hamlet* tend to be brief comments that establish a point for the audience, usually an expository point about "some necessary question of the play" (3.2.44–45). We have already noticed the King's aside—"It is the poisoned cup; it is too late" (5.2.293)— by which we know that Claudius will tough it out to the end and make no unnecessary compassionate gestures. This example makes a clear distinction between public and private discourse; the King cannot afford to make any public declarations or to intervene to save the Queen. The aside is a convenient acknowledgment of "purposes mistook / Fall'n on th' inventors' heads" (5.2.385–86).

Polonius has a series of explanatory asides in the Fishmonger Scene with Hamlet by which he asserts both his platitudinous wisdom and his patronizing superiority to the "mad" Hamlet. One key point is that Polonius is impervious to wordplay. In his asides he appeals to the lowest common denominator of the audience to help him make out what Hamlet might be saying. To Hamlet's "Conception is a blessing, but as your daughter may conceive, friend, look to't" (2.2.185–87), Polonius can only reply by missing the point of the pun:

> How say you by that? Still harping on my daughter. Yet he knew me not at first. 'A said I was a fishmonger. 'A is far gone, far gone. And truly in my youth I suffered much extremity for love, very near this. I'll speak to him again. (2.2.188–92)

Notice how deliberately markers are put in to separate the aside from the dialogue that follows. Polonius makes a point of telling us, "I'll speak to him again." It is as if the old counselor in his asides needs to be in cahoots with the audience to whom the asides are directed. He speaks only with their implied permission and complicity because he assumes that they too are having trouble understanding Hamlet's wild and whirling words.

As the dialogue proceeds, however, Polonius becomes more and more convinced of the truth of his next aside: "Though this be madness, yet there is method in't" (2.2.207–8). In other words, Hamlet is more calculating than he previously appeared to be, less spontaneous and more artful—in fact, more like Polonius himself. This is the conclusion of Polonius's final aside in this sequence:

> How pregnant sometimes his replies are! A happiness that often madness hits on, which reason and sanity could not so prosperously be delivered of. I will leave him and suddenly contrive the means of meeting between him and my daughter. (2.2.210–15)

"Pregnant" means "loaded, charged" in the sense that Polonius is aware of satirical connotations he cannot explicitly identify, but the double entendre fits very nicely with the sexual fears of Polonius and Laertes that Ophelia will open her "chaste treasure" to Hamlet's "unmastered importunity" (1.3.31–32). In a similar exchange after "The Mousetrap" play, Hamlet twits Polonius with the cloud shapes—camel, weasel, whale—yet it is Hamlet himself who feels put upon and toyed with, as he exclaims in an irritable aside: "They fool me to the top of my bent" (3.2.392). Presumably he means that Polonius and other officious attendants of the King force him to play the uncongenial role of fool in order to protect himself.

Hamlet's asides with Rosencrantz and Guildenstern illustrate the mingling of what Beckerman calls solo and conversational asides, which are here analogous in function. Hamlet begins his dialogue with them in a friendly enough fashion, but his confidence is gradually eroded as his old friends begin to probe like spies. Hamlet wants to know if they "were sent for or no" (2.2.296). At this point Rosencrantz turns to Guildenstern for a classic conversational aside: "What say you?" (297). By the workings of dramatic convention, Hamlet cannot overhear this question, but he can observe the gesture that accompanies it: "Nay then, I have an eye of you" (298). We are just on the edge of the aside convention here, and Hamlet's remark to the audience is not much different in function from Rosencrantz's question to Guildenstern. Both assume that the audience is the ultimate repository and arbiter of the asides spoken on stage. Another conversational aside occurs in the scene between Osric and Hamlet and Horatio. Hamlet objects to Osric's affected word "carriages" for "hangers," so that Horatio's aside to Hamlet underscores the foppish diction: "I knew you must be edified by the margent ere you had done" (5.2.156–57). The margin ("margent") of a printed text explains difficult words and allusions. Osric, of course, cannot overhear the insulting badinage contained in the aside.

The conversational asides in *Hamlet* tend to occur in longer sequences in which one group of characters is set against another. These extended asides are sometimes labeled "apart," since the stage is divided into speakers and commentators. There are two long examples in act 5, scene 1, where Hamlet and Horatio observe the gravediggers, then join them in dialogue, then stand apart to comment on the funeral of Ophelia until Hamlet can no longer bear to listen to the public discourse without breaking in. The asides serve to insulate Hamlet and Horatio from the onstage action, so that they can function as observers before they become participants. Perhaps the aside convention also suggests a new role for Hamlet as a contemplative onlooker. These asides in 5.1 are remarkably explicit, especially in their indications of when Hamlet and Horatio move out of the apart position and join the general conversation.

Hamlet and Horatio enter *"afar off"* (5.1.56 s.d.) at the end of the Clown-gravedigger's conversation with his assistant, who exits at line 61. The gravedigger then sings various ballads and tosses up skulls, while Hamlet and Horatio comment on the "easiness" (69) of his employment. The gravedigger is an acknowledged straight man for Hamlet's meditations on mortality. Hamlet then comes forward with a specific comment to cover his action: "I will speak to this fellow" (119). This is followed by a wit combat with the Clown-gravedigger like that of the earlier match between the gravedigger and his assistant.

When the King, the Queen, Laertes, and others enter with Ophelia's coffin, Hamlet and Horatio again assume the apart position at one side of the stage: "Couch we awhile, and mark" (224). Hamlet instructs Horatio about the participants in the scene: "That is Laertes, / A very noble youth. Mark" (225–26). "Mark" indicates the act of attention demanded from observers apart. It takes Hamlet a remarkably long time to figure out that this is a funeral procession for the dead Ophelia, but once he does so he can no longer remain apart. There is an element of real danger for the newly returned Hamlet to discover himself, but he cannot tolerate Laertés's inflated rhetoric: "What is he whose grief / Bears such an emphasis. . . . This is I, / Hamlet the Dane" (256–57, 259–60). They are soon grappling in Ophelia's coffin, if we follow the stage direction of the First Quarto: *"Hamlet leapes in after Leartes."* This grotesque stage business is confirmed in an elegy on the death of Richard Burbage on 13 March 1618:

> Oft haue I seene him, leap into the Graue
> Suiting the person, which he seem'd to haue
> Of a sadd Louer, with soe true an Eye
> That theer I would haue sworne, he meant to dye. . . .[5]

Horatio speaks only one line, a wise one, in this part of the scene: "Good my lord, be quiet" (267).

Once they have revealed themselves, Hamlet and Horatio can no longer return to the apart position, and one wonders how the scene was staged to render them invisible to the Clown-gravedigger and his assistant and, later, to the funeral party. There must have been well-understood conventions about the privileged status of observers apart so that their actions and movements would not seem awkward or intrusive. It adds a significant dimension to have an onstage commentator to mediate between the play and the audience. The observer apart in his asides suggests how we should react to what we see before us.

The stage situation of the asides in *Hamlet* is generally more noteworthy than that of the soliloquies, although there is a strong continuity between the two types of discourse. Some of the longer asides, such as those of the King ("How smart a lash" 3.1.49–54) and the Queen ("To my sick soul" (4.5.17–20), are analogous to soliloquies in which characters make important revelations. The distinction is based on whether the speaker is alone on stage, although in some soliloquies the speaker may think he is alone but actually isn't. For all practical purposes, soliloquy and aside have the same dramatic function in relation to the audience. We are speaking, of course, of solo asides; conversational asides work differently. It is remarkable how many soliloquies end with couplets, especially scene-ending couplets, which would tend to emphasize the speech's rhetorical purpose. There are also many markers to set the soliloquy off from ordinary dialogue, like Hamlet's "Now I am alone" (2.2.559) that prefaces the "O, what a rogue and peasant slave am I" soliloquy. Throughout the play we are made distinctly aware of the soliloquy situation, which is often self-consciously prepared.

In Hamlet's first soliloquy, "O that this too too sullied flesh would melt"

(1.2.129), he is suddenly alone after a "Flourish" during which Claudius and his entire court exit. There is an enormous contrast between the King's boastful account of his "rouse"—the drinking of healths accompanied by the firing of cannon, which "the heaven shall bruit again, / Respeaking earthly thunder" (127–28)—and Hamlet's mournful contemplation of nonbeing. When Hamlet sees Horatio, Marcellus, and Barnardo entering, he knows that his soliloquy is over and that he must once more return to public dialogue: "But break my heart, for I must hold my tongue" (159). The soliloquy is identified as a freer and more expressive medium. Hamlet must hold his tongue not in the sense that he must be mute, but only that he must return to social discourse in which he cannot speak his heart. Hamlet has another brief soliloquy at the end of this scene that acknowledges the appearance of the Ghost. This ends with a ringing couplet of high resolution:

> Till then sit still, my soul. Foul deeds will rise,
> Though all the earth o'erwhelm them, to men's eyes.
>
> (1.2.257–58)

This four-line soliloquy is not meditative in any way but expresses with great vigor Hamlet's anticipation of the Ghost's report of "Foul deeds." This echoes the proverbial "murder will out."

"O, what a rogue and peasant slave am I" (2.2.560) is Hamlet's longest soliloquy—58 lines—and it goes through at least three distinct movements: his reaction to the Player's weeping for Hecuba, his revulsion against his own inflated rhetoric—"Why, what an ass am I! This is most brave" (594)—and his plan to "catch the conscience of the King" (617) with a play. According to popular psychology confirmed by various miraculous examples from real life, "guilty creatures sitting at a play" could be trapped to confess "by the very cunning of the scene" (601–2). The soliloquy projects a strong feeling of sequence and narrative movement. It is the greatest showpiece of all the soliloquies in the play, and it too ends with a memorable, ringing couplet:

> The play's the thing
> Wherein I'll catch the conscience of the King.
>
> (2.2.616–17)

Hamlet is riding high in this soliloquy. There is no sense in its vigorous exhortation that Hamlet is in any way inadequate for revenge.

Hamlet's "To be, or not to be" (3.1.56) soliloquy is unusual in its stage situation because he is not alone on stage. We are aware of the fact that Polonius and the King, "lawful espials," "withdraw" at line 55 and remain behind the arras. When they come on stage again at the end of the scene

(164), it is quite clear that they know all. As Polonius says to his daughter, "You need not tell us what Lord Hamlet said; / We heard it all" (182–83). Nothing explicit is said about Hamlet's soliloquy, and there is no verbal indication that they have overheard it, yet we are still conscious of the fact that they are concealed behind the arras. The King and Polonius are clearly observers of the Nunnery Scene with Ophelia that follows imme-diately after the soliloquy.

We tend to forget that Ophelia, too, is on stage for the entire time of Hamlet's soliloquy, making it one of the most crowded soliloquies in all of Shakespeare. Ophelia has been staged by her clever father with a prayer book, to "color," or give a pretext for, her "loneliness" (45–46) or aloneness waiting on stage to encounter Hamlet. What is she doing during the time of his soliloquy? Presumably she is so preoccupied with her devotions that she doesn't notice the very person she is looking for, and Hamlet is so eager to unburden himself that he isn't aware of his old girl friend stuck away in one corner of the stage. The very attempt to give naturalistic explanations for highly conventional stage situations reveals the absurdity of setting two kinds of theatrical reasoning against each other.

Ophelia is very much there, and we should certainly not be allowed to forget that Claudius and Polonius are behind the arras—perhaps the arras is made to stir lightly from time to time to remind us—while Hamlet delivers what he earnestly believes to be, confirmed by the judgment of posterity, his most important soliloquy in the play. At the end of the speech, he suddenly notices Ophelia: "Soft you now, / The fair Ophelia!" (88–89). "Soft" is an all-purpose Elizabethan exclamation to indicate mild surprise, and it means something like "what have we here?" Anticipating the Prayer Scene with Claudius (3.3), Hamlet also believes that Ophelia is really praying, making "orisons" (89), or formal devotions, in which Hamlet hopes that all of his sins will be "remembered" (90). Despite the ingenious theories of John Dover Wilson,[6] Hamlet seems to have no inkling that Ophelia's orisons have been staged and that her father and Claudius are just behind the arras. The staging ironies of this scene are strictly dramatic ironies for the benefit of the audience.

It is also worth noting that Hamlet's "To be, or not to be" soliloquy is set back to back with Claudius's confessional aside, "O, 'tis too true. / How smart a lash that speech doth give my conscience!" (3.1.49–50). It seems important for Shakespeare to juxtapose these two expressions of con-science—and the distinction between aside and soliloquy here is more one of length and formal staging than of context. The King's aside is the immediate context for Hamlet's matching soliloquy, as if one needed the other to complete its meaning.

Ophelia's soliloquy after Hamlet's violent diatribe against women in the

Nunnery Scene is elegiac in tone. It makes no answer at all to Hamlet's demands—"To a nunnery, go, and quickly too" (3.1.141–42)—but mourns the loss of Hamlet as he used to be, "Th' expectancy and rose of the fair state, / The glass of fashion, and the mold of form, / Th' observed of all observers" (155–57). It is a tragic lamentation for the disappearance of all that was once so beautiful, and Ophelia herself, like Desdemona in the scene of willow, can only grieve for what has happened: "O, woe is me / T' have seen what I have seen, see what I see!" (163-64). These must be among the most moving lines of the play, especially in the way that Ophelia sets herself up as a spectator and audience of the tragedy. We can only sympathize with her experience of loss, disintegration, and deliquescence. Nothing remains fixed. The highly formal, poetic language of this soliloquy is unusual in its attempt to establish personal loss. Through their common sorrow, Ophelia is made to sound like Hecuba and the Player Queen.

Hamlet's odd soliloquy at the end of the Play Scene, "'Tis now the very witching time of night" (3.2.396), also called the "Now could I drink hot blood" (398) soliloquy, is very different from the other soliloquies in its vaunting resolve to be cruel but not to commit matricide. Hamlet is closest to the heroic mode of Norse mythology in this soliloquy, which also ends with a resounding couplet declaration of purpose:

> How in my words somever she [his mother] be shent,
> To give them seals never, my soul, consent!
>
> (3.2.406–7)

The Prayer Scene with Claudius (3.3) intervenes between Hamlet's determination to test and punish his mother and his arrival at her "closet." On the way, he passes through the King's "closet," or private withdrawing room, and finds him at prayer. Hamlet's presence here is both accidental and incidental, so that his encounter with Claudius at prayer can hardly be the "great opportunity" that he either misses or refuses. Like the earlier juxtaposition in 3.1 of Claudius's aside and Hamlet's soliloquy, the Prayer Scene sets the soliloquies of Claudius and Hamlet against each other. It looks, formally, as if Hamlet's soliloquy is inserted into Claudius's soliloquy, which concludes with a neat couplet after Hamlet's exit:

> My words fly up, my thoughts remain below.
> Words without thoughts never to heaven go.
>
> (3.3.97–98)

These soliloquies turn on misperceptions and dramatic ironies. Although he is standing right there, Hamlet by convention cannot overhear what Claudius is saying. Shakespeare avoids any awkwardness by having

Hamlet enter at line 72 when the King is kneeling and trying to pray.
Claudius is conveniently unaware of Hamlet's presence. There is an air of
magic and mystification in the scene, since we in the audience are well
aware of everything that is going on. Hamlet honestly believes that
Claudius is praying, just as he believed that Ophelia was busy with her
orisons in 3.1. The characters are required to trust the visual indicators of
prayer unless they prove to be suspect. There are certain fixed rules in
highly conventional stage situations, so there is no way for Hamlet to
break into the audience's awareness.

Hamlet is remarkably jaunty and colloquial in his soliloquy, as he enters
on his way to his mother's closet with sword in hand. He feels that now,
after the triumph of "The Mousetrap" play, the initiative is his and he can
afford to be on the offensive. All of this bravado, of course, ends with the
slaying of Polonius, but for the moment Hamlet can indulge himself in a
swaggering style: "Up, sword, and know thou a more horrid hent"
(3.3.88). He can luxuriate in perfect scenarios for revenge:

> When he is drunk asleep, or in his rage,
> Or in th' incestuous pleasures of his bed,
> At game a-swearing, or about some act
> That has no relish of salvation in't.

> (3.3.89–92)

Claudius's final couplet soliloquy completely dashes all of Hamlet's fantasies: "My words fly up, my thoughts remain below. / Words without
thoughts never to heaven go" (97–98). Hamlet's assumptions have been
totally wrong: Claudius has not been praying at all, just as Ophelia's prayer
is only a "color." And Claudius, too, has been spared the sight of the
demonic avenger with sword in hand hovering over him. Nothing can
shake the King's complacency and self-satisfaction, especially not the
truth that the audience knows through dramatic irony. Claudius is already
sufficiently aware that his attempt at prayer is merely "shuffling" (61), but
he cannot muster any real penitence or contrition.

The King's soliloquy at the end of act 4, scene 3 presents us with
another expository bombshell when we learn that he is sending Hamlet to
instant death in England. We need to know more about Claudius the
murderer and how he operates, something we have only heard about in the
Ghost's narration in act 1, scene 5. We will be further enlightened by the
triple plot the King concocts with Laertes against Hamlet in act 4, scene
7. The Claudius of this soliloquy is a terrifying figure, racked with anxiety
and impatience, and the soliloquy itself has an impetuousness and desper-
ation we see nowhere else in the play:

> Do it, England,
> For like the hectic in my blood he rages,
> And thou must cure me.
>
> (4.3.65–67)

The soliloquy demonstrates the "sickly days" (3.3.96) Hamlet predicted for his uncle at the end of the Prayer Scene. In his final couplet, Claudius anticipates Macbeth's urgency to kill Banquo and Macduff:

> Till I know 'tis done,
> Howe'er my haps, my joys were ne'er begun.
>
> (4.3.67–68)

The King cannot rest easy and enjoy the fruits of his first murder until Hamlet is disposed of. Soliloquy allows Claudius full scope for his breathless malice. There is no need to equivocate or palliate his homicidal intent as there would be in the social, public dialogue form. It is important to think of this soliloquy in relation to the more sympathetic soliloquy of the Prayer Scene. In both there is a deadly clarity of purpose and style.

Hamlet's final soliloquy, "How all occasions do inform against me" (4.4.32), is very precisely prepared when Fortinbras's Captain exits and Hamlet gets Rosencrantz out of the way: "I'll be with you straight. Go a little before" (31). The speech itself is in some ways remarkably unrelated to the immediate context of Hamlet the prisoner being shipped to certain death in England. This soliloquy is the most markedly thematic and sermonic speech in the play, very close to a prepared oration on the nature of revenge and the dangers of delay. Its fortissimo couplet ending makes Hamlet's long exit from the play at this point seem like a grand finale:

> O, from this time forth,
> My thoughts be bloody, or be nothing worth!
>
> (4.4.65–66)

So saying, Hamlet the Exhorter disappears, and the homicidal mood of the middle of the play fades away without any lasting effects.

Offstage speech in *Hamlet* is related to asides and soliloquies in the sense that it stands apart from regular dialogue. The stage situation makes us aware of dimensions of reality beyond, behind, above, and below the stage itself, as if there were a world elsewhere pressing for recognition. The Ghost of Hamlet's father crying in the cellarage beneath the stage is certainly a portentous effect that, in other plays, is rendered by music. In the symbolic scene of the soldiers in *Antony and Cleopatra,* "*Music of the hautboys is under the stage"* (4.3.11 s.d.), and in *Macbeth* we hear *"Hautboys"* from offstage—most probably from under the stage—as the Witches' cauldron sinks (4.1.106 s.d.). In *Hamlet* the Ghost is a semicomic "old mole," "A worthy pioner," who is praised for being able to "work i' th' earth so fast" (1.5.162–63). The *"Ghost cries under the stage"* (148 s.d.) with great portentousness, "Swear" (149). This injunction from beyond the grave is repeated three more times: "Swear" (155), "Swear by his sword" (161), "Swear" (181). The Ghost's insistence is attributed to a "perturbèd spirit" (182) to whom the ceremony is extremely important and who cannot rest quiet without it. In this climactic scene of revelations, we are forced to listen to voices beyond and beneath the stage, as if the stage itself were inadequate to circumscribe all of reality.

In the Closet Scene, we hear Hamlet crying from offstage before he enters, "Mother, Mother, Mother!" (3.4.6). These lines are from the Folio and First Quarto (only two "mothers" there); they do not appear in the Second Quarto. Harold Jenkins omits them from the Arden edition as "a fairly obvious stage accretion,"[7] which he had previously inveighed against in "Playhouse Interpolations in the Folio Text of *Hamlet*." The reasoning is so violently antitheatrical that it is worth quoting at length:

> I infer that Q omits it because it was not in Shakespeare's manuscript and that the actors put it in. Indeed this is the sort of literalism in production from which we sometimes suffer in the modern theatre, as though we are not capable of imagining that the characters in their world of the play may see or hear things that are not made visible or audible to us. Such things are at best superfluous and at worst merely crude. What sort of prince is this who cannot come to his mother's chamber without announcing his arrival by calling "Mother" three times in the corridor? It is a small thing, but it degrades the play for a moment. . . .[8]

Another small thing that degrades the play is to call Gertrude's "closet" her "chamber," a distinctively different room. The next step after playhouse interpolations is to postulate that the actors and the physical production degrade a play that could be better read in the study.

Hamlet's offstage exclamations, with all of their slangy overtones in contemporary American speech, prepare us wonderfully well for the mood and tone of the Closet Scene. They are in the spirit of the soliloquy at the end of 3.2: "Let me be cruel, not unnatural; / I will speak daggers to her, but use none" (403–4). Speaking daggers sounds like a stage direction for intoning "Mother, Mother, Mother," with pain, anger, and sorrow. It is passionate and wrenching and hardly dispensable as a "stage accretion," whatever that may be. We don't know how these lines got into the Folio text, which shows signs of revision from the earlier Second Quarto text. If they are an actor's interpolation, we are fortunate that so effective a detail has been preserved in the Folio. Presumably someone must have thought it a valuable addition to the Second Quarto version.

"Mother, Mother, Mother" is analogous in function to two other off-stage exclamations in the Folio text, both of which have been more or less omitted from the Arden edition. In act 1, scene 5, Horatio and Marcellus, who have been avidly seeking Hamlet, call him from offstage (or *"within"*): "My lord, my lord!" (1.5.113). They then appear and find Hamlet, who is still reeling with excitement at the Ghost's revelations. Calling a character from offstage is hardly a portentous matter, but it serves to extend the limits of the stage action and suggest a larger dimension. In 4.2, several anonymous Gentlemen call Hamlet from offstage *("within"):* "Hamlet! Lord Hamlet!" (2). Their shouting immediately precedes the entry of Rosencrantz and Guildenstern, who, at this point in the action, have abandoned all pretense of friendship and politeness. They are now strictly police officers of the King. This deterioration of Hamlet's status after the murder of Polonius is obviously reflected in the tone in which the anonymous Gentlemen address Hamlet. Like "Mother, Mother, Mother," "Hamlet! Lord Hamlet!" is an acted line with its own spoken intensity.

In the Closet Scene, we have to remember that Polonius speaks from behind the arras where he is concealed, which functions as another offstage area. Like any offstage speech, Polonius's cries from behind the arras would necessarily be muffled or otherwise distorted by distance and physical obstacles. Polonius responds gallantly to the Queen's terror at Hamlet's forcing her to "sit down. You shall not budge" (3.4.19). The Queen feels helpless and genuinely threatened: "What wilt thou do? Thou wilt not murder me? / Help, ho!" (22–23). It is at this point that the hapless Polonius cries from behind, "What, ho! Help!" (24), and Hamlet runs him through immediately. His last comment, helpful for the exposition, is "O, I am slain!" (26). Both Polonius and the Queen correctly interpret the homicidal mood of Hamlet, who has already been steeling himself against matricide: "let not ever / The soul of Nero enter this firm bosom" (3.2.401–2). Gertrude, unfortunately, never heard these soliloquy resolutions.

There is one further example of offstage speech, the stage direction in both the Second Quarto and Folio for the entrance of the mad Ophelia: *"A noise within: 'Let her come in' "* (4.5.152 s.d.). The *"noise within"* that preludes Ophelia's entrance may include some generalized offstage shouting, but it obviously also focuses on the imperative demand: *"Let her come in."* This is like the various imperatives shouted by the mob in *Julius Caesar.* The mob in *Hamlet* is associated almost exclusively with Laertes and his successful rebellion against the throne of Denmark. In that scene, too, there is *"A noise within"* (4.5.108 s.d.) that announces Laertes's

disorderly rabble breaking into the very presence chamber of the King and
Queen.

The implications for staging of the asides, soliloquies, and offstage
speech in *Hamlet* are rich and various. We cannot simply attribute what
happens to staging conventions; we must also study these nondialogic
resources in their immediate context and stage situation. I have already
written about that highly expressive play we may call "*Hamlet* Without
Words,"[9] which represents a substratum of nonverbal theatrical expression. But the verbal-nonverbal distinction is artificial and does not do
justice to our experience in the theatre, when we are hardly conscious
whether points are made in language, gesture, stage business, or spectacle.
The fact that we can postulate a *Hamlet* without words suggests that a
good deal of the spoken play lies outside the confines of dramatic dialogue. There are other ways for the language to move. The asides, soliloquies, and offstage speech seem to constitute an internal play, but this is
also the wrong image, since even in Hamlet's "To be, or not to be"
soliloquy, Ophelia is clearly visible on stage and Polonius and Claudius are
not very far away behind the arras. This is hardly private, and there is no
reason to consider the privatization of the play a theatrical virtue.

Shakespeare has gone to a lot of trouble to intertwine Claudius's confessional soliloquy in the Prayer Scene with Hamlet's incestuous and
murderous fantasies of revenge. The two are counterpointed against each
other and cannot be interpreted independently. The stage situation of
asides, soliloquies, and offstage speech establishes a context within which
interpretation must function. None of the great speeches can be disembodied or thought of as private meditations. They all serve the needs of the
play, which are sometimes surprising. In the confessional asides of
Claudius, Gertrude, and Laertes, there is an expository intent that seems
to speak for the play and to override the immediate expressive requirements of the characters. We have no pure examples of asides, soliloquies,
and offstage speech in *Hamlet*. The fact that even these well-worn dramatic devices and conventions can surprise us is a tribute to the resilience
of the play.

Notes

This essay is a revised and expanded version of a seminar paper presented at the
International Shakespeare Conference in West Berlin on 2 April 1986 and published in *Shakespeare Bulletin* 4 (1986): 5–8.

1. See the reviews of *Strange Interlude* by Frank Rich and Walter Kerr in *The
New York Times*, 17 July 1984 (the London production), 22 February 1985 (the
New York production), and 3 March 1985, a Sunday retrospective by Kerr.

2. Francis Berry, *The Shakespeare Inset: Word and Picture* (London: Routledge and Kegan Paul, 1965).

3. *Hamlet* is quoted from the Signet edition, ed. Edward Hubler (New York: New American Library, 1963), which relies heavily on Quarto 2. Other plays of Shakespeare are quoted from *The Complete Signet Classic Shakespeare,* gen. ed. Sylvan Barnett (New York: Harcourt Brace Jovanovich, 1972).

4. See Bernard Beckerman, *Shakespeare at the Globe 1599–1609* (New York: Macmillan, 1962), 186.

5. Quoted from Edwin Nungezer, *A Dictionary of Actors* (Ithaca: Cornell University Press, 1929), 74.

6. See J. Dover Wilson, *What Happens in Hamlet* (Cambridge: Cambridge University Press, 1959).

7. Harold Jenkins, ed., *Hamlet,* The Arden edition (London: Methuen, 1982), 318.

8. Harold Jenkins, "Playhouse Interpolations in the Folio Text of *Hamlet,*" *Studies in Bibliography* 13 (1960): 35.

9. See Maurice Charney, "*Hamlet* without Words," *ELH* 32 (1965): 457–77.

Much Virtue in *As*

Elizabethan Stage Locales and Modern Interpretation

ALAN C. DESSEN

Although Hamlet asserts confidently that "the play's the thing," not all scholarly and critical audiences have been as susceptible as was Claudius to such a performance-oriented strategy. Among the various objections or qualifications that have emerged are a set of murky questions linked to "historical" or "historicist" issues. Yes, all the evidence suggests that Shakespeare wrote his plays for actors and spectators, not for readers; yes, he clearly thought in terms of spoken words, gestures, properties, and costumes. Nonetheless, he crafted his plays for actors and audiences that no longer exist. To what "performance conditions" should we therefore be sensitive or oriented today? To the assumptions and working methods of "our" theatres, actors, and spectators? Or to the assumptions and stage conditions that informed the original production? To what extent have performance-oriented interpreters taken into account the passage of time that has destroyed not only the Globe but also what stood *behind* performances at the Globe—a sense of theatre and theatrical language shared then but blurred or lost since the Restoration? Can such changes or losses be ignored today without risking distortion?

Few critics or scholars, whether performance-oriented or not, take a gloomy view of the depredations caused by what Leontes terms the "wide gap of time."[1] Indeed, scholars (and writers of glosses and footnotes in general) thrive on such situations. But if performance criticism is truly to come of age, practitioners should develop a heightened awareness of distinctions between what is "real" or verisimilar or logical for us versus what (apparently) was workable, even highly meaningful for Shakespeare, his actors, and his spectators. All interpretation involves acts of translation, but, given the nature of theatrical scripts, stage-centered criticism has within it the capacity to make (wittingly or unwittingly) radical adjustments, even without the problems introduced by the passage of time.

To bring such problems into focus, let me concentrate upon the issue of locale in Shakespeare's plays. For centuries, readers have conjured up images in the theatres of their minds of famous moments linked to specific places (so who knows not the "balcony scene" or the "forum scene"?). Few of these readers, however, are aware of how little we actually know about how such places and locales would have been presented at the Globe or other theatres of the period. To expand the available evidence, I have skimmed or read about four hundred plays, but I have come away with few facts (albeit many conjectures). For example, stage directions that call for figures to enter *in prison, in the forest,* or *in his study* are fairly common, but little evidence survives to indicate how such effects were realized. Like other scholars, I assumed at the start that the practical way to convey a sense of prison or forest or study would be to bring onstage or "discover" some property which defined the space (a grate, a tree, a tabl with books, a bush for an inn, ropes thrown down for a ship), but, to m surprise, I found little support for such a practice. Rather, the scatter evidence indicates that place was signaled primarily by means of costu the presence of a jailer to indicate a prison; a forester or woodsman f forest; a host or vintner for an inn; a distinctive nautical figure for a s

Any such conjectures or inferences must take into account the nat the evidence—in particular, the dearth of external evidence (e.g., ments by Elizabethan playgoers or dramatists). Rather, what vestigator is left with is the dialogue (with many references t castles, walls, bushes, gardens, and caves that probably were to ined by the spectator rather than introduced onstage) and t directions. Interpreting the latter is then complicated by a serie lems I have outlined elsewhere.[3] In particular, discussions of locale can go astray if the scholar does not take into accou Hosley's distinction between *theatrical* and *fictional* signals. same action can be signaled *"enter above"* and *"enter on th* former, in Hosley's terms, is a theatrical signal for an action out by an actor; the latter is a fictional signal in keeping with or the place to be imagined. Matters can get very sticky whe an Elizabethan playscript today cannot be sure whether a *his study," "in the shop,"* or *"in the forest"* is indeed th properties or a discovery are called for) or fictional (so th the theatrical annotator, or the actor drawing upon his m not in terms of what an audience would see but rath narrative).

To both complicate and simplify matters, let m wrinkle: the magical properties of *as* (in the spirit Inevitably, our reading of either dialogue or stage di ditioned by a wide range of assumptions, some c grained that we are not aware we hold them. There to read a stage direction that calls for a figure to enter *in prison, in his study, in the forest,* or *a-shipboard* without somehow drawing upon our experience as either readers of novels or spectators attuned to cinema, television, and modern stage pictures linked to properties, sets, and lighting. But what if that same stage direction read (or clearly implied) *as in* or *as if in?* Would such an adjustment change our view of both individual signals and the larger problem?

To cite some examples: in *Greene's Tu Quoque* a figure enters *"as in his study reading"* (B4v); in *Brennoralt,* Suckling has Iphigene enter *"as in a Garden"* (3.1.s.d.); Davenport has two figures enter *"as in prison"* (*The City Nightcap,* 5.2.s.d.); in *Coriolanus* the Folio calls for two officers to enter *"to lay cushions, as it were in the Capitol"* (2.2.s.d.). Several such signals are linked to a room or "chamber": *"enter Sir Thomas More, the Lieutenant, and a servant attending as in his chamber in the Tower"* (*Sir Thomas More,* 1728–29); *"enter Scudmore, as in his Chamber in a morning, half ready, reading a Letter"* (*A Woman is a Weathercock,* 1.1.1–2); enter three figures *"as in a chamber, and sit down at a table, consulting about their treason"* (*Sir John Oldcastle,* 2086–88). Although not as common as the *as from* stage direction, such *as in* signals are scattered throughout the period (the examples cited above range from the 1590s to the 1630s) and, at the least, should encourage us to tread carefully when drawing inferences about the stage properties "necessary" to present specific locales.[5]

These *as in* or *as if in* stage directions have further implications, especially in relation to Shakespeare's sense of metaphor. When a signal in a playscript cites a study, forest, prison, or tavern, the reflexes of a modern reader call forth an appropriate image, just as dialogue references to night and darkness conjure up for that reader an absence of light associated with a scene in a movie or an equivalent experience in the "real world." But neither modern sets or modern lighting was available at the Globe. Granted, some sizable properties were thrust or carried onstage upon occasion: beds, thrones, bars (for courtroom scenes), scaffolds (for executions). But most effects were linked to conventional signals provided by dialogue, portable properties (e.g., torches, hand-held drinks, hunting weapons, keys, manacles), costume (woodland green, nautical garb, a tapster's apron, nightgowns), and appropriate acting (groping in the dark, dressing or undressing, sewing, reading a letter). Such signals (or theatrical shorthand) could then supply information (about place, time, recently completed offstage actions) and also, especially on an otherwise empty stage, could heighten metaphorical or psychological effects. To treat such signals or scenes solely in terms of a modern sense of place or time is then to impose an anachronistic sense of naturalism and realistic thinking upon a different (and potentially richer) mode of theatrical presentation. In short, in such cases our logic of interpretation may be askew.

Consider as a revealing example the final scene of *Romeo and Juliet*. Experience with this scene in cinematic renditions and most stage productions has reinforced the impressions of generations of readers who "place" the scene at night, first in a graveyard and then in a tomb or monument. Such a locale and such darkness are crucial to the story and not to be denied, but usually not addressed is the much trickier question: what would an audience in the mid 1590s actually have seen? Thus, it is possible that some special structure or large property was introduced to serve as a tomb, but no such signals survive (here or in equivalent scenes in *The Second Maiden's Tragedy* and *The Widow's Tears*). Moreover, although Brian Gibbons concludes that "the scene requires that the bodies [of Tybalt and Juliet] are visible once the tomb is open" (see his New Arden edition, p. 225), the evidence in the quartos supports no such requirement. For example, does Romeo's reference to Tybalt ("liest thou there in thy bloody sheet"—97) "require" that a spectator see a "real" body or does Romeo "create" the corpse by conjuring it up in our imaginations (as Juliet had conjured it up before she took the potion)? In simplest terms, the tomb may have been represented by a stage door or trapdoor, and Juliet's body (on a bier) would then have been thrust forth at the appropriate time just as Desdemona would have been thrust forth on her bed in the final scene of *Othello*.

My main concern, however, is not with the presence of Tybalt's body or how Juliet gets onstage but with (1) the entrance of Romeo and (2) the opening of the tomb. Both moments are clearly signaled in the early quartos (with the most suggestive stage directions found in the First or "bad" Quarto), and those signals are usually reproduced in modern editions, with the First Quarto's stage directions often in square brackets (the New Arden is an exception). As a playgoer, however, I have yet to see a production that followed these signals. Several related problems converge here, but of particular interest are the differing conceptions, then versus now, of place and metaphor in this climactic scene.

Let me start where Shakespeare starts—with the entrance of Paris. The First Quarto stage directions spell out what is implicit in the Second Quarto dialogue: *"Enter County Paris and his Page with flowers and sweet Water"*; *"Paris strews the Tomb with flowers"* (I4v). The Second Quarto speech that accompanies the latter action begins: "Sweet flower, with flowers thy bridal bed I strew / (O woe! thy canopy is dust and stones)" (5.3.12–13). If the First Quarto stage direction is "theatrical" in Hosley's terms, then Paris here strews his flowers on or around some "real" structure. On the other hand, if the stage direction is "fictional" (so that an actor-reporter is recounting the story, not describing the visual effect), by strewing flowers and talking about a "canopy" Paris defines an otherwise unlocalized stage space as "the tomb" (so, in this "minimalist" interpretation, the spectator would *not* see a special onstage structure that represents *"the Tomb"*). Meanwhile, this figure shows himself to be a particular kind of lover, one obsessed "with tears distilled by moans" and "obsequies and true love's rite" (15, 20).

Next, according to the First Quarto, Romeo and Balthazar enter *"with a torch, a mattock, and a crow of iron,"* with those implements cited in both quartos' dialogue ("Give me that mattock and the wrenching iron"). In a major speech, Romeo then lies about "why I descend into this bed of death," threatens Balthasar if he returns ("I will tear thee joint by joint / And strew this hungry churchyard with thy limbs"), and characterizes "the time and my intents" as "savage-wild, / More fierce and more inexorable far / Than empty tigers or the roaring sea" (22–39). The contrast between the two lovers of Juliet, one with flowers and sweet water, the other "savage-wild" with mattock and crow of iron, could hardly be more striking.

At this point (before Paris intervenes), the First Quarto stage direction reads: *"Romeo opens the tomb"* (K1r); the Second Quarto speech reads: "Thou detestable maw, thou womb of death, / Gorged with the dearest morsel of the earth, / Thus I enforce thy rotten jaws to open, / And in despite I'll cram thee with more food" (45–48). What follows is familiar to everyone: the fight and the death of Paris (not in the source), the finding of Juliet in "this vault" (86), and the deaths of the two lovers. What is often glossed over, however, is the twin problem of (1) what does Romeo "open" ("Thus I enforce thy rotten jaws to open"—later to be closed: "Seal up the mouth of outrage for a while"—216) and (2) what is the function of the two tools? The answers seem self-evident to the reader with a naturalistic bent who imagines a "real" tomb that must be pried open by "real" tools. But, for a variety of practical and imagistic reasons, these implements are invariably omitted from modern productions (so of the six or seven renditions I have seen, the only one to include an actual mattock and crow of iron was the wildly hilarious version presented in the Royal Shakespeare Company's *Nicholas Nickleby*).

Let me sidestep the reflexes engendered by naturalism and pursue my minimalist interpretation. What if we conceive of the entrances of both Paris and Romeo (on a bare apron stage) *as in* or *as if in a graveyard?* In this staging, a sense of "the tomb" would be conveyed not by a physical structure thrust onto the stage but by dialogue references ("thy canopy," "this vault," "the stony entrance of this sepulchre"—141) accompanied by gestures to a stage door or trapdoor. Paris's flowers and sweet water (as objects that would be carried by a conventional mourner) further establish a sense of place (for an equivalent see *Much Ado,* 5.3), as do the digging or prying implements brought in by the inexorable, savage-wild Romeo. The latter's highly visible properties therefore function not as tools to be used for "real" prying but rather as signals or theatrical shorthand to convey a sense of a tomb. Just as we know it is "dark" when figures on a fully lit stage cannot see each other or we infer "in prison" when manacled figures are accompanied by jailers wearing keys, so we know we are at a tomb when figures enter with accouterments appropriate to a graveyard.

What then of the metaphorical potential I cited earlier? On an obvious level, we are presented with two contrasted lovers or sets of values, with one of them literally and symbolically destroying the other. Indeed, one reason for a director's cutting the mattock and crow of iron is to sustain a "romantic" view of Romeo undercut or qualified by Shakespeare's signals. Equally important, if Romeo uses "real" tools to pantomime an opening of an imagined tomb, his speech addressed to "thou detestable maw, thou womb of death," takes on added meaning, especially: "Thus I enforce thy rotten jaws to open, / And in despite I'll cram thee with more food." The metaphorical emphasis here is upon a forcing open, a violation, associated with death and appetite, for Romeo is forcing open the "jaws" and cramming himself into the "maw" that will devour him (and Juliet). If that violation, moreover, is of an imagined, not a "real" tomb, I find it easier to conceive of the moment in metaphorical or symbolic terms, so that Romeo is not merely performing an action necessary to the story (opening the tomb to reach Juliet) but, more important, is acting out his tragic error by breaking open what should be inviolate and thrusting both himself and, unknowingly, Juliet into the maw of death (with overtones perhaps of violated virginity), a choice presented in terms of savage-wild appetites out of control (a maw gorged with morsels, "cram thee with more food," "hungry churchyard").

My purpose in introducing this example is not to argue strenuously for my interpretation of this moment but rather to display the tangled connections between modern assumptions about place and the Elizabethan theatrical presentation of metaphors and symbols. Although I cannot "prove" my minimalist staging, unlike other interpreters of this or analogous moments I am adding nothing to the evidence in the two quartos but rather am keying my interpretation to the specific signals that have survived in those scripts, signals which many critics and directors, working in the vein of modern performance criticism, prefer to ignore. Have we faced up to the implications of "fictional" and *as in* stage directions? Does this scene actually *need* a "real" tomb? Do the conditioned reflexes that call for such a tomb stand as a barrier between us and the fullness of meaning in the scene as presented in the original production? What are the possible functions of "real" tools on the open stage, especially if there is

no "real" visible structure to pry open? Are we in our superior, enlightened state-of-the-art theatrical (and editorial) environment diminishing the range of meaning in Shakespeare's scripts by imposing upon them
a straitjacket of scenic naturalism? Perhaps most important, upon what
performance or what notions about performance is performance-sensitive
criticism to be based? As Falstaff puts it: "a question to be asked."

Notes

1. *The Winter's Tale,* 5.3.154. Citations from Shakespeare are from *The Complete Pelican Shakespeare,* gen. ed. Alfred Harbage (Baltimore: Penguin Books,
1969).
2. For a fuller discussion, see chap. 5 of Alan C. Dessen, *Elizabethan Stage
Conventions and Modern Interpreters* (Cambridge: Cambridge University Press,
1984).
3. See chap. 2 of *Elizabethan Stage Conventions.*
4. Richard Hosley, "The Gallery over the Stage in the Public Playhouse of
Shakespeare's Time," *Shakespeare Quarterly* 8 (1957): 16–17.
5. For the editions used and for a fuller discussion of the problem, see *Elizabethan Stage Conventions.*

Editing the Staging / Staging the Editing

A. R. BRAUNMULLER

With a few honorable exceptions, the editors of Shakespeare have treated the staging of his plays in one of two ways. Either the editor ignores the text as a theatrical script, a guide to performers and for performance, or the editor creates a performance of the play in notes, stage directions, and other commentary according to the theatrical conventions of the editor's own time, usually in fact the conventions of his or her youth. In explanation of the first choice—ignoring the text as a script—we may remember that Shakespeare's plays were originally edited to benefit the solitary reader, not the actors or other theatrical personnel. From the time Nicholas Rowe first added lists of the dramatis personae and indications of locale—"A Wood outside Athens" is his, along with such gems as "An open Place before the Palace" and "A desert Country: the Sea at a little distance"—most editors have considered their audience a reading audience, and rightly so, since the actors had their own scripts and their own traditional ways of handling, or mishandling, them.[1] During the eighteenth century and after, these theatre texts, often derived from promptbooks and omitting unperformed lines, also went into print and were frequently sold at performances as souvenirs.[2] Nowadays, although certain specialist publishers continue to issue texts designed for theatre professionals, the vast majority of Shakespeare editions assume an audience of one silent reader who does not contemplate performing in or staging the play.

Early twentieth-century theatrical experiments and decades of scholarly research into Elizabethan performance conditions gradually prompted some editors to help readers imagine at least *a* staging of the play they were reading. Even here, however, the editorial staging generally reflects performances the editor had experienced in the theatre, so that— for example—John Dover Wilson, a great editor by any account, tended to recreate productions of Beerbohm Tree–like sumptuousness, replete with fixed sets, variable lighting, perspective effects, and so on.

Contemporary editors, with bibliographical overconfidence, pride themselves on having left all that behind. Some resolutely continue the text-for-reading tradition; others offer hypotheses about Elizabethan staging, or they offer accounts of historical stagings, or they offer a mixture of both.

No matter which avenue an editor follows (and it is likely that few can follow any single choice consistently), there are occasions when the imagined staging of a scene will actually influence what the editor chooses to print, and I do not mean simply what stage directions the editor chooses to add or modify, but how the editor construes or distorts the ipsissima verba of the Bard himself. My two cases in point come from *King John:* a line in act 5, scene 2 and the opening dialogue of act 5, scene 6. Although the second and third quartos (1611, 1622) of a related play on John's reign, *The Troublesome Reign of King John* (originally published anonymously in 1591) bear ascriptions to Shakespeare, I will discuss only the very different play included in the Shakespeare Folio of 1623.[3]

As *King John* act 5, scene 2 opens, the rebellious English lords have just religiously confirmed their alliance with the Dauphin Lewis. Mixing sincerity and hypocrisy (one supposes), Salisbury laments that circumstances have forced the English into this treasonous union—"I am not glad that such a sore of time / Should seek a plaster by contemned revolt" (5.2.12–13). Lewis first compliments Salisbury upon his "noble temper," his "noble combat . . . Between compulsion and a brave respect" (5.2.41, 44–45; the latter lines themselves slightly slippery) and then moves to reassert the alliance and the benefits the English may expect. Here is the Folio text, with spacing normalized, long *s* modernized, and ligatures omitted:

> Come, come; for thou shalt thrust thy hand as deepe
> Into the purse of rich prosperity
> As *Lewis* himselfe: so (Nobles) shall you all,
> That knit your sinewes to the strength of mine.
> *Enter Pandulpho.*
> And euen there, methinkes an Angell spake,
> Looke where the holy Legate comes apace,
> To giue vs warrant from the hand of heauen,
> And on our actions set the name of right
> With holy breath.
>
> (TLN 2311–20)

What, the editors have wondered, does "methinks an Angell spake" (5.2.64/2316) mean? There's no difficulty showing that the phrase was a popular one from about 1590,[4] nor in noting that the phrase quibbles on *angel,* a gold coin bearing the image of the archangel Michael and worth about ten shillings.[5] The problem lies in understanding (1) the signification of the phrase itself and (2) to what Lewis refers when he speaks the line. If we assume that the quibble on coins is primary, we note that the angel was also known as a *noble* and then suppose that Lewis continues (perhaps *aside* as the editors of the old Cambridge text speculate) the wordplay of *purse* (61) and *nobles* (62), thereby attempting a witty commentary on the financial benefits the English aristocrats may expect. That is: avarice will triumph over loyalty, an *angel* will silence a *noble,* money talks. Alternatively, Lewis may be complimenting himself on his intelligent reassurance of the wavering English lords: "There spake an angel" quite clearly means "That was an inspired suggestion" in *Eastward Ho.*[6] In this interpretation, Lewis says (again, perhaps, *sotto voce*): "How clever I am to remind them of their financial stake in joining me against John."[7]

Unaware of these possibilities or unsatisfied with them, however, some editors have adopted a rather desperate expedient. They invent a flourish or trumpet call preceding line 64, claim that Lewis's line refers to that angelic sound, and place Pandulph's entry after line 64.[8] In Dover Wilson's slightly eccentric punctuational conventions, the relevant text appears thus:

> Come, come; for thou shalt thrust thy hand as deep
> Into the purse of rich prosperity
> As Lewis himself: so, nobles, shall you all,
> That knit your sinews to the strength of mine. . . .
> *[a trumpet sounds*
> And even there, methinks, an angel spake.
> *Pandulph approaches with his train*

Note, however, that Lewis's next line—"Look where the holy legate comes apace"—apparently suggests he did not recognize the sound (if sound there was) as Pandulph's personal signature. In support of this change, editors have pointed to the absence of a sound cue when the Bastard next enters, but there the cue is indisputably present in the verse: "What lusty trumpet thus doth summon us?" (117).

Is it likely that adding a stage direction before 5.2.64 restores a lost direction or fulfills an inferable pattern? One obvious test is to examine other occasions in Folio *King John* where there are such cues, or where there aren't and might plausibly be in an Elizabethan or modern production.[9] On six occasions, the Folio provides a sound cue: *Drum beats* (TLN 372; alluded to in dialogue); *Trumpet sounds* (504; ditto); *with Trumpets* (609; i.e., trumpeters, accompanying a herald); *with Trumpet* (622; ditto); *Allarum[s]* (1282, 1297, 2439; none mentioned in dialogue). There are numerous occasions when one might expect a sound cue and finds none: the ceremonial entrances of one or more royal figures at TLN 3–4 (John), 379–80 (John), 646–47 (John and Philip *with their powers*), 998–99 (John and Philip), 1382 (Philip, Lewis in defeat), 1717 (John, after recoronation), 2167 (John, after reconciliation with Pandulph and Rome). Similarly, since there are some sound cues for battles, we might expect them at TLN 2250 *(Enter (in Armes) . . .),* 2459 (a glimpse of the English lords during the final conflict), and 2524 (a parallel glimpse of the French side), but they do

not appear. These seem to be the indisputable examples. The tally is seven
cued sounds and ten uncued sounds, if we total cues for royal entrances,
for heralds and warlike approaches, and for battle.[10]

Consider the more problematic cases. As I have already mentioned, the
dialogue alludes to the trumpet call preceding the Bastard's entrance at
5.2.117/2370, although there is no stage direction for it. The Bastard serves
as John's messenger one other time (TLN 2018), and he arrives in haste to
witness John's death at TLN 2658. On neither occasion (both scenes set
out of doors, one may note) is there a directed sound cue or any mention
of sound in the dialogue. At TLN 2603, Prince Henry makes his first
appearance in the play, and there is neither cue for nor mention of sound.
Chatillon enters at TLN 343, bringing John's retort to the French demand
for territory, and again there is no sound cue, although Philip greets his
arrival verbally: "Lo, upon thy wish / Our messenger Chatillon is arrived"
(2.1.50–51). There remain only two further examples, both occasions
when Pandulph enters a scene already in progress. The first lacks a sound
cue (TLN 1061: *Enter Pandulph*), but Philip says, "Here comes the holy
legate of the Pope" (3.1.135); the second example is the disputed one in
act 5, scene 2 for which editors have deemed a direction necessary to
rationalize "methinks an angel spake."

We may conclude, I think, that the Folio is extremely haphazard in its
provision of sound cues. Since the Folio establishes no pattern, one may
hypothesize (or "restore") as one will,[11] but equally, the *presence* of a
sound cue in a direction or in the verse (e.g., at 5.2.117) cannot be
regarded as reason to insert a new cue at another point where there is no
incontrovertible evidence for one. If we restrict our attention to Pandulph's two midscene entries, we find perfectly conventional signals that
do not demand a sound cue: Pandulph's first entrance is greeted with a
formula ("Here comes") that implies nothing about sound (compare, for
example, Philip's response to Constance's arrival, "Look who comes
here!" 3.4.17), and his second entrance has a similar verbal formula:
"Look where the holy legate comes apace" (5.2.65), again with no suggestion of a formal sonic prelude.

The text's habitual treatment of certain cues cannot justify editorial
intervention here because there is no such "habit." Instead, the editor
may logically defend any addition only through justifying an unusual
semantic meaning for "methinks an angel spake." The phrase has sufficient contextual meaning within Lewis's own speech (and, indeed, within
the wider contexts of his cumulative "character" and *King John's* incessant verbal play) to allow an editor to forgo adding a direction.

In act 5, scene 2, the Folio's text sufficiently defines the performance,
the staging, of the moment when Pandulph enters, and it does not need to
be changed. My second example concerns a more imperious editorial

intervention: rearrangement, not addition. Perceived internal contradictions at the beginning of act 5, scene 6 have led editors to restage the Folio. I have appended a lightly modernized version of the Folio's text and five editorial versions of it.[12]

Let me set the scene briefly. A French army, led by the Dauphin Lewis, has invaded England; desperate and inconclusive battle has been fought, and King John, stricken with a previously undisclosed "fever" (5.3.3), has withdrawn from the battlefield "toward Swinstead, to the abbey there" (5.3.8). With the King, apparently, goes Hubert, who exits with his master when John commands, "Set on toward Swinstead. To my litter straight; / Weakness possesseth me, and I am faint" (5.3.16–17). To carry on the fight, John leaves Philip Faulconbridge, the Bastard. In the two scenes immediately preceding act 5, scene 6, we have seen some rebel English lords decide to return to their allegiance and have heard the dying Viscount Melun ask the English, "Commend me to one Hubert with your King" (5.4.40); we have also seen the Dauphin and his troops, wearied with fight, claim victory although the French soon learn (as John had earlier been informed) that their reserves have been lost, "cast away and sunk on Goodwin Sands" (5.5.13).

Now, onto the large and bare stage of the Globe enter two actors, "severally." Presumably they enter from opposite sides of the stage, perhaps through the two (or more?) entry doors in the wall of the tiring house. The watching audience and the musing editor, some standing, others seated at word processors, may recognize by costume, gait, or stance that the actors represent Hubert and the Bastard. They speak. Following the Folio's lineation, the first eight lines include five questions, two statements that may be answers, and one imperative. The actors, of course, arrive to "make their presence real by claiming position in th[e] field of force that the open stage represents," as G. K. Hunter puts it,[13] but the editor's decisions here determine the actors' presences—or, rather, the quality and nature of those presences. Reciprocally, assumptions about those presences will dictate editorial decisions.[14]

The questions in this passage have dismayed editors, and portions of the text have consequently been redistributed between the scene's two characters. Text 2, for example, takes "What art thou?" from the Bastard and gives it to Hubert, but then retracts the gift by taking "Why may not I demand of thine affairs / As well as thou of mine" from Hubert and giving it to the Bastard. This preposterous editorial hysteron proteron continues in Text 3, which takes "Whither dost thou go?" from the Bastard and gives it to Hubert, only to return the favor by relieving Hubert of "What's that to thee?" and giving it to the Bastard. And so it goes, an interrogative dance of changing partners and unvarying steps. Text 4, for example, allows Hubert to keep "What is that to thee?" but takes away the longer

"Why may not I demand of thine affairs, / As well as thou of mine?" Text 5, that of the redoubtable Dover Wilson, makes the most radical change of all and starts the entire dialogue with the Bastard rather than with Hubert as the Folio has it. Dover Wilson made his choice because "the impetuosity of the opening speech is clearly more appropriate to the B[astard]. than to Hubert."[15]

We should note at once that the Folio's lineation and assignment of speeches may be acted or read with few problems, and all editors agree that the Bastard says, "Hubert, I think" and that Hubert replies, "Thou hast a perfect thought." Some editors, however, have been troubled by the Folio's assignment of the following questions to a single speaker:

> What's that to thee?

> Why may not I demand of thine affairs
> As well as thou of mine?

The first question evidently responds to an earlier question ("Whither dost thou go?"), but the second question suits a speaker who has just sought information and failed to receive an answer better than one who has tried to avoid replying.[16] On this theory of conversational exchange (by no means the only one), editors have reassigned or conjectured reassigning one or the other question. Assigning "What's that to thee" to Hubert requires no further intervention, although editors have in fact gone on to propose all the likeliest permutations, including Dover Wilson's summary decision to have the Bastard open the scene.

Whether articulated or not, a variety of assumptions guides editorial treatment here, and those assumptions covertly—because silently—guide performance by the two actors or in the reader's imagination. If one supposes the Bastard impetuous (still?) and the first speech a rude or reckless threat, then the two seem made for each other. The scene is evidently set at night (as line 17 later confirms: "here walk I in the black brow of night"), but are we to imagine two individuals each moving cautiously through the night, or is one (Hubert) more scout- or sentrylike and hence more proprietary, more likely to challenge an intruder? This latter conjectural context for the scene makes the first question not "impetuosity," but loyal vigilance. Or should we suppose Hubert, seeking the Bastard, has left John, the English court, and Swinstead Abbey far enough behind to justify our imagining the stage an undifferentiated piece of ground, a place where either Hubert or the Bastard might plausibly challenge a moving shadow? Recent scenes, especially act 5, scene 3 and Melun's assumption that Hubert will be found "with your King" (5.4.40), would suggest to the audience that Hubert's attitudes and "location" coincide with John's while the Bastard, they might assume, has arrived from another place, the location of the battle itself. The scene eventually confirms this set of assumptions, but only *after* the opening interrogative barrage. Finally, these exchanges might be staged to produce the eerie effects of *Hamlet*'s initial lines, where Barnardo—coming to relieve the sentinel on duty—actually challenges him first, so that Francisco must reassert his duty and advantage: "Nay, answer me: Stand and unfold yourself" (TLN 5–6, modernized).

Deciding to change or retain the Folio, the editor (again, perhaps unconsciously) will answer at least two further questions. Does Hubert's "I will believe . . . Thou art my friend" echo the Bastard's "A friend," or does Hubert himself speak both lines? And how much must the Bastard hear before identifying the speaker as Hubert? While these questions, like some of the earlier ones, may appear overliteral, or overscrupulous, the answers to them manifestly affect editorial treatment of the passage and, presumptively, its staging. In passing, we may note that metrical analysis will not provide an unambiguous pattern for the dialogue: the opening speech is a pentameter, as are (together) the third and fourth questions: "Whither dost thou go? What's that to thee?" The next Folio line ("Why may not I demand of thine affairs") is a pentameter, but "Hubert, I think" might link with either "As well as thou of mine" or "Thou hast a perfect thought." Yet the Folio's lineation gives "Hubert, I think" a visual, perhaps rhetorical, emphasis befitting the drama of recognition and released tension.

My choices, represented by Text 6, follow those made by Text 4 and partly conjectured by William Watkiss Lloyd in Text 2. That is, Dover Wilson's claim of "impetuosity" seems unfounded, but I agree with many editors that the Folio has combined two speakers' separate questions into a single speech. The arrangement adopted here has the following advantages: it implies that Hubert has some locus standi, some right to challenge *any* unknown individual, even one who proves his social and military superior; it follows the play's insistent device of echo and repetition by giving "A friend" and "Thou mayst befriend me" (5.6.10) to one speaker and "I will upon all hazards well believe / Thou art my friend" (5.6.8) to another;[17] it supports the characterization (seen as recently as act 5, scene 2) of the Bastard as both maturely self-confident and humorous by giving him "Why may not I demand of thine affairs / As well as thou of mine?" as a preparation for "Who thou wilt" (5.6.9) later in the dialogue. This arrangement has disadvantages, I must admit: it may improperly stipulate a staging (Hubert more static, in command; the Bastard initially uncertain, at a disadvantage); it may undervalue "Hubert, I think" rhythmically and even syntactically; it may strike some audiences as requiring clairvoyance for the Bastard to recognize Hubert at first hearing. Right or wrong, however, I take comfort in the fact that the exigencies of space led me to end my excerpts with Hubert's line, "Thou hast a perfect thought."

Notes

1. Many very early Shakespearean promptbooks are based upon printed texts, of course; see Charles H. Shattuck, *The Shakespeare Promptbooks: A Descriptive Catalogue* (Urbana and London: University of Illinois Press, 1965), 7–8 and passim. Manuscript promptbooks probably lie behind some early printed texts. My point is that formally edited texts posit a solitary reader; theatre scripts are "edited" with different motives, for a different audience.

2. Shattuck, *Shakespeare Promptbooks,* 8, gives a condensed history of "acting editions" of Shakespeare, dating the practice from Bell's *Shakespeare* (1773); the earliest printed text I know that marks theatrical cuts, the *Hamlet* quarto of 1676, uses quotation marks at the beginning of lines that "are left out upon the Stage" ([A]2r).

3. All modern-spelling quotations of *King John* refer to my edition of the play, forthcoming in the Oxford Shakespeare. When citing the Folio, I employ the T[hrough] L[ine] N[umber(s)] of the facsimile prepared by Charlton Hinman (New York: Norton, 1968). When the TLN is relevant to a modernized quotation, it follows the act-scene-line reference after a slash.

4. See the entries in the *Oxford Dictionary of English Proverbs*, 3d ed., rev. F. P. Wilson (Oxford: Oxford University Press, 1970) and proverb A242 "There spoke an angel" in Morris Palmer Tilley, *A Dictionary of the Proverbs in England in the Sixteenth and Seventeenth Centuries* (Ann Arbor: University of Michigan Press, 1950).

5. The coin is illustrated in C. T. Onions et al., comp., *Shakespeare's England,* 2 vols. (Oxford: Clarendon, 1916), plate facing 1:326.

6. George Chapman, Ben Jonson, and John Marston, *Eastward Ho,* ed. R. W. Van Fossen, The Revels Plays (Manchester: Manchester University Press, 1979), 2.2.301 and n.

7. One proposed meaning for the phrase is wrong. Tilley's confusing entry (see n. 2) misled E. A. J. Honigmann into believing that Giovanni Torriano's gloss, "Ironically spoken oft times, as if one would say, There spake Wisdom it self," refers to "There spoke an angel"; see Honigmann's Arden edition of *King John,* 4th ed. rev. (London: Methuen, 1954), n. to 5.2.64. Torriano's remark refers instead to another proverbial phrase, "There spake a sybill"; see his *Piazza universale di proverbi italiani* (London, 1666), 259 and 276, n. 136).

8. Charles and Mary Cowden-Clarke were apparently the first to suggest a sound cue; see their edition of Shakespeare's plays, 3 vols. (London: Cassell, 1864–68). The addition is supported by H. H. Furness, Jr. in the Variorum edition of *King John* (Philadelphia: Lippincott, 1919). Dover Wilson adds the direction in his New Cambridge Shakespeare edition (Cambridge: Cambridge University Press, 1936), as does Robert Smallwood in the New Penguin edition (Harmondsworth, England: Penguin, 1974).

9. The BBC television production (recorded in 1984) preceded each of Pandulph's entries with monkish chant; I caught only the phrase "Salvator mundi."

10. Compositors B and C set *King John,* and there appear to be no obvious

variations between them in setting or failing to set sound cues: B set 4 sound cues, C set 3; B did not set sound cues where they might be expected on six occasions, C did not on eight (excluding TLN 2370, where the cue is in the verse).

11. It does seem a safe bet that whoever prepared a manuscript for performance use could assume that certain common and ritualized occasions (e.g., royal entrances and battles) would receive appropriate aural accompaniment without specific instructions in the script.

12. In addition to the Folio and my own edition, the textual examples come from the following sources: Alexander Dyce, ed., *Works of Shakespeare,* 2d ed., 9 vols. (London: Chapman and Hall, 1864–67), vol. 4; Dover Wilson's edition; Henry Halford Vaughan, *New Readings and New Renderings of Shakespeare's Tragedies [sic],* 3 vols. (London: Kegan Paul, 1878), 1:84; W. G. Clark and W. A. Wright, ed., *Works,* The Cambridge Shakespeare, 9 vols. (New York: Macmillan, 1891), vol. 4 (for William Watkiss Lloyd's manuscript conjectures).

13. G. K. Hunter, "Flatcaps and Bluecoats: Visual Signals on the Elizabethan Stage," *Essays and Studies,* n.s., 33 (1980): 21–22.

14. This situation is circular, but I see no way out of it.

15. N. to 5.6.1–6 in Dover Wilson's edition; he concludes, "the distribution of speeches in my text . . . seems unobjectionable."

16. Audrey Stanley, an experienced director of Shakespeare, has suggested to me that this second question ("Why may not I . . .") *could* belong to the speaker who asked the first question if we suppose that some nonverbal gesture (e.g., a "fig," or a dismissive wave of the hand) or some sound not represented in the text (e.g., a negative grunt) has occurred. That is, the Folio reading may be retained here on approximately the same grounds that were used to justify changing it in my first example: something happens on stage for which there is no unequivocal textual evidence. A gesture certainly *may* have occurred, but because there is no check, no logical restraint, upon such hypothesizing (and therefore no way to distinguish likely from unlikely invented gestures—or likely from unlikely additional sound cues, at least in the case of *King John*), I would prefer to edit the words and whatever action they stipulate rather than to imagine action and then to edit *that.* For enlightening remarks on the way dramatic texts do or do not stipulate stage action, see Raymond Williams, *Drama in Performance* (Harmondsworth, England: Penguin, 1968), chap. 8.

17. "Thou mayst befriend me" is probably the Bastard's joke on how frequently he and Hubert have used the word *friend;* "befriend" therefore may mean "call by the name *friend,*" or "dub with the title *friend.*"

Appendix

King John, 5.6.1–8 in the Folio and some modern editions and conjectured assignments

1. FOLIO

Hubert.
  Who's there? Speak ho, speak quickly, or I shoot.
Bastard.
  A friend. What art thou?
Hubert.
  Of the part of England.
Bastard.
  Whither dost thou go?
Hubert.
  What's that to thee?
Bastard.
  Why may not I demand of thine affairs
  As well as thou of mine?
Hubert.
  Hubert, I think.
Bastard.
  Thou hast a perfect thought.

2. WATKISS LLOYD

Hubert.
  Who's there? speak, ho! speak quickly, or I shoot.
Bastard.
  A friend.
Hubert.
  What art thou?
Bastard.
  Of the part of England. Whither dost thou go?
Hubert.
  What is that to thee?
Bastard.
  Why may not I demand of thine affairs
  As well as thou of mine? Hubert, I think.
Hubert.
  Thou hast a perfect thought.

3. VAUGHAN

Hubert.
  Who's there? speak, ho! speak quickly, or I shoot.
Bastard.
  A friend. What art thou?
Hubert.
  Of the part of England. Whither dost thou go?

4. DYCE, 2d ed.

Hubert.
  Who's there? speak, ho! speak quickly, or I shoot.
Bastard.
  A friend. What art thou?
Hubert.
  Of the part of England.

Bastard.
   What is that to thee?
Hubert.
   'What's that to thee?' Why may not I demand
   Of thine affairs as well as thou of mine?
Bastard.
   Hubert, I think.
Hubert.
   Thou hast a perfect thought.

5.   DOVER WILSON

Bastard.
   Who's there? speak, ho! speak quickly, or I shoot.
Hubert.
   A friend. What art thou?
Bastard.
   Of the part of England.
Hubert.
   Whither dost thou go?
Bastard.
   What's that to thee?
Hubert.
   Why may not I demand
   Of thine affairs, as well as thou of mine?
Bastard.
   Hubert, I think.
Hubert.
   Thou hast a perfect thought.

Bastard.
   Whither dost thou go?
Hubert.
   What is that to thee?
Bastard.
   Why may not I demand of thine affairs,
   As well as thou of mine? Hubert, I think.
Hubert.
   Thou hast a perfect thought.

6.   OXFORD SHAKESPEARE

Hubert.
   Who's there? Speak. ho! Speak quickly, or I shoot.
Bastard.
   A friend. What art thou?
Hubert.
   Of the part of England.
Bastard.
   Whither dost thou go?
Hubert.
   What's that to thee?
Bastard.
   Why may not I demand of thine affairs,
   As well as thou of mine? Hubert, I think.
Hubert.
   Thou hast a perfect thought.

Stage Images in *Troilus and Cressida*

R. A. FOAKES

In recent years stage-centered criticism of Shakespeare's plays, attending to the dramatist's directing hand and the various forms of action, has become established as an indispensable method of analyzing them. It is a development that began to gather impetus in the 1950s, at a time when, coincidentally, an important shift was taking place in our conception of the Elizabethan stage. The publication of *The Globe Playhouse* by John Cranford Adams in 1942 had established the image of a tall, octagonal theatre possessing a highly decorative stage area, overlooked by two handsome bay windows and fitted with a large inner stage curtained off from the main platform. As scholars exposed the inadequacies of Adams's methodology and showed how unreliable were the maps and views (notably the Visscher view), on which he based his reconstruction, a new image of the Globe emerged.[1] This new concept, based on a very much more cautious and rigorous assessment of the evidence, led to a rejection of the Adams version in favor of what may be called the Richard Hosley version, as summed up in the *Revels History of English Drama*, vol. 3, 1576–1613 (1975); in this he concludes that the stage and tiring-house at the Globe were "generally similar to the stage and tiring-house of the Swan" (181).

Our image of the Globe has thus tended to become identified with the De Witt drawing of the Swan, showing a bare stage, with two doors and no inner stage (see p. 176 of this volume). Although the drawing is a copy of a lost original and does not represent the Globe, and its pictorial conventions are related to the treatise by Justus Lipsius, *De Amphiteatro* (1584), on the colosseum at Rome, it has become a central point of reference in a new orthodoxy of belief about Shakespeare's stage. The visual prominence of this much-reproduced image has no doubt encouraged what might be called a minimalist concept of theatre in the age of Shakespeare. By the time Bernard Beckerman published *Shakespeare at the Globe* in 1962, he could present as unchallenged what had by then become, and has since remained, an accepted view that the audiences at the Elizabethan theatres were "not expected to identify the stage with a particular location but to understand that it functions as a token of Troy or the Danish palace or the Forest of Arden" (67). The stage locale, it is said, was created by the mere presence of actors: "to see Cleopatra on stage is to realize that we are in Egypt, and a royal entourage accompanying a king announces a presence chamber."[2] This recognition that the actor did much to create his environment on the Elizabethan stage "by projecting upon the neutral or generalised diagram of stage space the shape of his fictional life"[3] has led to some valuable exploration of the use of stage spaces, movements, costume, and gesture, especially in relation to Shakespeare's plays. At the same time, we have become accustomed to think of plays in relation to the spareness of the stage and facade as shown in the De Witt drawing of the Swan. This is to say that we have become accustomed to think that plays were performed as economically as possible, with a minimum of scenery or properties, and with the smallest number of actors made possible by doubling the parts.[4] Furthermore, this concept of staging supposes that unless a property or location or any production feature is specifically required by the text, it was not used.

I believe this view ought to be challenged on several counts. Leading companies in London now stage their plays as sumptuously as their resources permit, and it is reasonable to suppose that the Chamberlain's/King's men did so in Shakespeare's time, if only to maintain their status as the equivalent of today's Royal Shakespeare Company. They were competing with the Admiral's/Prince Henry's Men, who spent liberally on costumes and properties for plays they staged, laying out, for instance, more than £38 on coats, gowns, velvet, taffeta, satin, tailor's bills, and "divers things" for a two-part play on *Cardinal Wolsey* in 1601. Such lavish expenditure was perhaps unusual, but for an old play, *Mahomet,* worth as a promptbook only forty shillings, the company at this time laid out fifty shillings on making crowns and other things for it. By 1598 this company possessed an elaborate stock of scenes and properties, including the city of Rome, steeples, a rock, a stable, and two moss banks.[5] Henslowe's accounts seem to reflect a lavishness of production that is inconsistent with the image of the bare stage derived from the Swan drawing.

It is not an easy matter to relinquish conventional assumptions, and we have come to take for granted the idea of a small company, somewhat frantically doubling parts, playing as economically as they could on an unadorned stage, and avoiding the use of scenery, properties, or stage features like trapdoors and balconies, except where absolutely essential. Such assumptions shape our reading of plays and govern our perception of the way they were staged. I do not want to suggest that all our thinking has been wrong, but we have come to accept the idea that the landscape of these plays was one of persons, not of places, and that it was left to "the imaginary forces of the viewer"[6] to build on hints provided in the text. It seems to me worth looking to see what we might find if we imagine the Chamberlain's/King's Men, under the watchful eye of Shakespeare, using the most elaborate scenic resources they could muster in order to enrich their productions and illuminate the meanings of his plays. I suspect that the results might notably enhance our understanding of some texts. In what follows, I seek to illustrate the larger issue by considering some matters of staging in one play, *Troilus and Cressida.*

If the dialogue and the mere presence of actors can establish a setting, as presumably happens when Pandarus tells Troilus to "walk here i'th'orchard" (3.2.14),[7] then we could likewise be persuaded to imagine a door when, a few lines earlier, Troilus says, "I stalk about her door" (3.2.8). Since later in the scene Troilus and Pandarus, then Cressida, enter, it is natural to suppose that they do so through a practical stage door. We assume the orchard is imaginary, but the door is real. This assumption illustrates a recurrent problem of interpretation, neatly but arbitrarily resolved by the minimalist argument that the feature described is there only if its use is absolutely required. The trouble with this solution is that it simply ignores the many instances where such a rule of thumb does not work. Are objects specified in stage directions, for instance, but not in the text, to be present or not? In 4.1 of *Troilus and Cressida,* the Folio entry reads, "Enter at one door Aeneas with a Torch, at another Paris, Deiphobus, Antenor, Diomed the Grecian, with Torches." Diomedes greets Aeneas with "Good morrow" (7), and Troilus enters in 4.2 saying to Cressida "the morn is cold": the time of these scenes is early morning, and only the torches show that they begin while it is still dark, but torches are not mentioned in the text. In 5.1 Achilles enters to say "I'll heat his blood with Greekish wine to-night," but only when Thersites sees "fires" and Hector and others enter with "lights" (5.1.66) are we made aware of the presence of lights on stage. Searching for Achilles, the party goes astray until Ajax finds his tent, "There, where we see the lights" (5.1.68).

The stage directions say nothing about lights at Achilles's tent;[8] in the daylight at the Globe, lights were not necessary, and it could be argued that when Ajax mentions "lights," this establishes imaginary lighting at Achilles's tent, much as the mention of an orchard outside Cressida's house establishes an imaginary orchard there. However, since Diomedes comes on here with lights, and Troilus follows his torch (or torchbearer) to the tent of Calchas, it is a reasonable inference that the tent of Achilles, where the scene begins, is all along illuminated by torches or lights of some kind. If I seem to be laboring the point, it is in order to reveal the inconsistencies, even absurdities, involved in conventional assumptions about interpreting evidence for staging and stage images. When Troilus and Ulysses approach the tent of Calchas in 5.2, Ulysses advises, "Stand where the torch may not discover us" (5.2.5). Assuming, again, that this torch is real, it could be that carried by Diomedes, or his torchbearer, or one carried by Troilus, Ulysses, or their torchbearer, or, more probably, matching the lights at Achilles's tent, a torch mounted in a bracket (by Diomedes?) at the tent of Calchas. If so, then two tent locations seem to have had sconces or brackets where torches could be placed. How, then, were tents indicated on stage?

In *Richard III,* 5.3, the text requires first the setting up of a tent for King Richard, who enters saying, "Here pitch our tent, even here in Bosworth field," and then the erection of a tent for Richmond. Shakespeare seems to have had practical stage tents in mind for the pavilions (5.1.27) of Henry and the opposing French in *Henry V;* Brutus and Cassius debate in Brutus's tent in *Julius Caesar,* 4.2, and tents may have been used in *Henry IV.* In these plays tents could have been suggested by awnings stretched from existing stage doors, but in *Richard III* a procession of ghosts has to enter and go off, and they probably circled the stage, entering by one door and leaving by the other, which suggests that the tents were located on the stage. If our inclination is to argue from economy and from anxiety about possible sight lines that the logical place for tents would be at the rear of the stage, it is worth bearing in mind the plot of *2 Seven Deadly Sins,* staged at the Rose, which calls for a tent to be placed on the stage, with Henry VI asleep in it, while two dumb shows enter at different doors. We have no way of determining where this tent was placed, or for that matter any of Shakespeare's tents, but it seems clear that at various public theatres practicable tents which could be opened to display a scene inside were in use; a tent is opened thus to reveal characters in bed or asleep in *2 Tamburlaine* and in *Edward I.* Brutus's tent in *Julius Caesar* may have been of this kind, opening to permit the audience to see him conferring with Cassius, Titinius, and Messala, and then to permit Varro, Claudius, and Lucius all to fall asleep in it, while the Ghost of Caesar appears to Brutus. The tents in *Richard III* also open to allow us to see Richard and Richmond sleeping. If the single tent required in *2 Tamburlaine* and *Julius Caesar* could have been a canopy extending from a stage door or rear wall, the staging of *Richard III* would be easier if the tents were set up (as apparently the tent in *2 Seven Deadly Sins* was) downstage, leaving the doors free; were they perhaps erected against the stage pillars, in such a way that they could be easily made to collapse and be tied back against them?

The question is an especially intriguing one in relation to *Troilus and Cressida.* In this play there are more than thirty references to tents, beginning with the prologue describing how the Greeks have pitched their "brave pavilions" outside Troy. A pavilion (as in *Henry V,* 4.1.27) was a stately tent rising to a peak in the center. Throughout *Troilus and Cressida* the Greeks are located in relation to their tents. The Greek council scene, 1.3, takes place in or in front of the tent of Agamemnon; when Aeneas arrives bearing Hector's challenge, Agamemnon asks, "What would you 'fore our tent?" and Aeneas asks if he is at the commander's tent, apparently implying, as does his later call to his trumpeter,

> Trumpet, blow loud,
> Send thy brass voice through all these lazy tents,
>
> (1.3.256–57)

that more tents are visible. Some of the Greek tents could be imaginary, or painted cloth, but the tent of Ajax is the location for 2.1; and 2.2, 3.3 and 5.1 take place at or by the tent of Achilles, who is seen by Ulysses and others "at the opening of his tent" (2.3.84) in 2.3. At 3.3.37, Achilles and Patroclus "stand in their tent" (Quarto), or "Enter . . . in their tent" (Folio), while the Greek leaders pass by them. In 5.1 Thersites goes in to help Achilles trim his tent for a banquet, and the entrance, as noted earlier, is apparently marked by a torch or lights, since Ajax identifies this tent as being "There where we see the lights." The action moves in 5.2 to a location in front of the tent of Calchas, into which Cressida goes to fetch a token for Diomedes (5.2.60).

The Greek warriors, Achilles especially, are thus specifically identified in relation to their tents, and it is striking how often these are referred to in the plural. If there is no need to take literally Ulysses's remark to Agamemnon,

> And look how many Grecian tents do stand
> Hollow upon this plain . . . ,
>
> (1.3.79–80)

it is harder to shrug off Aeneas's command to his trumpeter to broadcast "through all these lazy tents" (1.3.257) or the invitation Ajax and Nestor give to Hector in 4.5 in welcoming him "to our Grecian tents" (4.5.151, 200). At the end Troilus cries out upon

> You vile abominable tents
> Thus proudly pight upon our Phrygian plains,
>
> (5.10.23–24)

and although these lines could be addressed to imaginary tents among the audience, they extend the visual connotations of the numerous other references to tents in the text. The play requires three basic locations, the Greek tents, Ilium or Troy (for Priam's palace and Cressida's house), and the plains or battlefield between; and if the text suggests that several Greek tents were somehow indicated, no scene takes place inside a tent, as in *Julius Caesar,* or even requires that we see inside one.

Scenes in Troy, like 1.2 and 2.2, are interspersed among scenes in the

Greek camp. However, the sequence of scenes that begins in 3.1 seems to require two recognizably different Trojan locations. Act 3, scene 1 takes place somewhere in Ilium, as Paris and Helen go off to "Priam's hall" at the end of it to greet warriors returning from the field of battle. The action then passes at once to the exterior of Cressida's house, where Troilus walks up and down ("I stalk about her door," 3.2.8) in anticipation of meeting her. There follows a scene in the Greek camp and a scene (4.1) of Trojan and Greek agents meeting somewhere between the Greek camp and Troy to begin the transfer of Cressida to the Greeks. In 4.2 the stage, or part of it, becomes the interior of Cressida's house, with Cressida wanting to call Pandarus down to "unbolt the gates" (4.2.3); a knocking at the door brings Aeneas in to summon Troilus to go with him and announce the decision to send Cressida back to her father. The brief 4.3 transfers us to the exterior of the house, where Troilus says to Paris,

> Walk into her house.
> I'll bring her to the Grecian presently.
>
> (4.3.5–6)

In 4.4 we are once again inside the house, with Aeneas calling from offstage "is the lady ready?" (4.4.49), and eventually, at line 108, Aeneas, Diomedes, and others enter to take delivery of Cressida, and they go off with Troilus determined to see her as far as the "port" or gate of Troy.

How were these scenes staged? The entry in 4.1 in the Quarto and the Folio calls for Aeneas to enter "at one door," Paris and a group including Diomedes "at another door"; Paris asks Aeneas to hasten to Calchas's (Cressida's) house to rouse Troilus and prepare him to yield up Cressida to Diomedes. These scenes call thus for the use of at least two stage doors, and it would have been convenient to use one door for Priam's palace in 3.1, and another for Troilus to stalk about in 3.2.[9] If stage doors were in constant use during these scenes in Troy, where did Achilles and Patroclus enter "in their tent" in 3.3? One possible arrangement would have been to have them stand in the opening of a tentlike structure projecting from the center of the rear wall of the stage, where there may well have been a third stage door at the Globe. If there were also collapsible tents attached to the two stage pillars, a sense of the Greek camp could have been created, justifying the references to tents in the text.[10]

It would not do to put much weight on such conjectures, but they relate to certain other features of *Troilus and Cressida* that I want to consider. Shakespeare seems to have thought out the staging, scene arrangements, and grouping of characters with considerable care. The play falls into two roughly equal halves, the first, a series of daylight scenes, much lighter in tone than the second. The night Troilus and Cressida spend together between 3.2 and 4.1 begins a change of mood, marked in the night scenes in which torches were used in the later part of the play. Each half ends with Pandarus addressing the audience, and there was probably an interval at the end of what is now 3.2[11] (act divisions were of course added by eighteenth-century editors). The passage of time is suggested with some exactness and the action occupies three days and two nights. The play is also structured so as to set off domestic or intimate scenes, like those involving Helen, Cressida with Pandarus, or Achilles and Ajax with Patroclus and Thersites, against larger groupings in council scenes, processions, and the like. These larger groupings are of great importance in the overall dramatic effect of the play.

The processions, for instance, establish a visual grandeur and a sense of group identity for Trojans and Greeks. When in 1.2 Cressida and Pandarus "stand up here" to watch Aeneas, Antenor, Hector, Paris, Helenus, Troilus, and others return to Troy from the battlefield, those Trojans are not merely identified by name, but as warrior-heroes, with their helmets hacked and swords covered in blood (1.2.205, 233), and, visually, as representing the "chivalry" of Troy (1.2.229). There is, perhaps, something of a parody of this scene in 3.3, when the Greek warriors parade in turn past the tent of Achilles, scorning him as he stands in the entrance of his tent; this little procession here images the discords among the Greeks. However, both sides meet formally in 4.5, in an encounter marked by some pomp and ceremony. The Greeks appear first, with Ajax armed and a trumpeter; then come the Trojans, with Hector armed. Aeneas and Diomedes act as marshals and arrange a ritual combat between Ajax and Hector that ends in a truce. It appears that Hector and Ajax fight center stage, with the Greeks watching from one side and the Trojans from the other; only after the fight ends do the parties of Greek and Trojan warriors approach and mingle (at this point the Folio has the stage direction for the Greek leaders, who are already on stage, "Enter Agamemnon and the rest," 4.5.158), and then Nestor welcomes Hector to the Grecian tents (4.5.200). The Trojan and Greek lords go off together eventually to Agamemnon's tent (4.5.271), leaving only Troilus and Ulysses to find their way to the tent of Calchas; but they return in procession, winding their way to the tent of Achilles by torchlight in 5.1. This brief mingling of the two sides precedes the battles of act 5 and the death of Hector. The play ends with two more processional scenes: first Agamemnon leads the Greek warriors as they march from the field of battle accompanied by the sound of drums (5.9.2), and then in the last scene the Trojan army marches onto the stage, with presumably as many as may be spared to swell the ranks, as Troilus discomforts "all the host" (5.10.10) with news of Hector's death.

These processional scenes need to be understood in relation to two other features of the play's action: the Greek and Trojan concern for appearances and public display, and the sense of characters' observing others or being observed. The procession of Trojan warriors in 1.2 is watched by Cressida and Pandarus, to whom all the heroes look alike in their armor. In 3.3 Achilles and Patroclus watch as the other Greek warriors pass by their tent. In 4.5 Achilles and Hector each stand to display themselves for inspection by the other. Such viewing links with Pandarus's voyeurism as he hovers over Troilus and Cressida, watching them make love in 3.2. Such scenes and, on a lesser scale, the viewing of Ajax by Achilles in 2.1 and the playacting of Thersites as Ajax in 3.3, watched by Achilles, build up a dramatic charge that gives a special force and poignancy to 5.2, in which Troilus replaces Pandarus as observer of Cressida, who is now making love to Diomedes, and is in turn watched by Ulysses and by Thersites. "Th'attest of eyes," in Troilus's phrase, is very important, both for the conviction it can give,

> The present eye praises the present object,
>
> (3.3.180)

and for the way the eye can mislead:

> The error of our eye directs our mind.
>
> (5.2.110)

So it is with Hector, whose eye is caught by the rich armor of the soldier he hunts for his hide, an error that leads to his death at the hands of the Myrmidons.

Nestor, praising Hector, describes how he has seen him fight in battle, sparing the defeated,

> And I have seen thee pause and take thy breath,
> When that a ring of Greeks have hemm'd thee in,
> Like an Olympian wrestling. This have I seen,
> But this thy countenance, still lock'd in steel,
> I never saw till now.
>
> (4.5.192–96)

The warriors do not reveal themselves in soliloquy and are alike in appearance when wearing armor and helmets; Nestor has never seen Hector's face, just as Aeneas cannot recognize Agamemnon unarmed in 1.3. Greeks and Trojans are known by their crests or colors on the field of battle. The emphasis here and elsewhere on observing reflects the peculiar nature of the play as concerned with male characters who exist primarily as public figures. In Troy only the women, Cressida and Helen, are seen in their private or domestic world; the warriors exist as it were to fulfill the roles expected of them, each concerned, as we now say, with his image.

This is one reason the play seems so modern, since we live in a world in which vast organizations devote their energies to creating the images politicians, presidents, and generals present to the public eye.

Perhaps all the features of *Troilus and Cressida* I have been commenting on can be related to yet another stage image, that of Hector hemmed in by "a ring of Greeks." In these lines Nestor ironically anticipates the death of Hector, slain by Achilles's Myrmidons in 5.8, when surely they should hem him in, forming a ring, or at least a semicircle around him as they all strike him together. This image would be still more powerful if it came as the climax to a series of such stage images, and the play presents several episodes that might be staged so as to prepare this climax. The first comes in 1.3, when Aeneas interrupts the council of the Greeks with his trumpet and appears before "great Agamemnon's tent" (1.3.216). It would be appropriate if Aeneas unexpectedly intrudes into a circle of Greek princes, who do not recognize him and who have never known a Trojan to appear thus before their tents. The council held by the Trojan lords in 2.2 is also interrupted by the extraordinary figure of Cassandra, "raving" (Quarto), and "with her hair about her ears" (Folio). It would again be fitting if she broke into and disturbed characters arranged in a semicircle, or some such grouping, with Priam at the head mirroring the figure of Agamemnon as chairman of the Greek council.

An analogous stage image could be presented at the end of 2.3, when the Greek lords seem more or less to surround Ajax as he preens himself, and they goad him, or comment in asides, on his swelling conceit. A sequence of such stage images would give a special poignancy and significance to the arrival of Cressida among the Greeks in 4.5. Here for the first time she is exposed to public view; in contrast to 1.2, in which she watched from the privacy of her house the Trojans returning from battle, she is now on display for inspection by a group of warriors and, like Hector later, is hemmed in by Greeks. We have seen them baiting Ajax, and they now bait her, their behavior constituting a kind of assault upon her, once Agamemnon, the "great commander" (1.3.55) has clasped and kissed her. Just as Aeneas and Troilus in 1.1 think of fighting their enemy as "good sport," so the Greeks here make sport with Cressida, whose silence may be taken as a sign of her bewilderment, before she catches on to the game being played and wittily puts down Menelaus.

Here then may be found a series of stage images in which characters intrude into a group (Aeneas, Cassandra), or a group surrounds a character to mock, bait, or kill (Ajax, Cressida, Hector). These incidents in which a group brings pressure, so to speak, on an individual, may be related to the series of processions; in the way that these are presented, individuals sometimes watch and comment on a passing parade, as Cressida and Pandarus do in 1.2, and as Thersites watches the Greeks accompanying Hector to the tent of Achilles in 5.1; sometimes the procession itself is designed to bring pressure to bear on an individual, as when the Greeks pass before Achilles in his tent in 3.3.

Such stage images may in turn be related to the use of tents. Most of the Trojan scenes in the play are imagined as interior scenes, taking place in Priam's palace or in Cressida and Calchas's house, and the pressure of public duty against private affairs is expressed through scenes in which warriors return from battle watched, so to speak, from within doors, in the council scene, and in Helen's going off to disarm Hector in 3.1. The Greek scenes all take place among their tents, and the clash of public duty and private interest seems to be visually established as an opposition between the space where the Greeks meet—to debate, to mock Ajax, or to welcome the Trojans—and the private enclosure of the tent, especially that of Achilles, who, with Patroclus, refuses to fight or attend the Greek councils, defending himself to Ulysses:

> Of this my privacy
> I have strong reasons.
> *Ulysses.* But 'gainst your privacy
> The reasons are more potent and heroical.
>
> (3.3.190–92)

The tent of Achilles is a visual embodiment of the privacy he maintains, and he must be able to withdraw into it, as he does to avoid encountering Agamemnon, in 2.3, and again in 5.1 when he invites Hector in, "Come, come, enter my tent" (5.1.87).

The next scene, 5.2, takes place at the tent of Calchas, and this shows another private encounter, of Cressida and Diomedes, who remain unaware that they are spied on by others; since it follows directly upon a group entering the tent of Achilles, it must be at a different stage location. The Greek tents thus have an important function in the stage imagery of *Troilus and Cressida,* marking the isolation of Achilles, much as the Trojan scenes convey a sense of the seclusion of Cressida. They also have a further ironic significance worth noting: while the events of the play take place during the Trojan war, Shakespeare, as numerous commentators have observed, took his material from medieval sources, and he gave the action a medieval coloring by treating the Greek and Trojan warriors as knights and Troilus as a courtly lover. In particular, the Trojan warriors are seen, or see themselves, in chivalric terms, Hector especially. If there is irony in Pandarus's calling Troilus the "prince of chivalry" at 1.2.229 and in Hector's boasting, "I am today i'th'vein of chivalry" (5.3.32), shortly before his death, Nestor's tribute to Hector in 4.5 is unequivocal, and this "gallant Trojan" (4.5.183) appears in sharp contrast to the surly Achilles, "lumbering giant of egotism, lasciviousness and pride."[12] If both sides refer to warriors as knights, and the fight between Hector and Ajax has suggestions of a medieval tourney to prove Greek women are after all "worth / The splinter of a lance" (Aeneas in 1.3.282–83), it is the Trojans who lay claim to chivalric ideals, as against the Greeks' concern with policy and what is expedient. The "brave pavilions" of the Greeks provide another layer of irony, for their tents visually suggest for the audience the most obvious link with the world of chivalry, still distantly recollected in such events as the meeting of Henry VIII and Francis I at the Field of the Cloth of Gold in 1520.

There are good reasons for believing that more than one Greek tent was visually represented on Shakespeare's stage and for claiming that the meaning of the action is bound up with the use of tents, torches, groupings, and processions. Examples from one play do not provide a basis for generalization about Shakespeare's drama as a whole; but in *Troilus and Cressida* we have something more than the use of what J. L. Styan called "scenic emblems",[13] or properties and scenic devices conveying no more than a sense of location (such as a moss bank) or time (like torches to indicate night). So perhaps it would be worth examining other plays on the assumption that the King's Men produced as lavish a spectacle as they could mount, much as leading stage companies do now; the implications of scenes, settings, and properties need to be studied more fully. Recent investigations of Shakespeare's stagecraft have been exciting and have provided excellent surveys of the use of gesture, costume, and other visual signals; critics are now beginning to question whether the "emblematic significance"[14] Ann Pasternak Slater and others find in such signals is really direct or can be subversive—whether Shakespeare is a maker or breaker of images. I suggest we need to gain a fuller understanding of stage images before we proceed far down that particular road.

Notes

    1. The story is briefly told in R. A. Foakes, *Illustrations of the English Stage 1580–1642* (Palo Alto, Calif.: Stanford University Press, 1985), xiii–xv.
    2. David Bevington, *Action is Eloquence* (Cambridge: Harvard University Press, 1984), 13.
    3. G. K. Hunter, "Flatcaps and Bluecoats," *Essays and Studies* 33 (1980): 33.
    4. So, for example, Glynne Wickham, in his exhaustive study of *Early English Stages 1300–1660* (London: Routledge and Kegan Paul, 1963) vol. 2, pt. 1, 204, 322, claims that we should accept "De Witt's sketch of the Swan Theatre at its face value without modification" as a representation of a typical Elizabethan stage; and although he lists a good many scenic items and pieces of stage furniture mentioned in plays or inventories, he assumes that "any move which could be made towards using the *mimorum aedes* itself for establishing locale in stage-action and thereby economizing upon the number of scenic emblems which had to be constructed,

paid for, set on the stage and subsequently stored was to be welcomed." On doubling, see Stephen Booth, "Speculations on Doubling in Shakespeare's Plays," in *Shakespeare: The Theatrical Dimension,* ed. Philip C. McGuire and David A. Samuelson (New York: AMS Press, 1979), 103–31, and John C. Meagher, "Economy and Recognition: Thirteen Shakespearean Puzzles," *Shakespeare Quarterly* 35 (1984): 7–21.

5. See *Henslowe's Diary,* ed. R. A. Foakes and R. T. Rickert (Cambridge: Cambridge University Press, 1961), 178–80, 319–20.

6. Hunter, "Flatcaps and Bluecoats," 24–25; Alan C. Dessen, *Elizabethan Stage Conventions and Modern Interpreters* (Cambridge: Cambridge University Press, 1984), 90.

7. Line references of quotations from Shakespeare's plays are to *The Riverside Shakespeare,* ed. G. Blakemore Evans (Boston: Houghton Mifflin, 1974).

8. Dessen, *Elizabethan Stage Conventions,* 79–80, comments incisively on the use of lights in *Troilus and Cressida.*

9. George F. Reynolds, in *"Troilus and Cressida* on the Elizabethan Stage," in *J. Q. Adams Memorial Studies,* ed. James G. McManaway, Giles E. Dawson, and Edwin E. Willoughby (Washington, D. C.: Folger Shakespeare Library, 1948), 229–38, argued that there were signs on two stage doors, one indicating that it led to Troy, the other to the Greek camp, but Bernard Beckerman in *Shakespeare at the Globe* (New York: Macmillan, 1962), 72–73, pointed out that the two doors specified in 4.1 both lead to Troy.

10. The use of tents seems to be a feature of public-theatre plays; see E. K. Chambers, *The Elizabethan Stage,* 4 vols. (London: Oxford University Press, 1923), 3:53–54, 106. I assume Shakespeare had the Globe in mind when writing *Troilus and Cressida.* G. F. Reynolds, who pioneered a minimalist interpretation of the staging of Elizabethan plays, was inclined to take literally the prologue's reference to two sides:

> Now expectation, tickling skittish spirits
> On one and other side, Trojan and Greek,
> Sets all on hazard.

This reference to the two opposing armies need not be taken as relating to the stage, and others have pointed out that the play cannot be staged with a simple division of the stage between the two sides; see n. 7 above.

11. See Emrys Jones, *Scenic Form in Shakespeare* (Oxford: Clarendon Press, 1971), 66–88, who argues that a number of Shakespeare's plays fall into two parts in this way.

12. G. Wilson Knight, *The Wheel of Fire* (1930, rev. 1949; Meridian Books: New York 1957), 71.

13. *Shakespeare's Stagecraft* (Cambridge: Cambridge University Press, 1967), 30.

14. Ann Pasternak Slater, *Shakespeare the Director* (Brighton, England: Harvester Press, 1982), 3; James Siemon argues the case for Shakespeare as iconoclast in *Shakespearean Iconoclasm* (Berkeley and Los Angeles: University of California Press, 1985).

The "State" of Shakespeare's Audiences

ANDREW GURR

John Weever may have known Shakespeare from his Lancashire days in the 1580s, if Shakespeare did work as a teacher there after his marriage. Weever certainly knew Shakespeare in London and recorded his acquaintance in the collection of epigrams he published in 1599. Shakespeare may also have been involved, directly or indirectly, in Weever's decision to write a poem celebrating the life of Sir John Oldcastle, the knight Shakespeare used for the figure of Falstaff before the Cobham family protested and forced him to alter the name to the one we all know. Weever composed his poem in about 1599, two years after Shakespeare's abandonment of the name Oldcastle, the year when the rival company to Shakespeare's put on its play *Sir John Oldcastle*. It was undoubtedly written to help the restoration of Oldcastle's reputation and to celebrate his status as a martyr, made secure long since in Foxe's *Acts and Monuments*. When published in 1601, two years after it was written, its title indicated its aim: "*The Mirror of Martyrs,* OR, The life and death of that thrice valiant Capitaine, and most godly Martyre, *Sir John Old-castle knight* Lord Cobham."

Weever, for all his possible connection with Shakespeare, is relevant here only as a member of a Shakespearean audience, a playgoer in the 1590s at the Curtain and the Globe when *Richard II* and *Hamlet* were first staged. He knew Shakespeare's poems and he knew Shakespeare's plays in performance. His poem on Oldcastle uses the stanza form of *Venus and Adonis* and makes references to Adonis in the text. About a third of the way through the poem, telling the story of England in Oldcastle's youth, Weever employs a familiar phrase from Shakespeare's poem together with an evocative image deriving from the play of 1595.

> Looke when the sun most bride-groome like doth rise,
> Soone as the morne unbarres her christall gate:
> So *Bullingbrooke* unto the gazers eyes
> Riseth in *Richards* royall chaire of state.
> (*The Mirror of Martyres,* 1601, C3v)

A flowery piece of imitative poeticizing, we might think. That indeed it rather obviously is. But it reveals a knowledge of Shakespeare's play in

162

performance, and of some features of that original performance, that are much less obvious and point to some of the things which modern viewers of Shakespeare in performance have lost. Such losses as these are a necessary preoccupation of performance criticism. They generate in turn the further question whether or not the losses are retrievable.

Bacon wrote about the theatre in *The Advancement of Learning,* a couple of years after *Hamlet* was first staged, that "the minds of men in company are more open to affections and impressions than when alone."[1] Experiencing Shakespeare in the theatre, either in 1605 or now, is a collective activity, very different in its nature from the solitary act of reading. The minds of men opened in company, the sharing of laughter or horror, the flow and accumulation of dramatic momentum, the shared experience of live theatre are all components of the performance text. Such a massively complex experience cannot readily be dissected into accessible components as can the word on the page. We kill to dissect much more thoroughly when we try to "read" a performance organism than when we read a poem, even a Wordsworthian poem. The audience experience is also inaccessible in its traditions, which are visual more than they are verbal. In performance criticism the source hunting of written texts has to be replaced by icon hunting, seeking the visual familiarities that have vanished along with the players and their playhouses. Those collectively familiar sights of the Shakespearean stage are one of the biggest obstacles to our rediscovery of the long-dead organism that is the Shakespearean performance text.

Starting from Weever's reference to *Richard II* I shall try to single out two of the components, or organs, from the performance organisms of *Hamlet* and *Richard II* in an attempt to measure the gulf between a Shakespearean audience and a modern audience for those two plays. This exercise may also help in identifying some of the ways in which the gulf might be reduced.

Probably the most difficult line for a modern actor in *Hamlet* to speak is Marcellus's comment on the confusing events of act 1, "Something is rotten in the state of Denmark."[2] It became a joke catchphrase in the nineteenth century and is so well known now that these days audiences hardly ever hear it. Actors deliver it in a mumble while rushing offstage, swords clanking and leather rustling in the panic and confusion of the Ghost's disappearance. The line worked differently in Shakespeare's day and so provides a clear measurement of the distance that lies between then and now.

Marcellus is a soldier, one of the guards who has himself seen the Ghost walking at midnight twice already before he brings Horatio to witness the sight in the opening scene of the play. Like most soldiers Marcellus does not know why he is doing his duty on guard at midnight—Horatio, the

outsider, has to explain about the invasion threatened by young Fortinbras—and he is a worrier. He is also a careful man. He does not rush
around broadcasting the story of the Ghost but cautiously broaches it to
Horatio, the scholar, and gets him to witness the sight before spreading the
story any further. Even then he does not go to the King but to the young
Hamlet. He is uninformed, a worrier, and wisely cautious.

He is not present at the scene at the royal court that follows the ghost's
first appearance. But this scene has a direct bearing on his embarrassing
line and needs some visual explanation. The stage platform at the Globe
for this scene would have been dominated by the royal throne, looking as
near as the players could make it to the canopied royal throne Elizabeth
used on state occasions.

The stage throne was a wooden, probably gilded chair on a dais, with a
canopy over it. No doubt the Globe's throne was far less impressive than
Elizabeth's, and it may have been no more substantial than the judge's
chair shown in the 1620 woodcut on the title page of the Red Bull's
Swetnam the Woman Hater.

This illustration cannot be a picture of the real stage scene at the Red
Bull, since it has windows in the rear wall where the playhouse had
hangings, but it probably reproduces the kind of chair used for playhouse
scenes representing either a royal courtroom or a judicial court. We know
the throne was portable and was set on a raised platform three or more
steps high.

In 1.2 of *Hamlet* Claudius the new king enters at the head of a procession, Queen in hand, courtiers following, all in their splendidly colorful
wedding clothes, and seats himself on the canopied throne to begin his
official speech. Hamlet in funeral black among the wedding clothes is the
only visible sign of discord. Claudius makes all the right noises about the
sudden death of the old king and his own equally sudden wedding to the
widowed Queen. Then he proceeds to the most urgent business of state,
the invasion from young Fortinbras that Horatio has already told us is the
cause of the midnight guard. Claudius tells the story (I use Harold
Jenkins's punctuation):

> Now follows, that you know young Fortinbras,
> Holding a weak supposal of our worth,
> Or thinking by our late dear brother's death
> Our state to be disjoint and out of frame,
> Colleagued with this dream of his advantage,
> He hath not failed to pester us with message
> Importing the surrender of those lands
> Lost by his father, with all bonds of law,
> To our most valiant brother, so much for him,
> Now for ourself, and for this time of meeting,
> Thus much the business is. . . .

(1.2.17–27)

Figure 1. Queen Elizabeth I at the opening of Parliament, 1586. A detail from an engraving in Robert Glover's *Nobilitas Politica vel Civilis*, 1608. (*Courtesy of the Trustees of the British Museum.*)

Figure 2. A woodcut on the title page of *Swetnam the Woman-hater*, 1620. (*Courtesy of the Trustees of the British Museum.*)

Claudius is being gently contemptuous of this threat from Fortinbras. To show his control of things, he makes a joke, a little politician's witticism. The throne he sits on is an emblem of his power. Here is young Fortinbras, Claudius might have said,

> Thinking by our late dear brother's death
> Our *throne* to be disjoint and out of frame. . . .

Throne was not a word the Elizabethans used for what we think of as a royal throne. What Elizabethans saw their ruler sitting on was what Weever called the chair of state, or the "state." Claudius offers a witticism based on his solid-looking throne. Fortinbras thinks our chair of state is coming apart at the joints, is askew and "out of frame." Visibly—on stage—the chair of state in which Claudius sits is not askew and falling apart. How could young Fortinbras be so foolish as to think it would be? Claudius makes his joke with a metaphor from carpentry. The "state" seems visibly to be secure. It is Hamlet a little later on who makes the point that seeming is at some distance from reality.

And it is the uninformed Marcellus, two scenes later, knowing all too little of what is really going on, the cautious worried soldier, who gives words to the reality and in the process changes the metaphor from Claudius's carpentry to Hamlet's own recurrent image of disease. The sickness at the head that destroys the whole of Denmark is an image launched by Marcellus in that line about the seemingly secure throne and its occupant, "Something is rotten in the state of Denmark."

That is a small verbal point, perhaps, which merely requires a footnote in our reading editions (although it has not appeared yet in any edition). We can learn the old terminology for physical objects on stage, and we can imagine them being quibbled on and the quibble coming to life in the performance text. But others of Shakespeare's uses of the stage throne offer problems of a different order of magnitude. The throne is a basic feature of stage furniture in *Richard II*. In that play it shows some of the problems that remain for us as modern audiences even after we have decoded the literal and routinely metaphorical connotations of the "state" as a throne.

Richard II opens with a Court scene—a Court in which the king is judge, his Court a courtroom, his seat a judicial chair of State.

Walter Hodges has drawn this version of the setting—actually its reprise in 1.3, when the two contestants are ready for the trial by combat. I think it has at least one mistake in its conception that I will come to later. The king's "state," which Holinshed called his "seat of justice" and which Gaunt in the play calls his "state of law," occupies center stage, as the focal point to which all stage action relates. The symbolic, iconic potency

Figure 3. A drawing by Walter Hodges of the duel scene, 1.3 in *Richard II*, made for the New Cambridge edition of the play, 1984. (*Courtesy of C. Walter Hodges and Cambridge University Press.*)

of this source of authority was enormous for Elizabethans, and it is, I think, quite impossible for us to see it the same way. And yet the staging and the language of *Richard II* depend heavily on this potent icon. The throne or seat of justice was the visible emblem of power. In act 1 Richard sits on it giving judgment. In act 5 Henry Bullingbrook sits on it giving judgment. In the central scene, when Richard deposes himself, the throne is there on stage, but empty. This scene, 4.1, had a tremendous power for Elizabethans, as we know because the central part, where Richard arrives to hand the crown over to Bullingbrook, was censored out from the three Elizabethan editions. It opens with a procession of Bullingbrook and the lords entering "*as to the parliament,*" according to the Quarto, in what must have been a deliberate imitation of the opening procession, when Richard enters to sit on his throne and pass judgment on the quarrel between his two subjects. Richard in act 1 heard an accusation against Bullingbrook. In act 4 Bullingbrook tries to hear—as judge—an accusation against Richard, over the murder of Gloucester. He even uses Richard's own words from the opening scene, "freely speak," to the complainants. But there is one vital difference. Bullingbrook is not yet crowned, and he does not ascend to sit on the throne. It therefore remains empty throughout the scene.

The attempt to enact a court of justice scene, with Bagot as witness to the question of who murdered Gloucester, is conducted with no judge in the central seat. Bullingbrook does say, "In God's name I'll ascend the royal throne," but the bishop of Carlisle intervenes, and after a load of distractions Bullingbrook puts off the act until his coronation. In 5.2 and 3 and 5.6 he does sit on the throne as Weever's image has it, and Northumberland arriving in the last scene salutes his "royal state." That itself is a loaded statement, saluting the "state" and not the person, and that, together with Bullingbrook's occupation of it after we have seen it empty in act 4, is a comment on the concept of the king's two bodies, the divinely authorized body which occupies the throne and the changing human bottoms that do the occupying. The throne, first occupied by Richard, then seen vacant, then occupied by Bullingbrook, is a powerful visual emblem of the change of power in the play.

The state in *Richard II* is also a basic feature of the imagery of the four elements—earth, air, fire and water—that orchestrates the play. It stands on and over the earth represented by the stage platform, up on high, closer to the heavens painted on the underside of the stage cover than the seats of ordinary mortals. It is not merely a seat of justice but a symbol of the higher elevation, nearer heaven, that was thought (by some) to be natural to a king. Movement by Richard and Bullingbrook on and off the state with its dais and its steps reflects the upward and downward movement that is basic to the elemental imagery of the play. When Richard chooses

Figure 4. A drawing by Walter Hodges of the deposition scene, 4.1 in *Richard II*, made for the New Cambridge edition of the play, 1984. (*Courtesy of C. Walter Hodges and Cambridge University Press.*)

to sit upon the ground of England, which he has just kissed as his beloved property, to tell sad stories of the death of kings, he is renouncing the status that separates kings from ordinary beings and claiming that he is an ordinary mortal.

The ruling imagery, and its cross-patterning that sets Richard's fall against Bullingbrook's rise, is based precisely on the four elements. Richard, the sun-king of fire, contends with the flood of Bullingbrook's waters, which invade the earth of England. Their stormy meeting—thunderstorms were thought to be the elements of fire and water in conflict—drowns Richard's fire in the water of tears, brings him down, and by the contrary upward movement changes Bullingbrook into a sun. Fire and water struggle on the earth of England and conduct their fight in the airy breath of words.

This image pattern is so pervasive through the play that it hardly needs to be identified by quotation. It saturates the language of the two scenes, 1.1 and 3.2, that mark the beginning and end of Richard's dominance. In 3.3, the scene in which falling Richard descends past rising Bullingbrook, Bullingbrook invokes all four elements in a speech reverberating with self-conscious artifice:

> Methinks King Richard and myself should meet
> With no less terror than the elements
> Of fire and water, when their thund'ring shock
> At meeting tears the cloudy cheeks of heaven.
> Be he the fire, I'll be the yielding water;
> The rage be his, whilst on the earth I rain
> My waters—on the earth, and not on him.
>
> (54–60)

The overt artifice in that run-on line, "whilst on the earth I rain . . . My waters" with its blatant homonymic hint that the new man will reign on the earth of England after the storm, evokes some natural suspicions about the way in which the pattern of the elements so neatly fits the story of Richard's deposition. In part this reflects the structure of the play as metadrama, a challenge to the way people conceive reality and the words people apply to those conceptions. Accounts of *Richard II* as a meta-drama about the destruction of language should mistrust the imagery too, especially when it is invoked as grossly as Bullingbrook invokes it in this speech and as Richard does when he calls himself a sun-king.

The elements themselves are constant. What shifts in the dynamism of the play is their application as images. Both protagonists use the sun image in the pivot scene, 3.3. Bullingbrook describes Richard's appearance on the battlements of Flint Castle as like

> the blushing discontented sun
> From out the fiery portal of the east,
> When he perceives the envious clouds are bent
> To dim his glory. . . .
>
> (63–66)

But Richard has already given the order to discharge his followers and allowed them to go "From Richard's night to Bullingbrook's fair day" (3.2.218). When he accepts "King Bullingbrook" (3.3.173) and descends to the "base court" on a level with his rival, he describes himself as not the sun-king but "glistering Phaëton," the pretender who could not control the horses of the sun and scorched the earth before Jove killed him with a thunderbolt. That role also fits Bullingbrook. He is "hasty as fire" at the beginning of the play (1.1.19), and by the final scene his usurpation of the throne has consumed "Our town of Cicester in Gloucestershire" (5.6.3) with fire as if he too were a Phaëton. Unlike the water that is embedded in his name (a pun initiated by Daniel and deployed in the play at 3.2.106–10) and which moves naturally downward, Bullingbrook consistently aspires upward, like fire. The pattern is not the simple picture of his elements speech at 3.3.54–60. Fire and water images interact in intricate ways within the outline of Bullingbrook's water putting out Richard's fire and leaving the one with the sun's fire and the other with watery tears, an elemental role reversal.

Fire mounts upward. Water descends. The water images develop through references to the coming storm (2.1.263–69, 2.4.19–22 and 3.3.43–47) that culminate in Bullingbrook's presentation of the four elements (3.3.54–60). The first two of the earlier references to storms are by minor characters. Bullingbrook elevates the concept into a conceit. But by then Richard has already taken up the water image for himself and has deployed it even more histrionically than his rival. From Aumerle's innocent question at the beginning of 3.2, "How brooks your Grace the air / After your late tossing on the breaking seas?" Richard squeezes the elemental images for all they have. He weeps for joy to be standing on the earth of his kingdom again, the very stones of which will prove soldiers to fight off Bullingbrook. When the bishop of Carlisle reminds him of God's support for his title and Aumerle sensibly translates the bishop's praise of the Lord into an appeal to pass the ammunition, Richard deploys his own more prolix version of the elemental imagery.

> Discomfortable cousin, know'st thou not
> That when the searching eye of heaven is hid
> Behind the globe, that lights the lower world,
> Then thieves and robbers range abroad unseen.
>
> . . . .

> But when from under this terrestrial ball
> He fires the proud tops of the eastern pines
> And darts his light through every guilty hole,
> Then murthers, treasons, and detested sins,
> The cloak of night being pluck'd from off their backs,
> Stand bare and naked, trembling at themselves?
> So when this thief, this traitor Bullingbrook,
> Who all this while hath revell'd in the night,
> Whilst we were wandering in the antipodes,
> Shall see us rising in our throne, the east,
> His treasons will sit blushing in his face,
> Not able to endure the sight of day,
> But self-affrighted tremble at his sin.
> Not all the water in the rough rude sea
> Can wash the balm off from an anointed king;
> The breath of worldly men cannot depose
> The deputy elected by the Lord.
>
> (36–39, 41–57)

Richard is the sun. Bullingbrook is the rough rude sea. But that conceit does not outlast the scene. By the end it is "Bullingbrook's fair day," and Richard's talk is of "woe" (102, 178, 210) and graves in the earth (145–54). The exchange of roles with Bullingbrook takes place in the next scene, at Flint Castle (3.3). On his next appearance, in the deposition scene (4.1) his talk is of tears, water, and earth. He is the heavy bucket in Fortune's well, "down, unseen, and full of water." He applies the conceit to the upward and downward tendencies of the elements.

> That bucket, down and full of tears, am I,
> Drinking my griefs whilst you mount up on high.
>
> (187–88)

Richard and Bullingbrook both know how to exploit the concept of the elements.

The third element, earth, is the most consistent feature of the image pattern, as constant as the stage platform that represents it. Earth is the land of England, this other Eden, which when things are in their proper places is warmed by the sun and watered by the rains, both of which are the gift of heaven. Richard is said to abuse the land by his injustices, to give it out to lease "like to a tenement, or pelting farm" (2.1.60), because he will not use his heavenly authority properly. "Landlord of England art thou now, not king," Gaunt tells him (114). For the same reason Northumberland withholds from him the proper homage due to authority, the gesture of kneeling on the earth in front of him (3.3.72–74). The play is full of people kneeling to the different kings, to the point of parody in 5.3. In act 3 Richard's overindulgence in the sweets of his earth bring him to a surfeit so that the earth only gives him sour and bitter tastes and its poisonous venoms and caterpillars (3.2.12–22, 129–36, 3.4.37–47). As he "tastes grief" in 3.2 his title to the earth shrinks to the compass of a grave. At his death he asks that his body sink to the earth of which it was made while his soul, made of more airy substance, mounts upward (5.5.111–12).

The fourth element, air, is the least readily identifiable component in the pattern. The many commentators on the play's imagery have been slow to include it, and most have remained content with the fire and water elements. Air is present, however, both implicitly and explicitly along with the others. It is the "breath of worldly men" that Richard insists cannot depose God's anointed deputy (3.2.56). It is the "breath of kings" that Bullingbrook sarcastically acknowledges as the power which removes four years of exile (1.3.215). It is the same breath that Bullingbrook lacks as he goes into exile,

> When the tongue's office should be prodigal
> To breathe the abundant dolour of the heart.
>
> (1.3.256–57)

In short it is language, that gift which God gave uniquely to humankind, and that like air itself aspires upward to the heaven it came from. Just as Richard and Bullingbrook misapply the elemental images of fire and water, so language is abused throughout the play. The first scene opens with two declarations of truth, one of which, as Richard himself notes (1.1.25–26) must be false. Even names, the most stable form of language, shift under the pressure of events. Bullingbrook first falls into the nameless state of tongueless exile (1.3.159–73), then rises to Lancaster and eventually becomes King Henry. Aumerle, cousin to the two principals and supporter of the loser, finds his name lowered to Rutland. Richard falls from king to nothing. Language is the great betrayer when even names can shift like this. No wonder the wordy Richard falls to the "silent king" Bullingbrook.

In all the carefully orchestrated imagery of the elements, while Bullingbrook moves upward with fire and language and Richard falls downward with tears into his grave in the earth, there stands one dominant and unmoving icon, the "state." It stands center stage, itself unmoving as the storm shifts the characters around it. It is a royal "state," the name Northumberland upholds when he hails Bullingbrook's occupancy of it in the final scene. The "state" stands oblivious to its changing occupants throughout the play, from the fire of Bullingbrook's choler in the opening scene to the tears of his penitence at the close.

When John Weever wrote his poem about Oldcastle he knew the elemental imagery and the potency of the "state" better than we ever can. His lines about Bullingbrook rising like the new sun in the royal throne,

> So *Bullingbrooke* unto the gazers eyes
> Riseth in *Richards* royall chaire of state,

had a resonance in 1601 that can never be completely recaptured. We might repossess the image of the rotten "state" of Denmark, but not the force of the iconic rituals of kingship that dominated the staging of *Richard II*. In modern productions kings wander around without hats, let alone crowns, and subjects turn their backs, fail to kneel, and use their hats freely in ways that might have cost them their heads in Elizabeth's time. It might be possible with judicious program notes to make the point about subjects kneeling on the earth in fealty, but we cannot retrieve the force of Richard's instruction to his subjects to put their hats on in his presence in act 3. The iconography of hats—wearing them normally, indoors or out, doffing them in the royal presence—is as far gone as the collective awe for crowns and thrones.

An engraving made in 1641, the equivalent of a modern news photograph, shows some of the distance needed to cover the gulf between us and the reverence for the "state" that held sway under seventeenth-century monarchies. In 1641 Parliament impeached the earl of Strafford, Charles's most loyal minister. The king refused to act as judge of his minister. The trial therefore became notable for the empty seat of judgment, as Wenceslas Hollar painstakingly recorded. And the execution of the royal actor eight years later became an extension of that iconic act of vacating the chair of state. The minds of men in company, as Bacon understood it, can be seen in their collective responses to the "state" in *Richard II,* in Weever's poem, and in Parliament in 1641. We are unlikely to be able to make that recur in the modern theatre.

That iconic potency is not our only loss. Even if there were modern theatre directors who read their subtexts carefully enough to register when to supply thrones and crowns and willing to instruct their actors in the rituals of respect for kings, we should not come much closer to the mental constructs or "mindsets" (as Bernard Beckerman aptly named them) for which Shakespeare prepared his texts that require the minds of men in company to open. Audiences would have to acquire such mindsets collectively too, and audiences are less biddable than actors or even directors. The original performance texts, all that intricate interaction between poet's mind and collective audience mind, mediated in the familiar structures of the Globe and its players, can never be reconstructed.

There is no such thing as perfect criticism of any kind, and it would be idle to hope for performance criticism to differ. But the dissection of poems has its uses, however imperfect, and the dissection or reconstruction of performances has its uses too. Some things can be done with modern staging to recover the lost Shakespearean nuances, where we can

Figure 5. The trial of the earl of Strafford in Westminster Hall, 1641, from an engraving by Wenceslas Hollar (Pennington 551). The king is shown sitting in a spectator's box behind the throne. (*Courtesy of the Trustees of the British Museum.*)

identify them, and a great deal can be done with that much underrated influence on mindsets, the physical structure of the stage and auditorium. Even a brief scrutiny of that much-scrutinized picture, Van Buchell's copy of De Witt's sketch of the Swan, can show some of the things that still wait to be properly registered.

De Witt's picture has provoked a lot of dispute, partly because it is so oddly inconsistent. The trumpeter summons latecomers for the start of a play already in full swing. The stage platform and *frons* do not fit the enveloping galleries. There are no stage hangings and no visible discovery space. Each element in the sketch seems to represent a feature that does not properly match its accompaniments. It is not a trustworthy illustration of a playhouse interior. And yet it is all we have, and it represents a playhouse built on the Bankside only four years before Shakespeare's Globe was built as its neighbor and rival. It is even possible that Shakespeare's company used it for their plays when the Theatre was closed. As Walter Hodges's drawings show, *Richard II* could easily have been performed on a stage like the Swan's. Whatever the reservations about its

Figure 6. Arend van Buchell's copy of Johannes De Witt's sketch of the Swan, made in 1596. The original is in the library of the Rijksuniversiteit, Utrecht. (*Courtesy of the Bibliotheek der Rijksuniversiteit, Utrecht.*)

details, some of its features offer useful lessons about Shakespearean staging.

Its most obvious feature is its stage open to the sky, with the surrounding yard for spectators to stand in. There is natural light not only for the stage but for the auditorium, an emphatic difference from modern theatres. The audience not only flanked the stage platform by standing around the three sides but sat behind as well in the balcony's "sixpenny rooms." From whatever position in the auditorium you looked at the players the audience was visible behind them. Performances took place in the center of a crowd that was as visible as the players. Hamlet's soliloquies must have been very different events when spoken on a platform in broad daylight to an audience quite literally at the speaker's feet and as visible as he was. In a theatre familiar with the clown who commonly held "interlocutions with the audients" and in a play where the hero doubles the roles of prince and clown, the soliloquies were not at all the private musings of a solitary actor who is the only lighted figure in a dark room, the stock modern staging. Hamlet is prince ("Hamlet the Dane") and clown (assuming an antic disposition), rightful occupant of the chair of state and exploiter of backchat to the galleries and groundlings, figures of earth. His was a three-dimensional composition that our long immersion in proscenium arch staging and the two dimensions of the cinema screen has still not allowed us to recover.

It is, perhaps, regrettable that De Witt chose to draw his picture of the Swan from where the projection booth would nowadays stand. Even his three-dimensional stage can be seen all too easily in the two-dimensional terms that characterize the modern mindset. Walter Hodges's drawings for *Richard II,* in the composition of which I must admit a more responsible role than mere connivance, reflect the readiness with which we push central features of Shakespearean staging against the rear wall. On belated reflection I think that the "state" could never have been relegated to the back of the platform. It must have occupied center stage, probably a little further back than the bench on which the ladies sit in De Witt's sketch, allowing the courtiers room to present themselves in front of it, but much further forward than in the two illustrations for *Richard II* reproduced above. The judicial chair in the *Swetnam* illustration is better positioned for stage purposes. None of the three thrones from the early illustrations was backed up against a wall. Putting the "state" there reflects our (I should say *my*) two-dimensional mindset all too clearly.

The trap that lies in wait through such a search for the details of a performance text is our ignorance over what we are ignorant of. We do know something of what we do not know, of course. About the "state" we do not know whether it was brought out for court scenes and then taken into the tiring house again. There are some stage directions that specify *"bed put out,"* but none about states. It may have stood center stage throughout both *Richard II* and *Hamlet,* or it may have been carried out, mobile as the *Swetnam* chair evidently was, for each separate scene. We know that scenes were localized enough for characters to exit before the end of a scene if they are to reenter to start another scene in a different location, as Gaunt does near the end of the court scene in 1.1 of *Richard II,* before reentering with the widowed Duchess in 1.2. But we do not know if the scene with the Duchess was then played in front of the vacant "state." There are many recent discoveries about Shakespearean staging that could be applied to the performance texts and even some about the mental constructs which the audiences brought with them to the performances. But the real problem is always likely to be that we cannot identify what more there may be hidden. Many features of an original performance will never be retrievable. It is part of our loss that we are unlikely to know even the scale of our ignorance.

On such a darkling plain there is some point in concentrating on the more tangible features, those which there is some chance of retrieving. The physical structure of the Globe, for instance, is not such a distant chimera as it has often seemed to be. The limited evidence can be extrapolated and a replication made that can satisfy the available evidence. Such a physical structure would extend the possibilities of retrieval some way into the darker realm of the mental constructs that Elizabethans carried with them into the Globe. It is evident that *Hamlet* opens, according to any reading of the text, after midnight in freezing cold on Elsinore's battlements. It can also be made clear, with some scholarly effort, that the play would originally have opened at two o'clock in the afternoon in broad daylight in summer or early autumn, which even in London would have been a long way from being dark or even freezing. Even in winter in the early afternoon three thousand people crammed into an amphitheatre barely one hundred feet in outside diameter would have generated enough steam to make Francisco's complaint that it was bitter cold seem either a joke or an insistent demand laid on the audience's imagination to wrench themselves into another world. The Elizabethan response to such a demand must have predetermined the reaction a few moments later to the sight of a ghost walking in broad daylight. Without seeing the play in broad daylight, the surrounding audience a constant reminder that the play is a fiction, a staged entertainment, it is hardly possible even to conceive how much credulity, how much generous participation in the game of agreeing to pretend that the fiction is real, could have been expected of an Elizabethan audience. It may not be possible to reconstruct the precise shape of the mindset in an Elizabethan playgoer like John Weever when he went

Figure 7. The second Globe, built in 1614 on the foundations of the first. A detail from Wenceslas Hollar's "Long View" of London, 1644, (Pennington 1014), this version restores the caption that in the original was misplaced on the Hope, a nearby bear-baiting amphitheatre. (*Courtesy of the Trustees of the British Museum.*)

to see *Richard II* or *Hamlet*, but experience of the appropriate physical conditions would take us much further than we can go at present.

Notes

1. Francis Bacon, *The Advancement of Learning* (London, 1605), bk. 2, chap. 13.

2. Line references to Shakespeare's plays are to the New Arden Shakespeare, ed. Una M. Ellis-Fermor et al. (London: Methuen, 1951–).

Looking Back to Front

The View from the Lords' Room

DEREK PEAT

"I tell you that which you yourselves do know."
—Julius Caesar, 3.2.226

One of the most notable changes in the acting of Shakespeare's plays since the Second World War has been in the performance of soliloquies. It is now rare to see an actor "thinking aloud" and allowing an unacknowledged audience to "overhear" this internal musing. Nowadays, actors address their auditors directly, and doubtless this new form of delivery owes something to the rediscovery of the potential of open stages and the recovery of what we believe to have been the intimacy of the actor-audience relationship in Elizabethan theatre.

At Stratford-upon-Avon in 1984, Roger Rees, playing Hamlet for the Royal Shakespeare Company, achieved a great rapport with his audience through direct delivery of the soliloquies. When, for example, he asked his audience if he was a coward (*Hamlet,* 2.2.582) he spoke his lines as if he expected an answer. It therefore came as a surprise when Rees later revealed to the International Shakespeare Conference that he did not think much of the idea of building a New Globe on the London Bankside. He said he found it somewhat old-fashioned to rebuild an Elizabethan theatre, but he admitted that he would not mind working there, provided that he did not have to move when addressing soliloquies to the audience.

The last point perhaps needs explanation. Rees had been performing Hamlet in the main house at Stratford. This theatre began life as a reasonably conventional proscenium arch setup, but because of the constant modification to both stage and auditorium, the original point on the stage from which an actor could dominate the house, by containing the audience within his angle of vision, no longer exists. Nowadays, the actor must come down through the arch to the lip of the apron, raising his head to see the gallery and lowering it to address the stalls. This is what Rees had in mind, and he admitted he did not like it. What he hadn't realized was that in an "Elizabethan" theatre an actor is surrounded by audience looking up at him from below and down at him from above. Moreover, there is *no* point on an Elizabethan stage from which the actor can see all of his audience, or even two-thirds of them, so it is highly unlikely that he will stand still when addressing a soliloquy to them.

Rees was merely doing what we all do, working from his own experience of theatre and his response was a nice example of the situation Bernard Beckerman once described using his well-known metaphor of the "spectacles." Beckerman suggested that when we read a playscript we also don a pair of spectacles, that their frames are made of history and their lenses of "preconceptions about what constitutes drama and how it produces its effects."[1] The point is an obvious one, but easily forgotten, that whatever we see in a play, or whatever we imagine a performance was like in an Elizabethan theatre, is determined by our preconceptions.

When we look now at scholarly work on the Elizabethan theatre that postulates the existence of an "inner stage" for interior scenes, we can see that the idea was not based on the requirements of the known facts about the stage, but on the scholars' preconceptions based on experience of proscenium arch theatres. Indeed, here we may perceive the next part of the process, in which preconceptions are sifted according to preference and the resulting decisions are based upon taste. As C. Walter Hodges once noted, in reconstructions of Elizabethan theatres facts are "insufficient in themselves" so decisions are made "in accordance with influences of taste of which the scholar concerned may not even have been aware."[2]

We see what our preconceptions allow and we choose what we want, and this essay is concerned with a piece of information that most critics, either consciously or unconsciously, have chosen to ignore. As the epigraph to this essay suggests, I'm not revealing new knowledge about the nature of Elizabethan theatre, but rather developing some implications of what we already know.

The area of the theatre in which I'm interested is the gallery above the stage. We know that this gallery was used for acting, and we also know that later, in the Jacobean period, it was probably used for musicians, but the fact that fascinates me is that contemporary references suggest it was the "lords' room" (or rooms, since it may well have been partitioned). Like most things concerning Elizabethan theatre the evidence is far from unambiguous, but on the balance of probability the lords' room was located in the tiring-house gallery. W. J. Lawrence was, I think, the first to suggest this in an essay of 1908.[3] He pointed out Ben Jonson's reference in *Every Man Out of His Humour* in which a character is described as speaking to the lords "as familiarlie as if hee had . . . ta'en tobacco with them *over the stage i' the Lords roome*" (italics added). The other famous reference is in Dekker's *Gulls Hornbook* where we find "I mean not into the Lords roome (which is now but *the Stages Suburbs*). No, those boxes, by *the iniquity of custom,* conspiracy of waiting-women and Gentlemen-Ushers, that there sweat together, and the covetousness of Sharers, are contemptibly *thrust into the reare,* and much new Satten is there dambd by being smothred to death in darkness" (italics added).

While it may be objected that "above the stage" could refer to virtually anywhere in the galleries, the only gallery *directly* above the stage is the one in the tiring-house wall. Taken together with Dekker's reference to "thrust into the reare" and "the Stages Suburbs," which, however it may be being used pejoratively, here presumably means, as in the *Oxford English Dictionary*'s principal definition, "parts . . . that lie *immediately outside and adjacent to* [a city's] walls or *boundaries*" (compact edition, 1982), it appears, as I suggest, that on the balance of probabilities the gallery above the stage was the lords' room.

Moreover, while contemporary illustrations of theatres remain ambiguous on many points, a common element in at least three of the most important—the *Roxana* title page (fig. 1), *The Wits* frontispiece (fig. 2), and the De Witt sketch of the Swan (see p. 176 of this volume)—is that people appear in the gallery "behind" the stage. In the *Roxana* and *The Wits* it is fairly obvious that they are members of the audience. In the De Witt sketch it is much less obvious, but I suspect that the reason De Witt chose to show people in this, rather than in any other, part of the auditorium was probably because this was *the most important part.*

I have only touched on a small part of the documentary evidence concerning the lords' room. Those who require a comprehensive analysis should consult the series of articles, to which this essay is indebted, by Richard Hosley that appeared in *Shakespeare Survey* and *Shakespeare Quarterly* in the 1950s.[4] We know that seats in the lords' room were the most expensive in the theatre, but nevertheless Peter Thomson in a recent book suggests "we do not know which would have been considered the prime seats by an Elizabethan theatregoer."[5] All I can say is that I know of no theatrical setup in which the best seats are not considered to be those which cost the most, at least by those who purchase them. I can't envisage a situation in which the lords would purchase expensive seats with a bad view, and I assume that the actors, mindful of economic values and the benefit of court performances, were unlikely to ignore this part of their audience. And yet this is precisely what most commentators have managed to do. The existence of any audience "behind" the stage, let alone a very special part of the audience, has rarely been taken into account. Most commentators, placing themselves in the position from which De Witt viewed the stage of the Swan (ironically enough not at all a bad place to be in a proscenium arch theatre) assume *they* are in the best seats and comment on imagined stage action accordingly. Thus we usually find that

Figure 1. The *Roxana* title page, 1632. The play itself, by William Alabaster, is a Latin version of Luigi Groto's *La Dalida* (1567). Alabaster's play was performed at Trinity, Cambridge, ca. 1592, and was later registered and published—with this important title page—in 1632. (*From S. Schoenbaum*, Shakespeare, the Globe and the World [*New York: Folger Shakespeare Library; Oxford University Press, 1979*], *93. By permission of the Folger Shakespeare Library.*)

commentators refer to the audience at "the front" and "the sides" of the stage, but rarely, if at all, do they mention the audience "behind."

Hosley's work on the lords' room is some thirty years old, and he has drawn upon it in successive publications.[6] How is it that critics managed to undervalue the importance of this part of the audience? The points Hosley made, back in 1957, explain a good deal. He suggested that because most people's idea of theatre depended on their experience of proscenium arch theatre, in which the audience were in front and clearly separated from the stage, it was difficult for them to conceive of audience

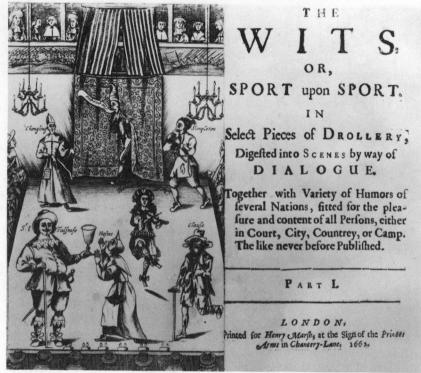

Figure 2. *The Wits* frontispiece, 1662. This depiction of a stage during performance appeared in 1672 in a publication by Francis Kirkman. It forms part of a collection of drolls entitled *The Wits; or Sport upon Sport*. (*From S. Schoenbaum*, Shakespeare, the Globe and the World [*New York: Folger Shakespeare Library; Oxford University Press, 1979], 94. By permission of the Folger Shakespeare Library*.)

"behind" the stage in an area that could also be used simultaneously by actors. Beckerman's idea of the "preconceptions" was clearly at work, and even Hosley succumbed by suggesting that the "visibility" of the stage from the lords' room couldn't have been too good.[7] He was still thinking in terms of a performance seen from "front of house," but I suspect there is another and a more important reason why many critics and scholars have tended to forget the lords rooms.

Our perception of Elizabethan theatre is not created by the work of scholars and critics alone, it is also, and perhaps more forcefully, created by the work of theatre practitioners. In this regard Tyrone Guthrie has been of enormous importance. His personal rediscovery of the Elizabethan stage coincided with a revival of scholarly interest and resulted in the creation of new "thrust" or "open" stage theatres. Yet while Guthrie was rediscovering and recreating the virtues of Elizabethan staging, there was one important element that he left out—an audience behind the stage. In the theatres for which he was largely responsible, at Stratford Ontario and Minneapolis, there are no members of the audience behind the stage. A gallery area can be used for acting, but the audience are essentially on three, not four, sides of the stage. It is therefore not surprising that the audience "behind," which in his theatres did not exist, should have been forgotten. This is not to say that there were not attempts to surround the stage with auditors. In the fifties Bernard Miles tried this, and in the seventies, the Royal Shakespeare Company, unhappy with the main house at Stratford, built "Elizabethan" galleries behind the stage.[8] In the sixties and seventies too there was an increasing interest in "theatre in the round," but rarely did Shakespearean plays find themselves in such venues (one exception was Tony Richardson's production of *Hamlet* in the Roundhouse at Chalk Farm in London), and even when they did the preconceptions were apparently too well established to be easily overborne.

And so it was that the increasing number of books that appeared from the mid-fifties onward dealing with Shakespeare's plays in performance and concentrating on the possibilities of original staging conditions paid little or no attention to that very important element of the auditorium, the lords' rooms. This is not to say that there was not a clear recognition of the difference between proscenium staging and what was conceived to be Elizabethan staging, for indeed there was. I have selected an apt illustration from John Styan's *Shakespeare's Stagecraft*[9] that shows the difference between the two kinds of theatre (fig. 3). Styan goes further than most in remembering that those arrows in his Elizabethan theatre need to go, not sideways, but backward, but I would suggest he still doesn't go far enough. There needs to be another arrow (the one I've added) going straight back to the tiring-house wall, because in an Elizabethan theatre the actor was surrounded by audience. This is *not* to suggest that Elizabethan theatre was "theatre in the round," because in such a theatre the best seats are everywhere and anywhere. In an Elizabethan theatre I suspect the best seats were behind the stage in the lords' room.

In theatre an idea is only valuable if it will work, and for the remainder of this piece I will therefore describe the effects of a series of practical performance experiments in a recreation of an Elizabethan theatre.

The theatre is the New Fortune on the campus of the University of Western Australia in Perth. The theatre was built in an existing quadrangle, because members of the staff of the English Department, which was housed there, realized it would accommodate a theatre with the dimensions of the Fortune contract. That proved to be almost true, but in that "almost" lies a substantial problem. As can be seen from the illustration (fig. 4) the courtyard wasn't quite wide enough to take the full twelve-

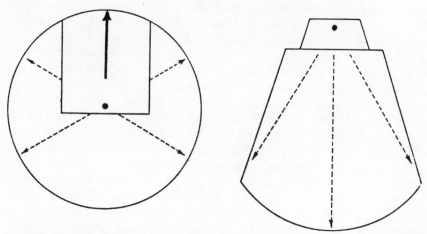

Figure 3. The Elizabethan and Victorian actor-audience relationship as indicated by J. L. Styan. The bold arrow on the left figure is my addition. (*From J. L. Styan, Shakespeare's Stagecraft [Cambridge: Cambridge University Press, 1967]. Courtesy of Cambridge University Press.*

foot-six-inch depth of the side galleries, so they had to be cut down by about two-thirds. To compensate, the depth of the front gallery was increased at ground level, and the yard used for seating. Ironically enough, the overall effect has been to create a theatre where the temptation to play to the front of the stage is encouraged (note, for example, where the side seating ends), and much of the potential for rediscovery of Elizabethan actor-audience dynamics has been lost. Of course it may be that the original Fortune, with its square shape and side galleries close to the stage, encouraged such forward playing, but our experiments with the lords' room tend to contradict this view. The illustration reveals that in this reconstruction the lords' room has a considerable "juttey forwardes" and is lower and much more open than the area the De Witt sketch shows. These modifications may have improved this area as an acting space, but they created worse sight lines for the lords than would have obtained if the area was flush with the tiring-house facade.

The experimental work was undertaken almost by accident. I and some colleagues, who are also friends, were attending a conference at the University of Western Australia, and we took the advantage to explore the potential of the New Fortune Theatre. The group contained people with a combination of scholarly and practical experience: Joanna Gibson, who teaches voice at the Victorian College of the Arts, and also works as a professional actor; Gareth Griffith, head of Drama Studies at Macquarie University, who has a good deal of directing experience as has Graeme Henry, head of Drama Studies at La Trobe University; and David Ritchie,

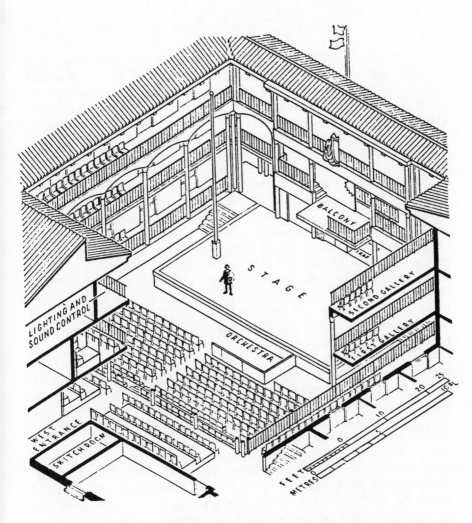

Figure 4. Drawing of the New Fortune Theatre, Perth, Western Australia, by Richard Leacroft. (*From Richard and Helen Leacroft, Theatre and Playhouse [London: Methuen, 1984]. Courtesy of Methuen.*)

who is a senior lecturer at Macquarie University, who also works as a professional actor and director. My account may give the impression that we were working on my ideas, testing out a thesis. This wasn't the case. As we workshopped several scenes, each member contributed from a wealth of previous experience, and I would like to acknowledge the debt I owe to my colleagues. I am simply reporting and commenting upon what I saw.

I had been much impressed with John Orrell's idea that Elizabethan theatres were built on ad quadratum principles.[10] My previous work on soliloquies had convinced me that Shakespeare seemed to write with the awareness that an actor addressing the surrounding audience would need to move from segment to segment of the auditorium. I wondered whether the ad quadratum idea could also have an effect on stage movement. The square Fortune, which Orrell admits is the odd one out compared to the general shape of Elizabethan theatres, was an ideal venue for such an exploration. During soliloquies the dynamics of the relationship between actor and audience should be most obvious, and the actors were simply asked to remember that the lords' room was in the tiring-house wall and that they should therefore play to that side of the theatre with equal weight.

I had expected a fair degree of awkwardness, even with actors who had previously worked and thought in terms of recreating Elizabethan conditions. I was surprised therefore to see the speed with which they took to the concept and the excitement that it generated. The actors found that working in this way liberated them to use the whole of the stage, bringing a new fluidity and often a circularity to their movement. Previously, they had been worried by movements that ranged across an arc of 180 degrees. They would get so far, for example, to the audience closest to the tiring-house on stage right; then they either had to work their way back or wheel around to address the opposite side of the house. Taking the lords into account meant the movement could be continuous. Rather than there being a strong point stage front and center, as has sometimes been suggested, from which an actor could address the audience, we found that the strongest points on the stage were the downstage corners. A common movement on entering was to cross down to one or other of the corners and subsequently turn to look back up to the lords' room and then around to the side and front galleries. Later, when working on dialogues we found it was in no way unnatural for the actors to be located one in each corner and to address each other across twenty-seven feet and six inches of stage.

The fluidity of movement was repeated in gesture. A movement of the arm toward the lords room was sometimes carried on, leading the actor's eye up into the side galleries. I want to emphasize the fluid nature of all this because what I am about to suggest may sound programmatic and formal. I noticed that in some soliloquies, especially when it appears that the

actor addresses a specific member of the audience, there did indeed seem
to be ad quadratum patterns involving groups of four. *Macbeth's* Porter
(2.3), for example, finds: "a farmer, that hanged himself on th' expectation
of plenty"; "an equivocator, that could swear in both the scales against
either scale"; "an English tailor come hither for stealing out of a French
hose"; and is about to find his fourth customer, "What are you?" when he
decides "this place is too cold for hell."[11] The speech was entirely suited
to a movement from one quadrant of the New Fortune to the next.
Falstaff's "honour" soliloquy (*I Henry IV*, 5.1) contains four questions
about honor with the answer "no," four further questions and answers
and four further questions, three with the answer "no" and one, the trick
question, with the answer "yea." There are other examples, but I don't
wish to make too much of the point; after all, Shakespeare was writing
with a rather different theatre in mind, and my points may best inhabit the
realm of coincidence.

A comment from David Ritchie seemed to imply that Orrell may well be
right when he argues that the Globe stage was larger than the Fortune
contract dimensions. Having worked in the flat-sided theatre for several
hours he announced, "If those walls were curved, this stage wouldn't be
big enough." Considering that at first he had been impressed by the size of
the New Fortune's stage, the comment suggests how much we have to
learn from reconstructions.

Thomas Platter said of the "gentlemens roomes," which Hosley argues
were situated in the first gallery indicated as "orchestra" in De Witt's
Swan sketch[12] that they were a place from which "he not only sees
everything well, but can also be seen." Sitting in the lords' room at the
New Fortune I knew exactly what he meant. The view of the stage was
excellent, giving the spectator the impression that he was almost a part of
the action and that the play was being acted almost exclusively for his
benefit. From this vantage point it was possible to view most of the
audience, and, even allowing for Dekker's comment in *The Gull's
Hornbook* about the "darknesse" of the room (supported by Orrell's work
on the orientation of the theatres), I imagine the room had considerable
convenience. If a spectator wished to be seen by occupying "a window,"
he could be. Alternatively a position slightly further back rendered him
less visible while providing him an excellent view of the stage. I should
emphasize that the view from this part of the theatre, even allowing for the
problems created by moving the area forward in this reconstruction,
appears to be excellent in all respects but one, which I'll discuss in a
moment. However, I must admit that the New Fortune does not possess
stage posts nor a stage canopy, and it may well be that experience in other
reconstructions will therefore produce different results.

The major problem of visibility from the lords' room is that the inhabitants of this area of the auditorium are the last to see characters entering the stage, since the entrance doors are located immediately below their station. I wonder if this is why so often in plays of this period characters onstage look toward the entrance doors (that is, they face the lords) to announce who is entering. This certainly gives added point to a piece of dramatic business that I've always thought was a somewhat crude way of establishing who was coming on, either for audience or actors, and it would help explain why such comments are found not only at a character's first entrance, but also at subsequent entrances.

When attention has been paid to the lords' room, it has usually been given to the way this space operated as an acting area. However, the implications have been little considered of the probability that when it did so, the lords were still present. Let me suggest some of them.

Since the lords watch the stage from their elevated vantage point and may, as I've suggested earlier, choose not to be seen, we should not be surprised if characters within the plays choose such a situation to watch and hear when they wish to be unseen. In *Henry VIII*, 5.2, this is required as Henry and Buts watch Cranmer, and in *The Tempest* I assume that this is the point designated "on the top" (3.3) from which Prospero watches the action below. I am sure David Ritchie was correct when he suggested that this is also an entirely appropriate place for Polonius and Claudius to spy on Hamlet and Ophelia (3.1) and that this goes some way toward explaining the speeches which cover their ascent and descent. It must have seemed perfectly natural to an Elizabethan audience to see player lords and kings observing events from the lords' room, surrounded by nonfictional lords. I wonder whether it is fanciful to suggest that this use of the gallery may be where we get our modern meaning for the word "overhear." *The Oxford English Dictionary* notes that the original meaning from Old English was either "hear" or "not listen, disregard, disobey" but that the modern English meaning was apparently "a new combination in the sixteenth century" (compact edition, 1982).

The presence of those real lords may have given certain moments in the plays added power. As I suggested earlier, an actor in an Elizabethan theatre can never see his entire audience, but I've also suggested that the lords have an excellent view of much of the auditorium. A character who is giving a formal public address might therefore be aptly located in the lords' room. I suspect that this is "the pulpit" to which Brutus and Marc Antony "go up" in *Julius Caesar* (3.2). It seems to me that *Julius Caesar* had considerable topical interest for Shakespeare's contemporaries as their childless queen neared the end of her life. If so, and if the authority figures within the play are surrounded by real figures of authority as they make their orations not just to the actors onstage, but to the entire audience at the Globe, the connections between Caesar's Rome and Elizabeth's Britain are intensified.

In other plays, the fact that scenes were played with the actors surrounded by the lords may have given them a certain satirical or political edge. Take for example Richard pretending piety on the battlements (*Richard III*, 3.7), surrounded by actors playing bishops and real lords. Or consider the impact of Richard II coming down, down "like glist'ring Phaëton" (*Richard II*, 3.3.178) from a space on which he was surrounded by real lords to be eventually deposed by Bolingbroke.

It is not only when a scene is played amid the lords that their presence gives an added satirical edge to the plays. The fact of having a place within the theatre where there was a high degree of social definition may have allowed the actors to point certain comments in an unexpected fashion. The contemporary actors working in the New Fortune found that the social focus provided by the lords was a great temptation in performance. I'll give two examples, one minor and one major. De Flores after his scene with Beatrice Joanna (*The Changeling*, 2.2—earlier in the scene he had spied on Beatrice Joanna and Alsemero from the lords' room) confides this piece of homespun wisdom to the audience:

> Hunger and pleasure, they'll commend sometimes
> Slovenly dishes, and feed heartily on 'em—
> Nay which is stranger, refuse daintier for 'em.
> Some women are odd feeders.[13]
>
> (2.2.151–54)

The actor, enjoying his triumph as De Flores, delivered the final lines with a rather pointed gesture toward the lords, and his next words were a mock apology—"I'm too loud"—which positioned him looking toward the entrance for the line following as he spies Alsemero, "Here comes the man goes supperless to bed." This is a small instance, but in other scenes the potential for the intensification of already pointed social commentary could be great. Many of Lear's lines in act 3, scene 4 are explosive enough without added pointing, but consider the following possibility as Lear tells the blind Gloucester about the relativity of power structures:

> See how yond justice rails upon yond simple thief. Hark, in thine ear: change places and, handy-dandy, which is the justice, which the thief?
> (4.6.153–56)

On "justice," Lear points to the lords' room with his right arm, and his arm remains outstretched as on "thief" he stretches out his left arm to indicate a thief down among the groundlings. On his next line he whispers in Gloucester's ear and simultaneously changes places with him, so that on the line following it is his left arm which points to the groundlings on the word "justice" while his right points to the lords on "thief."

Perhaps this is going too far and suggesting altogether too much; we know that the Elizabethan-Jacobean theatre was a dangerous place in which to criticize authority. And yet, in this scene, Shakespeare is the one who appears to go too far, allowing his king under the guise of madness to make comments that must have rocked the contemporary audience. It leads me to wonder if, in examples like those above, we may be dealing with a phenomenon akin to certain Berlin cabarets in the time of Hitler. Could those in power be criticized within the confines of the theatre while they were simultaneously paid court as respected and lucrative patrons?

I leave this as a question. Our work in the New Fortune was exploratory, and it seems to me that much of our work in Elizabethan theatre must necessarily remain so. When I advanced the views in this paper at the International Shakespeare Institute Conference in 1986, there was a measure of informed disagreement. Of several counter-points, there was one that had unquestionable force: "What about the discovery space?" If, as we have always assumed, this space is immediately below the gallery, how could the inhabitants of the lords' room see it? Unless it was in some way built *in front of* the tiring-house facade, perhaps on the semicircular pattern of the upper gallery enclosure in *The Wits* frontispiece, then the simple answer is, they couldn't. Long ago Lawrence suggested that this may have been the reason for the lords' vacating this space, which he takes to have happened by the time of Dekker's *Gull's Hornbook* description.[14] He may be right. Certainly as visual and then scenic effects become more important, the whole dynamic of the stage-audience relationship will change. In his plan for the *Cockpit at Court,* for example, Inigo Jones will locate his most important auditor, the king, center *front.* I have to admit that I have no answer to this "discovery space" objection. It is little consolation to note that such discoveries are found in only nine of the thirty plays performed at the Globe between 1599 and 1608[15] and that they are usually static. Why locate any important dramatic moments where significant members of the audience can't see them unless, perhaps, you are making a point by so doing? My tentativeness here is a useful reminder that our work is never done. The existence of a reconstruction like the New Fortune, even though it has demonstrable imperfections, allows us to test our theories in practice, to see if they will work. The building of reconstructions, such as the New Globe on the Bankside, which will profit from more recent scholarship, will obviously advance the development of this knowledge. The object is not to recover some modern equivalent of "the way it was really done in Shakespeare's time." We can never now for certain how scenes worked in an Elizabethan theatre, and this is not a matter for regret. Through experimental work like that detailed above we can, as we get a clearer idea of how the theatre may have worked, deepen our understanding of the potential of the primary material, the playscripts we have inherited. In Bernard Beckerman's terms, we can never remove the "spectacles" through which we view those scripts, but as we change and learn more, the "invisible panes," their lenses, are themselves changing and enabling us to see things we couldn't see before. As I said above, our work is never done—a fact that for me is both the joy and the challenge of performance studies.

Notes

1. Bernard Beckerman, *Dynamics of Drama* (New York: Alfred A. Knopf, 1970), 3.
2. C. Walter Hodges, "The Lantern of Taste," *Shakespeare Survey* 12 (1959): 8.
3. W. J. Lawrence, "The Situation of the Lords' Room," in *The Elizabethan Playhouse and Other Studies* (Stratford: Shakespeare Head Press, 1912), 29–40.
4. See: "Shakespeare's Use of a Gallery over the Stage," *Shakespeare Survey 10* (1957): 77–89; "The Gallery over the Stage in the Public Playhouse of Shakespeare's Time," *Shakespeare Quarterly 8* (1957): 15–31; "Was There a Music-room in Shakespeare's Globe?" *Shakespeare Survey 13* (1960): 113–123.
5. Peter Thomson, *Shakespeare's Theatre* (London: Routledge & Kegan Paul, 1983), 40.
6. In, for example, his excellent section on "The Playhouses" in *The Revels History of Drama in English, vol. 3 1567–1613* (London: Methuen, 1975) and his thinking on the lords' room as embedded in the various documents and planning statements about the New Globe.
7. Hosley, "The Gallery over the Stage," 25.
8. For details of Bernard Miles's experiments see Bernard Miles and Josephine Wilson, "Three Festivals at the Mermaid Theatre," *Shakespeare Quarterly 5* (1954): 307–10. The R.S.C.'s "galleries" weren't very successful because, as might have been expected, the actors felt a first allegiance to the majority of the audience who were "out front." Significantly, the seats behind the stage were the cheapest in the theatre.
9. John Styan, *Shakespeare's Stagecraft* (Cambridge: Cambridge University Press, 1967), 15.
10. John Orrell, *The Quest for Shakespeare's Globe* Cambridge, Cambridge University Press, 1983).
11. *Macbeth,* The Arden Shakespeare, ed. Kenneth Muir (London: Methuen, 1967).
12. *Revels History of Drama in English,* vol. 3, 1536–1613, 154. There is a good deal of evidence that "the Lords" and "the Gentlemens" rooms were not one and the same, but they did share one important feature: they were "behind" the stage—the lords directly, the gentlemen at the side. This supports the idea that the best seats were not considered to be those in front of the stage.

13. *The Changeling* in *Elizabethan and Stuart Plays,* ed. Baskervill, Heltzel, and Nethercot (New York: Holt, Rinehart and Winston, 1962).

14. Lawrence, *The Elizabethan Playhouse,* 30.

15. The figures are once again from Hosley, "The Discovery Space in Shakespeare's Globe," *Shakespeare Survey, 12* (1959): 35–46. Although he has done work on both the lords' room and the discovery space, as far as I know, Hosley hasn't really come up with an answer to the "objection" either.

Stage Space and the Shakespeare Experience

J. L. STYAN

A target for performance criticism must be the recreation.of the authentic
qualities present in the play performed, recapturing its special spirit, its
best style, its own mode of working on an audience. Such an attempt at
recreation is not to pin the butterfly, but to enable it to fly. Yet whatever
aspects of drama and performance we may choose—the quality of speech,
its use of music and song, its symbolism of gesture and movement,
properties and costume, the degree of realism in characterization, any of a
hundred and one elements of drama—at some point discussion will turn
on the problem that besets all dramatic representation: what kind and
degree of "illusion" must its audience undergo if the relationship between
actor and audience is to be the most appropriate, and if the manipulation
of stimulus and response is to be at the maximum subtlety? In the case of
Shakespeare and his contemporaries, we shall best hope to answer this
sort of question when we have an authentic replica of the Elizabethan
Globe Theatre in which to work and play.

For many years we have spoken of dramatic conventions as the key to
understanding a play from an earlier theatre or from another culture, as if
the identification of prologues and epilogues, soliloquies and asides, elements of characterization and plotting, time and place, and other details
would solve the problems of comprehension. Some part of this is true: if
we knew, say, how a soliloquy was delivered by an actor to an audience in
its own time, we might begin to assess what was important for its success
in performance. But conventions per se are as nothing unless we also
know their place in the general aesthetic of performance—what and how
far the audience accepted, assimilated, and believed at that time.

A valid starting point could well be the "empty space" occupied by the
actor, with what is done and said in it. Peter Brook's celebrated empty
space[1] is both an acting area and a region of the mind, and both of these
are the focus of the spectator's attention. It is as if Shakespeare exemplified some such theory of performance and response by his use of the
empty stage of the Elizabethan theatre, thrust aggressively into its au-

ditorium, demanding full attention, rich with imminent possibilities for direct communication, awaiting its spokesman, and until he came magnetizing its viewer. The space was neutral until it was engaged, of course, but its very neutrality was a challenge. Coleridge insisted that the very nakedness of the stage was an advantage, since it gave the playwright his liberty to do what he wanted in the *form* that he chose, as well as liberating the imagination of the audience to accept or reject what it saw and heard.

While we think of the bare Elizabethan stage as a battleground for the action of the play, actor set against actor, it is more accurately the battleground where the playwright can pit the actor against the spectator. It is natural for us to think of the Elizabethan space in terms of the localizing and temporal conventions, for it is in the modern style to fill any space with indications of place and time. So it is quick and easy for us to accept that "This is Illyria, lady" or "This is the forest of Arden," and for us to hasten in our minds to populate and decorate the new territory from such light and glancing references. We are as ready to adopt Shakespeare's clock upon hearing "'Tis now struck twelve, get thee to bed, Francisco" or "Get me a taper in my study, Lucius." Nevertheless, it is less natural and more true to remember that there are rarely any constant reminders of Shakespeare's place and time, and his stage is primarily and properly the target area for imaginative thought and emotion.

The actor in his or her space, through voice and gesture and movement, soon asserts dominance and takes charge of the region of our mind, and for most of the action of the play this is occupied by the promptings of human relationships, those between actor and spectator. The less the audience concentrates on where the actor *is,* the more it will accept what he is standing *for:* the neutrality of the platform's space implies the strongest commitment by author, actor, and audience to the particular relationships of the play. *Hamlet* takes place in the castle of Elsinor, yes, but where is "To be or not to be"?—to affect us this speech may need space, but hardly any place. "This is Illyria, lady"—very good, but of course it is still the same old stage we know well, and the line becomes almost a private joke between Shakespeare and his audience. Occasionally a localizing line is even more metatheatrical: "When shall I come to the top of that same hill?" asks Gloucester on Dover Cliff, and in this instance Shakespeare, the audience, and the character Edgar all know there is no cliff at all. We may conclude that the convention of localizing on the Elizabethan stage seems rather nebulous and, as a theory of Elizabethan dramaturgy, even a kind of nonsense. At one point there appear to be four men in Desdemona's bedroom—Iago, Roderigo, Othello, and Lodovico—who, by the arguments of localizing, if not of modesty, must leave before she can undress for bed.

So it is with the convention of time. When the spectators need to check the clock or the calendar, it seems that they are so advised. In *Measure for Measure,* 4.2, the Provost announces, "Tomorrow morning are to die Claudio and Barnardine," and a little later he says to Claudio, "'Tis now dead midnight, and by eight tomorrow / Thou must be made immortal," while after a few moments more Angelo advances the deadly hour to "four." In *All's Well That Ends Well,* 4.3, both the plot and the subplot seem to come to a head at midnight: just before this hour is set the time for Parolles to be ambushed by his friends, and at midnight also is Bertram instructed to come to Diana's bed in preparation for the substitution of Helena: a busy night for all concerned, but especially the audience. Of course we are never asked to confirm these times, only to feel their urgency. Or night passes (in *A Midsummer Night's Dream, Henry V, Antony and Cleopatra*), lovers will stray, soldiers prepare to die, and yet the stage conveniently remains its usual daylit self. As an audience we are indulgent; and without our general tolerance the story of the play could not go forward. By keeping the stage free from the clutter of place and time, we are again the sharers who enable the actors to act.

From this principle of imaginative neutrality shared by author, actor, and audience all things theatrical can follow. Shakespeare and his contemporaries could pursue extraordinary dramatic freedoms: an acrobatic development of the chronicle play that leaped from one part of the realm to another, from court to camp, from the highborn to the low; pastoral fantasies like *A Midsummer Night's Dream* and *As You Like It* that compelled their audience to make and perceive plays within plays and roles upon roles in order to explore the human condition and its illusions; or by a series of devices of alienation those comedies that juxtaposed the realities of sex and war, sex and class, and sex and religion in the ambiguous persons of the problem girls Cressida, Helena, and Isabella. These innovations were the direct result of a fluid stage that encouraged not merely the leaps of place and time, but also the quick changes of tone and style designed to expose the areas of the mind where conflict and paradox lie.

The discussion of spatial relationships that follows is hesitantly outlined by a few examples chosen for analysis—hesitantly because no two instances in Shakespeare are finally alike. What I have to say nevertheless seems to fall into categories of a sort:

1. The space that relates the actor directly to his audience and calls for a recognizable intimacy of speech. This is the space that joins.
2. The space that distinguishes between an actor who is intimate with his audience and another who is not, so that the former appears to distance the latter. This is the space that divides.
3. The space that permits a double or triple intimacy, thereby setting

up a contrast and conflict of "simultaneous" staging. This space simultaneously joins and divides the stage and audience.

4. The space in which an actor is temporarily "upstaged" or denied
intimacy with his audience, while he may return with ironic force to urge
a contradiction. This is a deceptive division of space.

5. The space that cheats and deceives those on the stage and can be
seen to tell lies. This space is almost palpable and speaks to us like a
character.

First, the space that joins. "Soliloquy" is a late seventeenth- or eighteenth-century literary concept, and "speaking to oneself" was not a
device that Shakespeare or the Elizabethan stage would have recognized.
However, addressing the audience was a normal and constant activity
("The soliloquy always to the pit—that's a rule," insisted Mr. Puff in
Sheridan's *The Critic*). It was a convention by which an actor gave himself
completely to the house, putting him in direct touch with the spectators; it
was the primary device to encourage sharing. Alone on the great platform,
a solitary figure made a powerful statement to the spectator, one not so
much about the character's state of mind (the lines would do that), but
about the actor's need to reach out to his audience with intimacy and
immediacy. The play that jumps to mind by its abundance of soliloquies is
Hamlet, a tragedy in which the device perfectly exemplifies the actor's
urge to step outside his play, even outside his part, alone on indeterminate
space, and create a few moments of the highest excitement and attention.
In such a play, the playwright and the actor take their audience point by
point through the action, commenting on events, anticipating the future,
compelling us to think like the Prince, and indeed shaping the structure of
the play by making sure that we remain partners to the enterprise. In this
sense, word and deed, what is heard and what is seen, are essentially
inseparable in the spatial treatment of the Elizabethan platform.

In the case of a villain-hero in tragedy like Richard III or Macbeth, it is a
matter of the greatest importance that the actor get into immediate touch
with his audience lest its thought and feeling be allowed to drift and
escape. Whether Gloucester declares the winter of his discontent in the
shape of a catlike Emlyn Williams (Old Vic, 1937), a smooth-tongued
tyrant like Donald Wolfit (Strand Theatre, 1942), a chillingly ironic intellectual like Laurence Olivier (New Theatre, 1944), a leering Alec Guiness
jogging his legs as he sits on the balcony (Ontario, 1953), a giant crab like
Douglass Watson (Connecticut, 1964), a wounded spider like Donald
Madden (New York, 1970), or the beetle of Anthony Sher on his crutches
(Royal Shakespeare Theatre, 1985), the first perverse objective of that
remarkable opening soliloquy is to accommodate the monstrous "received
idea" that legend has imposed upon the audience to this play. *Richard III*

opens with its actor alone on the empty stage for a lengthy period of time to ensure that his audience learn to collaborate with villainy: the playwright and not the historian is to take possession of the action, and against all reason we willingly participate in the outrageous events of the play.

One scene in *Romeo and Juliet* (2.5) seems to have been a remarkable experiment in spatial organization because in it Juliet seems to win the audience by soliloquy and then surrenders the precious, intimate territory so gained in order to upstage the speaker. The scene has Juliet waiting for the Nurse to bring her the news of the marriage arrangements with Romeo, and immediately we are charmed by a conventional soliloquy that efficiently identifies the hour, the issue, and the character's state of mind:

> The hour struck nine when I did send the Nurse,
> In half an hour she promis'd to return.
> Perchance she cannot meet him. That's not so.
> O, she is lame. Love's heralds should be thoughts
> Which ten times faster glides than the sun's beams
> Driving back shadows over lowering hills. . . .
>
> (1–6)

Here Juliet has given us direct information about the clock, and then, alone on the stage, she at once conveys her anxiety by a broken, kinetic line ("That's not so.") designed to animate the player. By now she is within arm's length of the audience as her amorous desires are lyricized by a poetry of another order ("Love's heralds should be thoughts"), so that we share the quality of her anticipation, as well as laugh a little at her youthful impatience. Her anger finally overwhelms her softer feelings, and Shakespeare arranges that her lines actually serve as a stage direction, telling the Nurse how to make her entrance:

> But old folks, many feign as they were dead—
> Unwieldy, slow, heavy, and pale as lead.
>
> (16–17)

Juliet's own movement is the very opposite, since she runs upstage on

> O God she comes. O honey Nurse, what news?,
>
> (18)

and we are not to forget the great depth of the platform.

Begins the farce of having this Nurse refuse to disclose the information requested of her:

> I am aweary, give me leave awhile.
> Fie, how my bones ache. What a jaunce have I!
>
> (25–26)

Can she be as tired as she says? No, indeed—for we are soon given hints enough that she is enjoying her moment of superiority by deliberately prolonging Juliet's agony of mind. So the Nurse works her way downstage, fixing the audience with a wicked eye:

> Jesu, what haste. Can you not stay awhile?
> Do you not see that I am out of breath?
>
> (29–30)

The Nurse is now on the platform where Juliet was, probably sharing her joke with a wink or a nod, and no doubt breathing unnaturally heavily the while. For the joy in this scene lies in the fact that the audience knows all that there is to know about this marriage—it was after all party to the arrangement with Romeo—so that the plot per se has no need of this scene at all. A factor of possibly greater importance is nevertheless at work here in the mixing of the lyrical and the prosaic, the humorous and the pathetic, contrary ingredients that lie at the heart of this play. Both Juliet and the Nurse must have the chance to manipulate the audience, and the critical working space nearest the center of the playhouse must be occupied by both equally.

The space that joins has already given way to the space that divides, and given one character onstage who sufficiently shares his or her thoughts with us, there will be another who accordingly will be "distanced." Of many straightforward instances, Lady Macbeth's sleepwalking scene (*Macbeth*, 5.1) springs to mind. The sleepwalker addresses no words to us. On the abstract, open spaces of the platform lit only by daylight, Lady Macbeth carries her taper and gropes through her nightmare in a darkness of her own. The empty space is the tortured arena for the reenactment of her part in the murder of Duncan: her eyes are open, but their sense is shut, while we observe and witness like the Doctor of Physic and the Waiting Gentlewoman, who, like the audience, "observe" and "stand close." Are they hiding?—no, no more than is the spectator. For they, not the Queen, are our surrogates on the stage, and their comments throughout are for our ears: "What a sigh is there! The heart is sorely charg'd"; "I would not have such a heart in my bosom for the dignity of the whole body" (51–53). They are close, secret observers, standing still on the perimeter of the stage adjacent to the audience. But not only are our eyes open; so too is our "sense."

The distancing space is felt on countless occasions, and it always lends a judgmental and sometimes a comic perspective to the comparison between the selected characters onstage. The scenes between Orsino and Viola in *Twelfth Night* offer familiar instances. When, for example, in 2.4 the lovelorn Duke is mouthing his blustering sentiments about true love, the fact that Viola as Cesario is his audience, lovelorn herself and scarcely able to disguise her feelings as well as she can her clothes, must upstage him. He calls her to him:

> Come hither, boy. If ever thou shalt love,
> In the sweet pangs of it remember me:
> For such as I am, all true lovers are,
> Unstaid and skittish in all motions else,
> Save in the constant image of the creature
> That is belov'd. How dost thou like this tune?
> *Viola.* It gives a very echo to the seat
> Where love is thron'd.
> *Duke.*   Thou dost speak masterly.
> My life upon't, young though thou art, thine eye
> Hath stay'd upon some favour that it loves.
> Hath it not, boy?
> *Viola.*   A little, by your favour.

(15–25)

Whether the Duke is sitting or pacing, Viola is unable to take her eyes off him and must repeatedly turn away to save her modesty and her disguise. His every remark is registered in her expression, which is altogether a better exemplar of staid and unskittish motions. If Orsino touches her (and "My life upon't" warrants a playful slap on the boyish shoulder), Viola's reaction of amorous desire must positively convey a "constant image." All very amusing for us, but we are smiling at both of them in different ways, for they have been separated here, not by the depth of the platform, but by a relative space used flexibly to mark a physical relationship.

The physical relationship, conveyed on the Elizabethan stage by measurable distance from the center of the house, has here become a judgmental relationship, echoing our response to the spatially related actors on the stage. In *All's Well That Ends Well*, 1.3, the Countess of Rossillion invites the audience to observe the condition of Helena's unhappy love as she passes at a distance on another part of the stage, even the balcony, unaware that she is being watched. As we all look at Helena, the older woman explains with compassion just how it is with the younger: "Even so it was with me when I was young" (123). In *King Lear*, 1.4, Goneril stands on her entrance in threatening silence, accusing her father by her very stillness and absence of words, until he emphasizes her demeanor with an explosive, "How now, daughter! what makes that frontlet on? You are too much of late i'th'frown" (197–98). Thus the momentous confrontation between father and daughter awaits the spectator's verdict on relative guilt. In *The Winter's Tale*, 1.2, Leontes first indicates his jealousy of Polixenes after that gentleman has innocently led Hermione away upstage—or somewhere out of his hearing—so permitting the husband to misinterpret the behavior of his wife: "Too hot, too hot! / To mingle friendship far, is mingling bloods" (108–9). We know that he is wrong, since we heard clearly enough their simple courtesies when he did not. Thus we are made sharply aware how the eyes—and human behavior seen at a distance—cause mistakes to be made.

There are times when space seems to be almost visible, even self-conscious. Some forms of "simultaneous staging" (the arrangement by which two things may happen on the stage at the same time) encourage the audience to perceive and evaluate both together. This simultaneity, incidentally, presents difficulties for the film and television camera but is easily assimilated by the human eye. The opening court scene in *King Lear* demonstrates a brilliant sequence of contrasting spatial images, with so much happening on the stage spatially that the test for Shakespeare's mastery of his craft is whether he has not bewildered the spectator by the riches of the scene.

First, the discussion between Gloucester and Kent that opens the play is not merely to announce the division of the kingdom: it is alive with a sinister kind of comedy, marked by the cruel laughter which separates Edmund from his father and showing how easy it is to divide the loyalty of families as well as kingdoms. Nevertheless, an audience makes this perception only if Edmund enters and stands apart from the older men, seeing their laughter enjoyed at his expense when they jest about his illegitimacy:

> *Kent.* I cannot conceive you.
> *Gloucester.* Sir, this young fellow's mother could.
>
> (12–13)

General mirth—until we see the grim expression on Edmund's face. He is eventually called over to be introduced: "Do you know this noble gentleman, Edmund?" And now we hear the ice on Edmund's breath as he replies, "My services to your Lordship" (29). As the two parties are joined, the audience knows to hold them separate.

Second, Lear's throne (which may be presumed to be upstage center from the evidence of Jonson's *Every Man in His Humour,* prologue, line 16, where he jokes about how the "creaking throne comes down, the boys to please") must itself divide the stage again, between the sisters Goneril and Regan and their parties. For this part of the scene the most formal patterning is suggested, not only by the ceremonial occasion, but also by the outright rivalry of the sisters. Thus when Goneril speaks her smooth lines to Lear,

> Sir, I love you more than word can wield the matter;
> Dearer than eyesight, space and liberty . . .
>
> (55–56)

the issue of division in the family comes across most powerfully if she faces, not so much her father, but her sister, placed directly across the width of the platform, and seems to address her. Again, when Regan speaks her formal statement of love, the issue is visually reinforced if she too faces across the platform, lobbing her words at Goneril:

> I find she names my very deed of love;
> Only she comes too short . . .
>
> (71–72)

Once again we hear the icy tones of inbred hatred, and gesture and posture will match them.

Yet there is a third spatial statement made at this time. Three sisters on a square platform do not make for symmetry, and Cordelia is carefully placed on the perimeter of the platform for her two critical asides:

> What shall Cordelia speak? Love, and be silent.
>
> (62)

and

> Then poor Cordelia!
> And yet not so; since I am sure my love's
> More ponderous than my tongue.
>
> (77–79)

By her simpler words, her closer proximity to the house, and her more natural informality, sound and movement not only single her out but also identify her as the one to believe. Moreover, they also prepare the audience for the radical break in the apparent direction of the action, and for the next lesson in spatial exploration. To this point I take it that the audience has been chiefly an observer. At the first sign of direct address from the stage—that of Cordelia's "asides" (the term, of course, is not the one that Elizabethans would recognize, so we must think of such lines merely as remarks intended to be heard as external comments presented outside the action)—the audience will be drawn into collusion with the speaker. Thus to this point we have separated Goneril and Regan, and now separate Cordelia. The only major character who remains unplaced in our regard is Lear himself. He remains on his throne, allowing essentially no distinction of feeling, unless it be that "Now, our joy, / Although our last, and least . . ." (82–83) marks the first change in him, since here it could be argued that he speaks more like a father and less like a monarch.

Fourth, then, when he speaks more like a father, any test of the Elizabethan platform will ease him from the formal upstage position and carry him downstage to greet his youngest daughter personally, affectionately.

The naturalistic intimacy between father and daughter that follows in the shorter, more colloquial, broken lines ("Nothing, my Lord . . ." "Nothing? . . ." "Nothing" [87–89].) has in production been conveyed by having Cordelia make the next move, even to sitting on Lear's knee. However, the intimacy that is shared with the house for this crucial exchange, one that addresses the leading motif of the play, is of greater importance. If the moment is played out in the center of the house, not only are the actors able to speak their lines with more vocal and facial subtlety—and more realism—but the audience may receive the message about the bond of blood all the more forcefully for its being less formalized and more human.

It is interesting that Shakespeare's language usually signals the spatial relationships he appears to want between actor and actor, and between actor and spectator. Outstanding in its control of audience response and its differentiation between characters is the dialogue between Macbeth and Lady Macbeth during the scene of the murder of Duncan (*Macbeth,* 2.1). In this remarkable piece of dramaturgy, the two principals, each in turn, move from soliloquy to dialogue as if to prepare for their increasing separation in body, mind, and spirit. With the prompting of a tolling bell and a screaming owl, each character passes from the unreal regions of the sick imagination to the realistic business of murder, from witchcraft and "pale Hecate" to the grisly business of drugging the possets of Duncan's grooms and finding Macbeth's daggers laid ready.

Realism is at its peak in the scene when attention is drawn to the daggers and the blood on Macbeth's hands. Yet at this moment of greatest physical and visual horror, the dialogue suffers a striking change. As Lady Macbeth's lines grow shorter and more prosaic, her voice more shrill, so Macbeth's grow longer and more rhythmical, his voice more colorful.

> *Macbeth.* There's one did laugh in's sleep, and one cried, "Murther!"
>   That they did wake each other: I stood and heard them;
>   But they did say their prayers, and address'd them
>   Again to sleep.
> *Lady Macbeth.*   There are two lodg'd together.
> *Macbeth.* One cried, "God bless us!" and "Amen," the other,
>   As they had seen me with these hangman's hands.
>   List'ning their fear, I could not say, "Amen,"
>   When they did say, "God bless us."
> *Lady Macbeth.*   Consider it not so deeply. . . .
>
>   (22–29)

It is clear that these two are moving in different realms of the mind. What may be less clear to the *reader* is that the lines also separate man and wife physically. On the one hand, Macbeth is off into his living nightmare, his feet not quite on the ground, moving into the neutral area of the platform, close to the center of the playhouse, to the audience, and to the skies.

> Methought, I heard a voice cry, "Sleep no more!
> Macbeth does murther Sleep,"—the innocent Sleep;
> Sleep, that knits up the ravell'd sleave of care. . . .
>
> (34–36)

On the other hand, Lady Macbeth is powerless against the terrifying poetry of the murderer's mind, nor can she follow him into his private hell. She must remain where she is, unable to reach him, fixed and transfixed in the inner play. The audience, meanwhile, continues to share his thoughts to the end, rejecting those of his lady.

We have previously touched on a fourth use of responsive space, when a character is upstaged by another and temporarily denied the direct sympathy of the audience. Think of Beatrice's eavesdropping scene in *Much Ado about Nothing*, 3.1, carefully arranged so differently from that of Benedick. Where Benedick commented upon what his deceivers were saying throughout, poor Beatrice is allowed not a word. Thus Hero takes the opportunity to lambaste her friend with

> But Nature never fram'd a woman's heart
> Of prouder stuff than that of Beatrice.
> Disdain and scorn ride sparkling in her eyes. . . .
>
> (49–51)

Beatrice can only hear these words with pain, unable to respond, although we may know from her demeanor that she is upset. "She is so self-endeared" is quite a challenge, and we may guess that Lady Disdain has a softer heart than she has shown before. When she is finally alone and free to address us, she does so in a joyful soliloquy of lyrical rhyming verse, closing upon her audience in a short confessional sonnet:

> What fire is in mine ears? Can this be true?
> Stand I condemn'd for pride and scorn so much?
> Contempt, farewell, and maiden pride, adieu!
> No glory lives behind the back of such.
>
> (107–10)

Her true and passionate nature are here revealed to everyone's satisfaction, and this time without laughing we confirm our impressions of her sincerity.

In this instance the upstaging has been redeemed. When Ulysses pronounces judgment on his victim Cressida in *Troilus and Cressida,* 4.5,

> There's language in her eye, her cheek, her lip—
> Nay, her foot speaks; her wanton spirits look out
> At every joint and motive of her body,
>
>   (55–57)

it is left to the audience to choose between the man who has just engineered her rough treatment at the hands of the Greek army officers and the girl who was in tears when she was dragged from Troy and from Troilus. If we take Ulysses's words at their face value, we may well choose to recognize "her wanton spirits" and think she simpers upstage to the exit—and so, indeed, have many critics and actresses unfamiliar with the ambiguous ways of the Elizabethan stage. However, if an audience senses the ambivalence, the "indeterminacy," that so deliberately informs the problem comedies, it will claim the privilege of deciding for itself and will not believe everything it is told.

A fine instance of such spatial indeterminacy introduces that unusual tragedy of seesaw values, *Antony and Cleopatra*. The Roman soldiers Demetrius and Philo are granted the first lines of the play: they enter talking and talk their way downstage. There the audience can more readily hear the veteran Philo tell the rookie Demetrius of the problems that beset the army now that their general has taken up with his gypsy. And all this criticism of "this dotage of our general's" may be assumed to echo the received idea of both Plutarch and the Elizabethan audience about Antony. Then, unexpectedly perhaps, we are commanded:

> Look, where they come:
> Take but good note, and you shall see in him
> The triple pillar of the world transform'd
> Into a strumpet's fool: behold and see.
>
>   (10–13)

The "look where" tag directs all eyes to an upstage entrance where the subjects of the conversation may be seen. And the Folio has the unusually rich stage direction, "*Flourish. Enter Antony, Cleopatra, her Ladies, the Train, with Eunuchs fanning her,*" as if the King's Men wanted to contradict Philo's censure of Antony visually, sensuously. The audience is confronted with a sharp incongruity, and its idea of the magnificent, legendary love of a weak, degenerate Antony notwithstanding, the play catches fire. It does so because we are shown a glimpse of both sides of the story, "the bellows and the fan / To cool a gypsy's lust" as well as intimations of "new heaven, new earth" (9–10, 17), the two not only contrasted in imagery and tone, but also divided by space. Our sympathies are evoked, balanced, and engaged—by the contradictory evidence of our eyes and ears on two parts of the stage.

Fifthly and finally, the Elizabethan platform encourages a stage space that demonstrates how well the eyes can deceive the ears. This kind of illusory space is implicit in every eavesdropping scene, every speech "aside," every address in which the actor appears to step outside the inner action in order to embrace his audience. It was remarked how in *The Winter's Tale,* 1.2, Shakespeare arranged it that Hermione and Leontes be heard, then seen, alternately: a curious, mechanical, and highly experimental pattern by which the audience is invited to compare and accommodate the information of the ears with that of the eyes. When Leontes misreads the signs ("paddling palms, and pinching fingers" [115], "making practis'd smiles / As in a looking-glass" [116–17], "to sigh, as 'twere / The mort o'th'deer" [117–18], "Still virginalling / Upon his palm?" [125–26]), the audience knows his wife to be innocent. Yet it hears the heated words of Leontes's "*tremor cordis*" and has the urge to cry out advice at Hermione's puzzled "He something seems unsettled" when she returns to that part of the stage where she can be heard as well as seen. At this moment Shakespeare anticipates Pirandello's manipulation of appearance and belief among the townspeople and the audience of *Cosi è, se vi pare!*

As with Pirandello, we are led to the edge of the irrational, and space becomes excessively self-conscious. *Othello* is a play rich in such spatial effects, for not only is the hero regularly upstaged by the villain (Iago's soliloquies begin with the first scene of the play, while Othello's first soliloquy proper is not heard until the last), but two of the major scenes of Othello's deception (3.3, that of Cassio's request to Desdemona for his reinstatement, and 4.1, that of Othello's eavesdropping) use the full length or depth of the platform in order to stress the error of the eye. These are two notable scenes of experimental theatre.

During the Cyprus scene of 2.1, the audience is prepared for spatial illusion to come. As Desdemona addresses Cassio, so Iago in his aside, certainly downstage of them, describes their innocent gestures and indicates how he will contrive to "ensnare" Cassio:

He takes her by the palm; ay, well said, whisper: as little a web as this will ensnare as great a fly as Cassio. Ay, smile upon her, do: I will catch you in your own courtesies. . . . (167–70)

Iago's threat is heard again a moment later in a second aside, this time undercutting the greeting of Othello and Desdemona:

O, you are well tun'd now,
But I'll set down the pegs that make this music,
As honest as I am.
                                                    (199–201)

Iago goes on to confirm his plan in the soliloquy at the end of 2.1. Thus the audience is dragged into the ugly conspiracy and is cunningly put on the alert for further signs of the error of the eye.

The audience has not long to wait. As soon as Desdemona has given her assurance to Cassio, their dialogue conducted in intimate and urgent tones as they stand close together in one part of the platform, any audience might anticipate the husband's entrance in the classic sequence of comic cuckoldry.

> *Emilia.* Madam, here comes my lord.
> *Cassio.* Madam, I'll take my leave.
> *Desdemona.* Why, stay and hear me speak.
> *Cassio.* Madam, not now, I am very ill at ease,
>   Unfit for mine own purpose.
>
>   (29–33)

Cassio's hurried exit and Desdemona's attempt to restrain him, perhaps by touching his arm, his hand, is "guilty-like" by any convention of behavior, and the two also present Iago with the opportunity to hint that all is not innocent, so that the audience soon hears in Othello's voice that a first doubt has been planted in his mind:

> *Desdemona.* I have been talking with a suitor here,
>   A man that languishes in your displeasure.
> *Othello.* Who is't you mean?
> *Desdemona.* Why, your lieutenant, Cassio, good my lord. . . .
>
>   (43–46)

He was of course almost sure who it was; all he needs now is to hear his wife seem to confess that it was indeed Cassio. And soon after we again hear the small voice of doubt and distress: "when I love thee not, / Chaos is come again" (92–93). The jealous brain begins monstrously to misinterpret the smallest tone or gesture.

There follows the long and subtle scene of verbal temptation (3.3), until Othello demands his "ocular proof." Iago will supply it in the scene (4.1) where he can make barracks-room suggestions to Cassio about his mistress Bianca. He will laugh with him and have Cassio show how she falls about his neck, "hangs, and lolls, and weeps" upon him, "hales, and pulls" (137–38) him—all the time confident that on the other side of the stage Othello, observing but not hearing, will identify Desdemona with this Bianca. To Othello and to the audience every laugh will sound coarser, every gesture more obscene than it is, until the Moor is ready to kill. Iago has one moment of anxiety when, unexpectedly, the real Bianca approaches, for she is not at all the "poor caitiff" of the earlier conversation, but a far more independent creature. However, as luck (and Shakespeare) would have it, she brings with her the very handkerchief that Othello gave Desdemona, and taking it to be "some minx's token" (151), she throws it in Cassio's face. For his part, Othello sees only what he wants to see, further incriminating evidence: "By heaven, that should be my hand-kerchief" (155). Thus Bianca's dangerous entrance has most conveniently exacerbated all his worst suspicions. So, again, space has served the play: in Cressida's words,

> The error of our eye directs our mind.
> What error leads must err; O, then conclude,
> Minds sway'd by eyes are full of turpitude.
> *(Troilus and Cressida,* 5.2.109–11)

Space at such times is seen and heard—but hardly invisible, scarcely silent. The days of the two-dimensional Victorian picture-frame stage are passing, and the proscenium-arch protesters who sustained the public debate that followed Tyrone Guthrie's thrust stages in Ontario, Chichester, and Minneapolis have fallen silent. It is everywhere acknowledged that the shape of the stage affects the acting and the response to it, even controls the play and the experience of it. Wherever Shakespeare is played in the Elizabethan way, the medium is the message, and we must now believe that actors are reassuming their former importance. Especially it is for us to learn to perceive the new old dramatic values. They have much to do with our rediscovery of spatial relationships between actor and audience; and the amazing fluctuation that space can create between, on the one hand, illusion and belief and, on the other, nonillusion and reality has yet to be experienced. Like Troilus, "enkindled" by his eyes and ears, which he calls

> Two traded pilots 'twixt the dangerous shores
> Of will and judgement,
>
> (2.2.65–66)

we the audience may hope to be at once more caught up in the essential spirit of the Shakespeare play and more aware and sensitive as its auditors.

Notes

1. Peter Brook, *The Empty Space* (London: MacGibbon and Kee, 1968).
2. All quotations from Shakespeare are from the Arden Edition (London: Methuen).

Reflections Arising from Recent Productions of *Love's Labour's Lost* and *As You Like It*

GLYNNE WICKHAM

In a short article for *Shakespeare Quarterly*[1] I suggested that a source, hitherto lacking, for *Love's Labour's Lost* was to be found in *The Four Foster Children of Desire; or, The Castle of Perfect Beauty,* edited for printing by Henry Goldwell from verses by Philip Sidney and published shortly after the entertainment that Sidney himself and three other chivalrically minded courtiers presented to Queen Elizabeth I and the French ambassadors in the tiltyard at Whitehall Palace in 1581.

This entertainment had been devised in the most courtly and diplomatic style to inform the duc d'Alençon—duke of Anjou and Brabant, and heir to the throne of France—who was at that time seeking, through his ambassadors, the queen's hand in marriage, that he was wasting his time. Shakespeare, as I argued in that article, when writing *Love's Labour's Lost,* had a copy of Goldwell's edited text of this notorious entertainment before him. From it he took his own "four foster children of desire"—Navarre, Berowne, Dumaine, and Longaville and then substituted for the figure of Queen Elizabeth I and her maids of honor (the impregnable "castle of perfect beauty") the Princess of France and her three maids of honor, Rosaline, Katherine, and Maria.

To alert the play's first audience to these allusions, he then proceeded to arrange for Rosaline and Katherine to claim in the dialogue of act 2, scene 1, that it was in Brabant, and more specifically at a dance given by the duc d'Alençon, that they had first met Berowne and the young Dumaine. Lest this broad hint toward a recognition in the auditorium of the original state occasion that he was about to parody in his comedy miss its mark, Shakespeare allows Don Armado, when embarassed by his unworthy passion for Jaquenetta, to lament the fact that he cannot "take desire prisoner and ransom him to any French courtier for a new devis'd curtsey" (1.2.56–63).[2]

Directing this play again for a third time this summer (1986) in an open-air production at the University of the South, Sewanee, Tennessee, I was struck by other peculiarities in this text that, once again, help as I believe to unravel the mystery of how this highly sophisticated play first came to be written and performed.

The most singular of these peculiarities is the "antic," or "bergomask," of *Hiems* and *Ver*, winter and spring, respectively represented on the stage by the owl and the cuckoo. This charming musical epilogue is stuck onto the end of the play with a view to translating the pathos of the final farewells between the departing princess and the chastened young men left behind at Navarre's court for a year and a day to ponder their mistakes into a jollier and more lighthearted atmosphere befitting a comedy before the audience exchanges the world of the play for the real world. But why "Winter" and "Spring"? Why "a twelvemonth and a day"?

This deliberate contrast of winter with spring, heightened and made visible in song and costume, strongly suggests a need on the author's part to take note of a particular calendar festival traditionally associated with the winter solstice; in other words, a need to link a festive comedy to the no less festive occasion responsible for the commissioning and writing of the play—the twelve-day feast of Christmas. If this premise is granted, then the Princess's choice of a year and a day as the penitential period to be imposed upon Navarre before he may challenge her by his gift of diamonds to marry him not only ceases to be arbitrary and whimsical but fixes the date of the calender festival in question as New Year's Eve, or Twelfth Night.

This deduction, while it cannot be proved, at least has the virtues of tradition and precedent behind it stretching back into the past to John Lydgate's *Mumming at Hertford*, ca. 1425.[3] In that courtly disguising, presented to the young King Henry VI when he was spending the Christmas holiday at Hertford Castle in Essex, six lusty tradesmen complain to the king through the poet-presenter about the rough treatment each has received, on returning home from his labors, from his wife; they demand that a law be placed on the statute book guaranteeing them "maistry" in their own homes. The six wives then retaliate by delivering a spirited reply through one of their own number to justify their conduct. The piece concludes with an appeal to the king to grant them "the maistry," the king's "sentence and iugement" on "þe complaynte of þe lewed husbands with þe cruwell aunswers of þeyre wyves." This is delivered on the king's behalf by a pursuivant (a junior herald) who states that the matter in question, being too serious to permit an instant verdict, is to be passed to a committee for rigorous "examynacyoun" and "inquysicyoun": this committee will then report back to the king who will deliver his verdict to the husbands and their wives if they will return to receive it at the same time next year. Thus, where both playmaker and actors are concerned, the

poet's formula has provided neatly for a return visit to court at this same
calender feast a year hence. This formula, moreover, accords appropriately
with the winter solstice when life itself appears to be precariously balanced between between decline and renewal, death and rebirth, malev-
olence and goodwill.

Within this context, it strikes me as particularly significant that
Berowne, in *Love's Labour's Lost,* when referring to the treatment ac-
corded by the Princess to his own Masque of Muscovites (5.2) should say
to Navarre that it had been "dashed like an old Christmas comedy": for
this, of course, is exactly the fate that is to overtake Don Armado's and
Holofernes's *Pageant of the Nine Worthies.* Such boisterious, if ill-man-
nered, audience participation was thus something that actors had learned
to anticipate as a normal occurrence during the twelve-day feast of Christmas, presided over throughout by a Lord of Misrule, himself a vestigial
survivor from the Feast of Fools (1 January).

In *Love's Labour's Lost* Shakespeare has cleverly protected himself and
his actors from this fate by using the "Pageant of the Nine Worthies" as a
lightning conductor to abstract such mockery as they might otherwise fear
would be visited upon them by an arrogant, if sophisticated, audience
fortified in its sense of its own cleverness and self-esteem by wine: "not
generous, not gentle; not humble" (5.2.626), as Holofernes so succinctly
observes.

The fortunate survival of the *Gesta Greyorum* provides us with a full
account of how the festive Christmas holiday period, with its insistence
upon inversion of normal social order, was celebrated at the Inns of Court
in London in Shakespeare's own lifetime. The case argued by Leslie
Hotson for regarding *Twelfth Night* as a play commissioned for and
presented on Twelfth Night in Middle Temple Hall is a strong one.[4] The
case I am now arguing for *Love's Labour's Lost* likewise to have been first
presented before a highly sophisticated audience of lawyers and young
courtiers at one of the Inns of Court is at least as strong as his. In that
environment all the allusions to *The Four Foster Children of Desire* of
1581 would have been instantly picked up and greatly enjoyed. Morever,
anticipation by author and actors of such an audience at once justifies and
explains the emphasis placed by Shakespeare within this text upon oaths,
perjury, and the highly legalistic twisting of patent vice into apparent
virtue exemplified by the recourse taken to the entry of a plea of "neces-
sity." That word, first dropped by Navarre in the opening scene, is seized
upon by Berowne as an expedient loophole to extract him, should this
become desirable, from the oath to which he is being asked by Navarre to
sign his name. Yet so preoccupied has the young king been with his own
dream of a utopian Platonic Academy established within his own Court
(itself a mirror image of the Inns of Court) that he has failed to remember,

when issuing his proclamation forbidding cohabitation or consort with women, the imminent arrival of the Princess of France on a diplomatic mission concerning the future of the adjacent Duchy of Acquitaine.

> *Navarre.* What say you, lords? Why this was quite forgot.
> *Berowne.* So study evermore is overshot.
> . . . .
> *Navarre.* We must of force dispense with this decree:
>   She must lie here on mere necessity.
>
> (1.1.139–40, 145–46)

Berowne immediately leaps upon this word as offering the escape clause that he and his fellows need to protect themselves against the consequences of their rash vow.

> *Berowne.* Necessity will make us all forsworn
>   Three thousand times within this three year space;
> . . . .
>   If I break faith, this word shall speak for me:
>   I am forsworn on mere necessity.
>
> (1.1.147–48, 151–52)

On this explicit understanding, he signs.

This idea then lies dormant until after all four young men have exposed their own hypocrisy in their private dealings with the Princess and her ladies in the sonnet scene (4.3). The king appeals directly to Berowne.

> *Navarre.* . . . good Berowne, now prove
>   our loving lawful, and our faith not torn.
>
> (4.3. 280–81)

This is a direct appeal to an able barrister to enter a plea that black is white and white black—a brilliantly calculated device to whet the appetite of an Inns of Court audience both for the case that is to be pleaded and the manner in which the orator will handle it. For the next seventy-six lines—a speech of quite exceptional length by Shakespeare's standards—Berowne settles to his task. Step by logical (if emotional) step, he leads his case to the desired conclusion.

> *Berowne.* Then fools you were these women to forswear
>   Or, keeping what is sworn, you will prove fools
>   For wisdom's sake, a word that all men love;
>   Or for Love's sake, a word that loves all men;
>   Or for men's sake, the authors of these women;
>   Or women's sake, by whom we men are men
>   Let us once lose our oaths to find ourselves

> Or else we lose ourselves to keep our oaths.
> It is religion to be thus forsworn;
> For charity itself fulfils the law,
> And who can sever love from charity?

$$(4.3.351–61)$$

As a peroration designed to sway the sympathy of the jury in the defendant's favor, little could be better judged—or, indeed, better calculated to win applause from spectators at the back of the Court.

From here I move on to more speculative territory—to that of the sequel to *Love's Labour's Lost,* the return visit of the company with the supposed *Love's Labour's Won* which, as the company had itself suggested, might follow to celebrate the same Christmas festival a year later. *Much Ado About Nothing* has proved to be a favorite candidate among critics; and, indeed, Beatrice and Benedict, in the swift thrust and parry of their bouts of wit, do provide some grounds for this supposition, granted the more mature versions of Rosaline and Berowne that the play contains. Dogberry too, with his pretentious use of his own illiteracy, bears some resemblance to the earlier Costard; but there is little else to support this contention. In my own view, *As You Like It* makes a much stronger candidate.

This is a view I have reached while directing this play for the Hartke Theatre in Washington, D.C. Both *Love's Labour's Lost* and *As You Like It* share predominantly woodland settings. In the latter, here again most strikingly we find the four girls and the four young men central to the former—this time decked out as Rosalind, Celia, Audrey, and Phebe, and as Orlando, Oliver, Touchstone, and Silvius. They are all very different from the original "four foster children of desire" and their matching ladies; but in their own ways they are all nevertheless love's victims and love's prisoners: moreover, in *As You Like It,* love's labors are finally won for all eight of them. As Duke Senior puts it in the closing moments of the final scene,

> First, in this forest let us do those ends
> That here were well begun and well begot;
> And after, every of this happy number
> That have endured shrewd days and nights with us
> Shall share the good of our returned fortune,
> According to the measure of their stakes.
> Meantime forget this new fall'n dignity
> And fall into our rustic revelry.
> Play, music, and brides and bridegrooms all,
> With measures heaped in joy, to the measures fall.

$$(5.4.164–73)$$

Here, then, is a faithful fulfillment of a promise to translate a festive Christmas comedy in which four "Jacks" failed to win their "Jills" (to use

Berowne's terminology) into one in which all eight Jacks and Jills are led by Hymen into wedlock. Can this be attributed merely to coincidence? If so, there are other striking similarities of structure, characterization, and dialogue to be accounted for.

The first among these is the lively reduction (if not repetition) of the famous sonnet scene in *Love's Labour's Lost* (4.3) in the form of the sonnets addressed to Rosalind that Orlando hangs on forest trees and which are read aloud by Orlando himself, Rosalind, and Celia (3.2). The closing bergomask of *Love's Labour's Lost* is also repeated in *As You Like It,* where it is now fully incorporated into the fabric of the final scene as part of the "rustic revelry" ordered by Duke Senior to celebrate the quadruple wedding ceremony; and it is to Jaques that the final valedictory lines are given, just as in *Love's Labour's Lost* they are entrusted to Don Armado.

These correspondences are further reinforced by the dramatization in both plays of the winter solstice with its message of renewal in the songs provided within the texts. For the owl and the cuckoo as the representatives of winter nights and summer days of *Love's Labour's Lost* we are offered, "Blow, blow thou winter wind" with its contradictory refrain of "Then heigh-ho the holly / This life is most jolly," and "It was a lover and his lass" with its complementary refrain of "Sweet lovers love the spring."

Against this, it may be objected that where *Love's Labour's Lost* contains five female parts, *As You Like It* provides only four; but here, we must remember, Shakespeare had a practical problem to contend with that critics tend to overlook or to forget. Unlike most plays written today, Shakespeare's were carefully planned to fit the talents of a company whose membership was known to him before he set pen to paper and whose skills and talents played a major part in his thinking about the number of roles and the individual personalities of his stage characters. The one serious variable year by year was the time at which a trained boy actor's voice might break, thereby depriving the company of his services in female roles. Thus where in *Love's Labour's Lost* he had been able to count on the availability of five trained boys—two of exceptional ability who could be trusted with the taxing roles of Rosaline and the Princess— by the time he began to write *As You Like It* there were only four. When the cast lists of the two plays are set side by side it is fairly easy to judge what had happened. The boy whose voice had broken, and who could no longer be used (at least where female roles were concerned), was the one who played the Princess of France. Take her/him away and the use of the other four can readily be discerned. Rosaline becomes Rosalind; Katherine and Maria graduate to the larger roles of Celia and Phebe; and that leaves Jaquenetta free to take on Audrey. This raises the interesting question of the two Pages attendant on Duke Senior in *As You Like It* who appear in a single scene (5.3) with two lines each and as singers of a single song. Are these two new apprentices being given their first chance to appear in public and thus groomed to replace the boy already lost and the boy expected to drop out next?

This strictly theatrical problem may have sufficed in itself to deter Shakespeare from scripting a *Love's Labour's Won* for the same group of characters that had peopled *Love's Labour's Lost;* but it is also hard to imagine how the later could have been spun out into another full-length play ending with a quadruple wedding without any obvious narrative source material out of which to fashion it. Thomas Lodge's romance, *Rosalynde, Euphues's Golden Legacy* of 1590 supplied an alternative that offered an equally rich and varied group of stage characters and the possibility of the desired quadruple wedding.[5]

While that, however, can at best only be regarded as hypothetical, there is much firmer evidence to support this case within the text of *As You Like It* and to prove that *Love's Labour's Lost* was still vividly alive in Shakespeare's mind as he was writing it. This is at its clearest in the characterizations of Jaques, Le Beau, and Audrey.

Jaques is so much himself as to be a role still greatly coveted by actors. Yet Jaques unmistakably carries within himself much of Don Armado and a touch or two of Holofernes, just as Sir Oliver Martext echoes Sir Nathaniel in his inadequacy to his priestly pretentions. Duke Senior retains Jaques as an amusing companion in whose company to spend leisure time just as Navarre employs Armado. Both are gentlemen born but having fallen on hard times have become dependent on a wealthy patron; both are said to have been great travelers and, like all tourists, to possess as a result a fund of strange and amusing anecdotes; both are bachelors and singular in their appearance, deportment, and language. This singularity, combined with their respective affectations and pretentions, makes them vulnerable to attack as laughing stocks to others who are more confident and secure in their knowledge of themselves and of their status in society. It is surely no coincidence that both Armado and Jaques should, in their isolation from the mainstream of daily working occupations, fall back on singers and music for solace and comfort—Armado on Moth, Jaques on Amiens. Armado never makes any pretensions to being a philosopher and professional cynic; nor does Jaques claim to have been an army officer or to be well versed in the latest literary fashions. They are thus interestingly different; yet both are clearly grafted of the same stock.

The only repetition of Don Armado's linguistic gymnastics in *As You Like It* is given to Touchstone in conversation with William.

William. Which he sir?
Touchstone. He, sir, that must marry this woman. Therefore, you clown, abandon—which in the vulgar is leave—the society—which in

the boorish is company—of this female—which in the common is woman—which together is: abandon the society of this female: or, clown, thou perishest: or, to thy better understanding, diest. . . .

(5.1.42–49)

Similar affinities link Le Beau in *As You Like It* to Boyet in *Love's Labour's Lost;* for while Le Beau disappears from the text of the former by the end of act 1, never to reappear, he serves the same purpose at Duke Frederick's court as does Boyet in the household of the Princess of France—a highly placed official whose foppishness is matched by the precision of his wit and his diplomatic skills. Both, it is to be assumed from the dialogue, are bachelors and ladies' men. Le Beau is drawn as no more than an echo of Boyet; but all viewers seeing *As You Like It* who had already seen *Love's Labour's Lost* would instantly recognize where they had met him before.

Audrey, likewise, is a recognizable redaction of Jaquenetta, cut down from a figure appearing in five scenes to a character confined to three scenes in the latter half of the play. Both are farm girls—Jaquenetta a dairy maid, Audrey a keeper of goats; both are as spirited and robust in their fleshy feminity as the sun-kissed harvest wenches depicted in the paintings of Peter Paul Rubens; and both are as sharply perceptive in recognizing a situation that they can exploit to their own advantage as they are naïve and illiterate in their command of language. Shakespeare even equips Audrey with the same joke about Touchstone's physical appearance as he had previously given to Jaquenetta concerning Don Armado's.

Armado. I do betray myself with blushing. Maid!
Jaquenetta. Man!
Armado. I will visit thee at the lodge.
Jaquenetta. That's hereby.
Armado. I know where it is situate.
Jaquenetta. Lord, how wise you are!
Armado. I will tell thee wonders.
Jaquenetta. With that face?

(1.2.126–33)

In As You Like It it recurs as,

Touchstone. And now, Audrey, am I the man yet?
   Doth my simple feature content you?
Audrey. Your features, Lord warrant us. What
   features?

(3.3.2–4)

The conclusions I have drawn from the chances given me to direct *Love's Labour's Lost* and *As You Like It* in sequence and within six months of each other persuade me forcibly that the latter play proved to be the fulfillment of the promise made in the concluding scene of the former to supply the same audience with a *Love's Labour's Won* after an interval of "a twelvemonth and a day." Some readers may feel that this is just so much moonshine; but I remain confident that directors, actors, and actresses who have become aware of these structural parallels, correspondences of characterization, and even direct repetition of snatches of dialogue, are more likely to wish to hang onto them than to reject them.

Notes

1. "*Love's Labour's Lost* and *The Four Foster Children of Desire*, 1581," *Shakespeare Quarterly*, 36 (1985): 49–55.

2. The quotations from *Love's Labour's Lost* are from the New Penguin edition, ed. John Kerrigan (Harmondsworth, Eng.: Penguin, 1982).

3. See Glynne Wickham, *English Moral Interludes*, Dent's Everyman Library (London: Dent, 1985), 204–9.

4. Leslie Hotson, *The First Night of Twelfth Night* (New York: Macmillan, 1954).

5. The quotations from *As You Like It* are from the New Penguin edition, ed. H. J. Oliver (Harmondsworth, Eng.: Penguin, 1981). Thomas Lodge's *Rosalynde* is printed in Geoffrey Bullough, *Narrative and Dramatic Sources of Shakespeare*, vol. 2 (London: Routledge and Kegan Paul, 1958).

Peter Quince Directs *Romeo and Juliet*

HUGH M. RICHMOND

Romeo and Juliet "has probably been the most popular after *Hamlet* of all Shakespeare's plays on the English stage," according to C. B. Young's stage history.[1] Unfortunately, this simple assertion invites the retort; "But whose *Romeo and Juliet?*" I would like to argue that we hardly ever see an authentic Shakespearean interpretation of the play. From the very start there has been controversy about the various texts, including views that "the First Quarto represents a first draft by Shakespeare or some other dramatist, or at least a pirated version . . . corrupted and perverted by certain actors who had performed it . . . or that the Second Quarto contains layers of text composed by Shakespeare at different times."[2] Anyone familiar with stage production will recognize that the bad First Quarto version of the fight between Mercutio and Tybalt reflects the more limited practical opportunities for speech in live production of the fight than the fuller, more literary version of the more authentic Second Quarto. I have tested this assertion through direct demonstration by members of the Berkeley Shakespeare Festival to the scholarly audience that celebrated the publication of the collected Shakespearean Quartos.[3] The pirated First Quarto version is briefer, leaving more scope for physical action than the more formal and elaborate Second Quarto text. Thus from the start of the play's history we can detect a discrepancy between script and performance. Unfortunately "no actual record of performances before the Restoration survives," despite the First Quarto's affirmation of its reception "with great applause."[4]

When the play was revived at the Restoration, Pepys considered it to be "a play of itself the worst that I ever heard, and the worst acted that ever I saw these people do,"[5] comments seeming to put that production in the same league as Quince's *Pyramus and Thisbe*. Inevitably, therefore, some years later, "it was altered by James Howard so as to end happily with the lovers alive," which seemingly required "the inclusion of Count Paris' wife."[6] Even this drastic adaptation failed to preserve the original play, which was replaced until 1735 by "a strange hotch-potch of garbled Shakespeare matter and new invention, Otway's *Caius Marcus,* first shown in Dorset Garden in 1680. This stole, as the Prologue admitted, half its material from *Romeo and Juliet;* but the conflict of Marcus and Sylla in Republican Rome took the place of the Montague-Capulet feud in Verona."[7] While Garrick reverted often to Shakespeare's text, he still made many drastic alterations: "the last act opened with a funeral procession for Juliet inside a church with much pompous solemnity. But his chief crime was to rewrite the scene in the tomb in accordance with Otway's foolish idea of having Romeo linger, after drinking the poison, while Juliet awakens—a melodramatic notion that was used by Cibber, Kemble, many nineteenth-century actors."[8] In 1770 Francis Gentleman praised this version saying, "No play ever received greater advantage from alteration than this play, especially in the last act."[9] Granted this perverse rendering, it is perhaps hardly surprising that "the greatest actors between Garrick and Macready largely neglected the play."[10] However, soon even more bizarre innovations were to come. On Shakespeare's stage Juliet had been played by a boy, but on many nineteenth-century stages the casting was reversed in the spirit of the Principal Boy of popular pantomimes. Instead of two males playing Romeo and Juliet, the roles were enacted by two females— most conspicuously by the Cushman sisters, Charlotte and Susan. As Romeo, Charlotte achieved the highest acclaim: the London *Times* called her "far superior to any Romeo we have ever had," and another of Charlotte's Juliets called her "the best Romeo I ever saw or ever shall see."[11] Perhaps it is significant that around this time the play reached "the heyday of its popularity" in the U.S.A., for Charlotte Cushman created a rage for female Romeos for over thirty years beginning in 1839.[12]

Our own age is not exempt from such bizarre adjustments. Speaking of the notoriously abrupt termination of his production of the play, Bill Glover has justified to me the excision of the final ending of the feud as a proper punishment for his audience's toleration of the killing of youth in the Vietnam war. No less partisan is the currently best known and admired film version, by Franco Zeffirelli, which adds a nude bedroom scene, almost wholly avoids Rosaline, and cuts Romeo's killing of Paris. These adjustments were apparently intended to make it "a contemporary drama" overriding the youth audience's view shared by Leonard Whiting, Zeffirelli's Romeo, who found "Shakespeare very boring."[13] As recently as 1985 a Parisian production reflected a similar weariness with the text. At the Maison de la Culture in the Paris suburb of Bobigny, Daniel Mesguich's production of *Romeo and Juliet* "was haunted by Racine's Phèdre, Richard II, Hugo's Ruy Blas, Hamlet, Cyrano de Bergerac, and Molière's Don Juan, all of whom actually make appearances on stage."[14] There would still appear to be some anxiety about the adequacy of the original text.

The performance history of *Romeo and Juliet* thus often suggests the prescience of Shakespeare's presentation of the Quince production, *Pyra-*

mus and Thisbe. There is clearly often as much dreadfully wrong with the historical productions of *Romeo and Juliet* that I have mentioned as of this Shakespearean parody. Before isolating the causes of this misdirection and their remedy, it seems proper to seek any evidence concerning the author himself, by recreating the theatrical context of the development and rehearsal of the *Romeo and Juliet* script. There are numerous clues about attitudes, interpretations, and methods of performance of romantic plots in the earlier plays of Shakespeare, but obviously one play comes closest to review of the staging of classic romantic tragedy. In a recent address my colleague Donald Friedman has suggested that, as with almost every Shakespeare text, much of the production business of *A Midsummer Night's Dream* is not an improvisation but is based on precedent: in this case through a playful parody of the actual playing company's own personnel and rehearsal procedures.[15] In this light, according to Professor Friedman, the role of Peter Quince as script writer and director approximates Shakespeare's own, while the ever-intrusive Bottom closely matches the assertive clown, Will Kemp, indirectly censured also by Hamlet in that tragedy's anachronistic allusions to the problems of the Elizabethan stage (3.2.38–45). Personally, admiring Bottom as I do,[16] I am tempted to see Bottom's bizarre virtuosity as nearer to ·Richard Burbage's histrionic talents than Kemp's; but in any event there can be no doubt that *Pyramus and Thisbe* is a parody of *Romeo and Juliet,* as numerous cross-references affirm. The plays are roughly contemporary, and *A Dream* offers us a detailed commentary on how (or how not) to stage "a lamentable comedy" about "a lover, that kills himself most gallant for love" (1.2.11,23).[17]

The simplest observation about *Pyramus and Thisbe* is the impossibility of any deep empathy, identification, or acceptance of theatrical illusion by the interlude's supposed stage audience. This is not merely the result of the amateur actors' incompetence, for their own "Prologues" and interpolated "explanations" are overtly designed to destroy any pretence of plausibility. Their "audience's" wholehearted acceptance of this unrealistic mode ensures the play's success as comic entertainment for that audience. However, exploration of the play's larger Shakespearean context indicates that this disabusing of the stage "audience" is not only normative in all of Shakespeare's other "plays within plays" but is characteristic of his own approach to the real audiences in his theatre. The induction to *The Taming of the Shrew* indeed establishes that the whole following play has no more validity than the doubly artificial "aristocratic" environment created to delude Christopher Sly. Kate's "passion" is no more authentically feminine than the wifely charms assumed by the Page assigned to the role of Sly's "Lady." The continued presence of Sly and his entourage exploited in *The Taming of a Shrew* (1594), the anonymous and possibly pirated version of Shakespeare's play, suggests a likely purpose of sustaining this enforced awareness of artificiality in performance, as many modern directors continue to accept. This audience distancing does not always require structural recognition of stage artifice. In *The Two Gentlemen of Verona* the audience is systematically alienated from its dual heroes by comparable ridicule of their emotional convictions, but in this case by other characters nominally within the main action. These actually control the audience's perspective by their choruslike commentary. In our recent exploration of this antiromantic aspect of *Two Gentlemen*, in a production by the Shakespeare Program at the University of California at Berkeley, we found that our audience's amused reactions to the lovers were wholly governed by the parodies and objective censures of them offered by Speed (2.1), Launce (3.1), or even by one lover of another (2.4). As with the wry observations and manipulations of the young lovers in *A Dream* by Oberon and Puck, our audiences rejected identification with the romantic leads and any acceptance of their narrowly subjective reality.

If it be objected that comedy cannot provide a gloss for tragedy, it is easy to find tragic analogies of audience distancing (not to say alienation) from the most supposedly intense moments of Shakespearean tragedy. Some of these are almost willfully disillusioning, such as Macbeth's self-deconstruction into "a poor player, / That struts and frets his hour upon the stage" (5.5. 24–25); or the involuntary self-identification of the boy actor who would have played Cleopatra with "the quick comedians," who will have "some squeaking Cleopatra boy my greatness / I'th' posture of a whore" (5.2. 216, 220–21). More subtly, all audiences are cued by the villains to perceive the misreadings of artifice in Lady Anne's facile responses to Richard of Gloucester's manipulative courtship or in Othello's naïve passion at Iago's "staging" of Cassio's lecherous account of Bianca's love. Thus in the tragedies as in the comedies Shakespeare insists on the discrepancy between the audience's alienating awareness and the heroes' illusions, whether we talk of Lear or Othello, Orlando or Claudio.

In sum it is rare that Shakespeare leaves a lyric statement of feeling unchallenged by a critical context and emotionally unlimited by awareness of the artifice of performance. Where this does seem to occur—as in the soliloquies of Hamlet—a romantic misreading of the play has tended to develop in which the hero's perspective has usurped the critical balance and tension of forces that lies at the heart of drama. Romantic criticism has equated Hamlet with *Hamlet* in ways not characteristic of Shakespeare's dramaturgy and fitter for the fancifulness of the study than the reality of the stage. As scholars and critics inflate individual roles such as Falstaff's there has been a loss of dramatic tension and even a decline in performance, as happened in this case in the late nineteenth century.[18]

This I believe is what has happened with *Romeo and Juliet*. The play has been transformed into a sentimental icon for the literary imagination, and as such it has ceased to be a stageable play. Romeo's subjective perspective has preempted the necessary diversity of viewpoints required in truly dramatic performance, and this has been favored even at the price of mutilating the text itself for study purposes. The recent bitter controversy over the standard excision of several hundred lines from all the secondary school–text versions of *Romeo and Juliet* is a case in point. This achieves the same results as Zeffirelli's cuts, if for different motives: the diminution of ideas, personalities, and episodes inimical to Romeo's sentimentality. In the 1979 production of the play in the California Shakespeare Festival at Visalia (now defunct), the director Mark Lamos insisted on an "abstract" and "exalted" interpretation of the lovers that required radically suppressing much of the play's contrasting humor.[19] He apparently even replaced a Nurse who resisted this homogenization. In such glorification of the lovers, lyric sentiment is preferred to dramatic multiplicity of awareness.

This view of *Romeo and Juliet* derives from the private study, not the public stage. When John Donne returned home from seeing these early plays of Shakespeare, he recreated in private the sentiments of individual characters unlimited by their original objectifying contexts and humorous audience detachment.[20] This kind of private solemnizing of feeling recurs in scholars such as Caroline Spurgeon with her selective misreading of the play's imagery. She continually lists images of brightness and light without investigating why they correlate closely with allusions to explosions, violence, and destruction: "fire," "lightning," "gunpowder," etc.[21] Similarly, while correctly recognizing the moral tensions that limit our approval of Shakespeare's tragic heroes, Lyly B. Campbell almost willfully fails to apply her categories to Romeo, leaving the naïve reading of his role unchallenged.[22]

Now it is true that in comparison with the crudely didactic purposes of Brooke's version Shakespeare is far less openly censorious of youthful passion.[23] This should heighten our sense of the tragic cost of adolescent exuberance, but critics have swung from Brooke's approval of parental repressiveness to just as naïve an endorsement of adolescent idealism, enshrined in such textbook misrepresentations as this: "Shakespeare was never more patently the schoolmaster than in his repeated moralizing that love must destroy hate. . . . Nothing would remove the continuance of their parents' rage except their children's end. The moral lesson is so shaped formally that it becomes the main theme of the drama . . . the closing scene offers the sacrifice of innocents to wipe out in blood the cursed strife of the old partizans."[24] So dogmatic a reading involves factual misrepresentation, but it is also un-Shakespearean in its simplicity and undramatic, as are most sentimental readings of the play and the performances based on them. For example, every death in *Romeo and Juliet* is primarily attributable to the initiative of youthful males, above all of Romeo, who, far from innocent, is directly or indirectly responsible for six deaths. The elders repeatedly resist youthful bellicosity—above all old Capulet, who is also particularly anxious to assure Juliet's free choice of spouse until he is emotionally unbalanced by the youthful massacres. The simplifying of the play's tensions into one of youthful virtue versus intemperate age is wearisome and necessarily lacking in dramatic tension or even intellectual interest.

My ultimate purpose in this essay is to argue that the now normal transmutation of *Romeo and Juliet* into a pathetic lyric duet with sinister intrusions falsifies Shakespeare's well-established skepticism about the positive value of high sentiment.[25] The transmutation can only be made plausible by ignoring, or even excising, substantial parts of the play essential to its vitality in performance. With this antisentimental approach in mind I have staged not only *Romeo and Juliet,* but many of the relevant plays and scenes to which I have alluded here. The Shakespeare Program at Berkeley makes use of live and videotaped productions of Shakespeare by students precisely to test out the validity and value of such scholarly approaches and critical interpretations. The sequence started ten years ago with *Love's Labour's Lost,* which scandalized our audiences by the skeptical contempt with which the play's ladies greet their fickle lovers' amatory protestations. In the same sardonic mood we applied Kott's wry interpretation of *A Dream*[26] to a sixties version of the play set in northern California, with the young lovers as preppies, the fairies as an ecological commune of flower children, Egeus as a first-generation immigrant, Theseus as the local chief of police of a Mendocino township, and Hippolyta as his bellicose captive in the vein of Patty Hearst. The whole was played with an antisentimental verve that proved compelling to our audiences and probably recreated the "modern dress" mode of the Elizabethan stage.

The cumulative effect of these experiments has been to help to discredit the sentimental misreading of Shakespeare in general and *Romeo and Juliet* in particular, of which Zeffirelli's film is only one example in a series of productions beginning in the Restoration. Just as no Antony I have seen can stomach the audience's contemptuous laughter, which the author deliberately elicits when Antony botches his own suicide after Cleopatra's pseudosuicide, so no sentimental director can bear to expose Romeo to the censure that his fickleness, volatility, and homicidal moods invite us to balance against his seductive idealism. Yet it is just this kind of provocative balance of feelings about the similar mixed nature of youthful idealists that held our audiences' attention when my students performed *Love's Labour's Lost* ten years ago and *The Two Gentlemen of Verona* on May Day of 1986.

The solipsistic sentimentality of scholars and critics has corrupted actors and directors into misrepresenting the play in terms not only of its Shakespearean context but also of its very text, which is normally mutilated in the interest of suppressing its masculine reservations about a "feminized" hero such as Charlotte Cushman epitomized, and which the actor playing Zeffirelli's own Romeo clearly despised. This is not to say that Romeo should be unseductive, but that his resemblance to Longaville, to Lucentio, to Valentine and even to Proteus must be given full force if the play's dramatic tensions and vivacious diversity are to survive. That is why Shakespeare gave such humorous authority to Mercutio and the Nurse, who provide an earthly corrective to the sex-and-life rejecting elements in Romeo's textbook idealism.[27] The Visalia director resisted this undercutting of Romeo and the result was naïve, boring, and depressing: in a seminar after the production, cast members confessed that they invariably finished their sentimental performances of the play feeling enervated and alienated, while their more authentically Shakespearean twin production of *The Taming of the Shrew* left them happy and exhilarated.

I have personally explored this issue in numerous versions of both plays with student performances of every kind, and I have found that *Romeo and Juliet* can only be authentically and effectively performed when its relationship to *Pyramus and Thisbe* is recognized. This involves giving full play to Romeo's pseudo-loveaffair with Rosaline and to the satirical force of Mercutio and his shared awareness with the Nurse that mundane sexuality is the expression of true love. This is what high school texts have bowdlerized from the play, leaving the high Petrarchan sentiments uncorrected by the sexuality of the fabliaux, in a way antipathetic equally to the genius of a Chaucer or a Shakespeare. moreover, such a prissy reading bores audiences and leaves unintelligible the violence of repressed sexual energies that makes Romeo a killer. We have learned all too often on modern campuses that it is the superidealistic or sexually repressed student who turns most readily to murder. Thus in our productions we have found the text requires reinforcement of the didactic censures of Romeo by the friar via the ridicule of Mercutio, the Nurse, and Juliet herself. Their humorously critical observations provide variety of tone and perspective, while the latent death wish in Romeo from the start affords the justification for his fatal behavior in the end.

How exactly will these issues alter performance of the text? By stressing Romeo's limitations we shall, ironically, make it more modern—nearer to the mood of *Hedda Gabbler* or *The Seagull* or even *Madame Bovary*. More specifically we found it important to note the compulsive negative strain in Romeo's scarcely unconscious ambivalence in such phrases as "loving hate" (1.1.176); "Beauty too rich for use, for earth too dear!" (1.5.47); "love-devouring death do what he dare" (2.6.7); "let me be put to death, / I am content" (3.5.17–18), "How oft when men are at the point of death / Have they been merry" (5.3.88–89); "Thus with a kiss I die" (5.3.120). I observed earlier, concerning his Old Vic production of the play (in 1960, eight years before the film was made), that Zeffirelli largely anticipated these views: the hot lights of the opening scene evoked the ominous sultriness of *I Vitteloni,* the gang warfare appeared a symptom of adolescent boredom and restlessness, the balcony scene was more comic than romantic (a value that survives happily in the film). The whole production had an uneasy energy and volatility—alternately comic, as survives in the film's Mercutio, and violent, as in the first half of that film— that always disturbingly reminded us of Romeo's incompetence as a neces- sary corollary of his adolescent charm. This sheer incompetence is what the film willfully suppresses from the start—and even Romeo's killing of Tybalt in the film has a self-indulgent violence worthy of Rambo: its intensity is endorsed by the direction in a way the text resists. It would seem that Shakespeare (unlike Marlowe and Jonson) repudiates empathy with intense feelings either amatory or murderous.

Our goal then in Shakespearean Program production has been to dis- credit both delusion and illusion through open-air, unpretentious perfor- mance that admits the artifice of the staging, welcomes the unbelief in its reality, and hence questions the propriety of naïve empathy with an actor's feigning, as Hamlet perceives: "What's Hecuba to him, or he to Hecuba / That he should weep for her?" (2.2.559–60). Our conditioning by Victorian proscenium productions, reinforced by the specious realism of the cine- ma, must be broken if we are to recover the consciously artificial modes of the Elizabethan stage and the audience detachment that it implies. The behavior of Shakespeare's onstage audiences invariably suggests his ex- pectation of an alienation effect prefiguring Brecht's. Hence Shakespeare's willingness to cue his real audience to accept their own awareness of the artifice of staged passions and their falsity as good models for either performance or behavior. What is needed is a kind of "temperance," as Hamlet says: "Give me that man / That is not passion's slave" (3.2.7,71– 72). Romeo is not such a one, and to invite audiences uncritically to accept him as admirable is not only poor drama, it is un-Shakespearean. Romeo is nearer to Bottom's Pyramus than is usually allowed, just as Quince owes more to the professional values of his creator, and both may provide some precedents for modern direction of *Romeo and Juliet.*

Notes

1. William Shakespeare, *Romeo and Juliet,* ed. John Dover Wilson and George Ian Duthie (Cambridge: Cambridge University Press, 1955), xxxviii.
2. Ibid., xiv.
3. *Shakespeare's Plays in Quarto,* ed. Michael J. B. Allen and Kenneth Muir (Berkeley: University of California Press, 1981), 136–37, 178–79.

4. Shakespeare, *Romeo and Juliet,* xxxviii.

5. Ibid.

6. Ibid., xxxix.

7. Ibid.

8. Bernard Grebanier, *Then Came Each Actor* (New York: David McKay, 1975), 98.

9. Grebanier, *Each Actor,* 99.

10. Shakespeare, *Romeo and Juliet,* xliii–xliv.

11. Grebanier, *Each Actor,* 259.

12. Shakespeare, *Romeo and Juliet,* li.

13. Grebanier, *Each Actor,* 522.

14. Rosette C. Lamont, "Innovation Blossoms On the Fringes of Paris," *The New York Times,* 18 May 1986.

15. At the Western Shakespeare Seminar, University of California at Berkeley, 1984.

16. See for example, Hugh M. Richmond, *"A Midsummer Night's Dream,"* in *Shakespeare Criticism,* ed. Laurie Larzen Harris and Mark W. Scott (Detroit: Gale Research, 1986), 3 : 480–81.

17. Line reference to quotations from Shakespeare's plays are to *the Riverside Shakespeare,* ed. G. Blakemore Evans (Boston: Houghton Mifflin, 1974).

18. William Shakespeare, *The First Part of the History of Henry IV,* ed. John Dover Wilson (Cambridge: Cambridge University Press, 1968), xli–xliii.

19. Mark Lamos, "The Director's View," in *California Shakespeare Festival Inaugural Season* (Visalia: California Shakespeare Festival, 1979), 18.

20. Hugh M. Richmond, "Donne's Master: The Young Shakespeare," *Criticism* 15, no. 2 (Spring, 1973): 126–44

21. Caroline Spurgeon, *Shakespeare's Imagery and What It Tells Us* (Cambridge: Cambridge University Press, 1965), 310.

22. Lyly B. Campbell, *Shakespeare's Tragic Heroes: Slaves of Passion* (New York: Barnes and Noble, 1960), 115, 208.

223. *Narrative and Dramatic Sources of Shakespeare,* ed. Geoffrey Bullough (London: Routledge, 1966), 1 : 277.

24. Donald A. Stauffer, "The School of Love: *Romeo and Juliet,"* in *Shakespeare: The Tragedies,* ed. Alfred Harbage (Englewood Cliffs: Prentice Hall, 1964), 29.

25. This issue is explored more fully in Hugh M. Richmond, *Shakespeare's Sexual Comedy* (New York: Bobbs-Merrill, 1971), 102–22.

26. Jan Kott, *Shakespeare Our Contemporary* (New York: Anchor, 1966), 213–36.

27. Juliet accuses him, "You kiss by th' book" (1.5.110).

"Balancing at Work"

(R)evoking the Script in Performance and Criticism

THOMAS CLAYTON

> . . . Shakespeare, more than almost any other dramatist, responds to performances that balance the concrete reality of his characters' thoughts and feelings against the oft-stressed fancy of their situations. Strehler's production [of *The Tempest*] shows that balancing at work. By devising striking yet deeply relevant visual analogues to the circumstances of the action, he endows events and characters with a rare kind of magic.
> —Bernard Beckerman, "The Odd Business of Play Reviewing"

1

It is of course no coincidence that the late Bernard Beckerman was in the midst of the action in the recent (1985) special issue of *Shakespeare Quarterly* on *Reviewing Shakespeare* with "The Odd Business of Play Reviewing."[1] One always turned with interest and expectancy to what he would have to say on any subject, and I think very pertinent to performance criticism what he refers to as a "theatrical review" in commenting on the Royal Shakespeare Company's already famous 1984–85 production of *Richard III* with Antony Sher demonic and riveting on crutches, and on Giorgio Strehler's long-running Teatro Piccolo production of *The Tempest,* shown far from Milan in Los Angeles and New York in 1984 when I was still hapless enough to see it in neither place. In writing reviews of productions that readers can never see, he writes,

> it is extraordinarily difficult to give a reliable summation of a performance's contents. Even when the play is by Shakespeare and its script is not entirely strange to readers of a review, a writer still finds it tricky to give an adequate account of the style of production and nearly impossible to convey the character and quality of the acting. To do so the reviewer has to be a creative writer in some measure. He or she must translate a holistic perception into a concise verbal statement, and that translation requires a touch of the poet. Mere description, for a performance that readers can never see, is useless. Instead, the reviewer has to evoke the entire production obliquely. . . . Whereas a book of Shake-

spearean scholarship or criticism is inextricably immersed in the world of scholarship or criticism, a stage production is a fresh work of art. While our response to it cannot but be affected by our knowledge of earlier productions and by our attitude toward the play, it is not bound by either that knowledge or that attitude. A new rendition of a play can override our predispositions. It can assert itself as an absolutely novel endeavor, to be judged not as a Shakespearean revival but as an original creation.[2]

In a way, that distinction between a "revival" and an "original creation" is my subject here, though with a difference. My interest in the riddle "When is a production not a production?" and in the possible solutions continues, and my inquiry here is an extension of what I have written on "Theatrical Shakespearegresses at the Guthrie and Elsewhere: Notes on 'Legitimate Production' " in *New Literary History*.[3]

2

Michael Bogdanov's 1986 production of *Romeo and Juliet* was first performed on 31 March in the Royal Shakespeare Theatre. Owing to its Mafia-Italian setting replete with motorcycles, convertible sports car (hence the apt tag of "Alfa-*Romeo*"), and a central staircase often in motion in front of a large screen on which pictures and portraits were projected from time to time to complement, interpret, and not seldom compete with the action and dialogue, this production serves to focus differences in perception, interpretation, and evaluation—and half the story is told by the fact that lately we typically identify a major production by the name not of the playwright but of the director. Of a group of Shakespeare scholars who saw this production on 20 August 1986, some complained that the script was often radically at odds with the set and actions, and at least one applauded with his feet by leaving at the interval.[4] It is easy to dismiss such responses as superannuated and reactionary, but I think it is also precipitate and facile. How *do* theatregoers hear and understand the dialogue in such productions unless they know it well already? By fits and starts, and as through a glass—and hearing aid— darkly, one may suspect. But since in such productions the spectacle and score, in this case rock, seem as much end as means, it may be supposed that many members of the audience get what they "really" even if unconsciously came for: a "theatrical experience" with or without the contemporary attitudinizing that is characteristically widespread if not wholly collective in such productions.

In fact, the "curmudgeons"—critics resistant to Bogdanovation and its kin—seem to have had their finger on the pulse of an ailment unrecognized as such both by those who know a play extremely well (and tend to *assume* the efficacy of the script in delivery) and those who know it less than well or not at all. The former are likely to concentrate on and evaluate the novelty of the "production values" as such, the latter to attend to the spectacle, sound, and actions because that is mostly, sometimes solely, what they have to go on. The problem is at once semantic, moral, and ideological, and in more than one sense critical. It may well be—to borrow a term expressing a categorical criterion—that the language of the dialogue is "degraded" in productions that background it in favor of spectacle and supertext. I for one think it often is. But critics do not necessarily agree on what is or should be foregrounded in a contemporary production, and they may in fact not "see" the same production, even though they may be watching the same performance.

Stanley Wells's review of *Romeo and Juliet* appeared in the 25 April 1986 issue of the *Times Literary Supplement*. I had read it but did not have it in mind when I saw the production in August 1986. Productions characteristically evolve, sometimes extensively or even drastically, over time, but Wells's review is circumstantial enough for me to infer that not much and nothing crucial had changed between April and August: the description in his review recognizably corresponds with the performance I attended, and I am bound to agree in the main with his mixed evaluation. But we might almost have seen different but coextensive *productions* being performed simultaneously, with Wells attending more to the one and I to the other, a disparity this *Romeo and Juliet* all too easily accommodated. He saw Bogdanov employing "all the cliches of modern-dress Shakespeare," with "appurtenances [that] are tediously predictable, but the production displays some of the virtues of the mode. There is a serious attempt to root the dialogue in social reality." He concludes:

> As the play deepens into tragedy the production loses its grip and dwindles into self-indulgence, most blatantly in the elaborate carnival gratuitously introducing blown-up caricatures of current political leaders which can be excused only as a heavy-handedly ironic background to Romeo's reception of the news of Juliet's supposed death. After the lovers have died, there is a brief blackout; when the lights go up again, the bier has become a plinth bearing upright golden statues of Romeo and Juliet. The Prince speaks the play's opening Chorus (omitted earlier), transposed into the past tense, as an introduction to a public ceremony enacted before television cameras and press photographers. The lovers' tragedy has become a media event, and most of the publicity conscious survivors are interested mainly in the figure that they cut before the cameras. In its cheap cynicism, this ending epitomizes the production's worst elements: its cultivation of superficial theatricality, its shying away from the direct exploration of serious emotion, and its exploitation of Shakespeare's play for doctrinaire purposes.

That describes what I should call an "exploitation production," one way of using the script as a means to ends other than performing it in consonance with its own resources and intentionalities. Seen as I persistently saw it in the course of watching it, it was less an "exploitation production" than an "alienation production," one with an evidently deliberate ideological/satiric thrust, corresponding presumably with what Wells calls "doctrinaire purposes." If this *Romeo and Juliet* was intended by the director to be as it seemed to me to be, then what Wells faulted might well be praised—by some—for many of the same tokens differently perceived. In this perspective the young lovers were at odds with and destroyed by bourgeois capitalist society epitomized in one of its most virulent manifestations and synecdoches, the Mafia, or *Cosa Nostra,* in this case with the Prince as the *capo de tutti capi,* an Al Capone type that this Prince seemed to resemble if not indeed to represent, being referred to jokingly (but accurately) by T. P. Matheson of the Shakespeare Institute as "that well-known *Mafioso* Prince Escalus." Wells found "Capulet conceived as a brusquely successful, cigar-smoking business man, . . . a less rounded character than he should be; Lady Capulet is caricatured as his hard-faced, socially ambitious wife." She was also not much more than the twenty-eight she needs to be as Juliet's mother, and her obvious pleasure-loving indolence made it all too plausible that she would, as she was shown to, have something going on the side with Tybalt.

Many things fall into place in accordance with the quasi-Marxist perspective, from the generational class war through what Wells describes as the "gratuitously introduc[ed] blown-up caricatures of current political leaders" right down to the transposed prologue-become-epilogue and the "media event" memorializing Romeo and Juliet as a pair of negotiable golden "soulmates" at the end. And what Wells calls "its cheap cynicism" is, in this perspective, precisely the didactic epiphany the entire production has been preparing for, a strongly ironical conclusion to the play for (as it were) a now edified audience to take to heart and body politic. The same could be said of "the production's worst elements: its cultivation of superficial theatricality [versus its *characterizing* a superficial, cynical, greedy, and pleasure-bent society], its shying away from the direct exploration of serious emotion [which is all but impossible to feel, let alone express, in such an alienated world, except for an exceptional and accordingly doomed pair like Romeo and Juliet], and its exploitation of Shakespeare's play for doctrinaire purposes." On this concluding note there is not much room for disagreement, whatever the special premises of the production, which in my view did well what it apparently set out to do, with the director's hand very much in the designer's glove. Arguably a "successful 'production' ": novel, thoughtful, provocative, politically committed, and so on.

It is possible that the apparent ideological design was coincidental if not inadvertent, but that cannot be concluded merely on the basis that Bogdanov is known for theatrical "exhibitionism" in general and for motorcycles in particular, which figured prominently also—but much better attuned—in his RSC *Taming of the Shrew* (first performed on 19 April 1978). In any case, my considered view of the "production" is much like Stanley Wells's, because we evidently share some such assumptions as that the director (with the designer) has a particular obligation to the script—and in general to the playwright's (other) work, since a script is known for what it is by the entire corpus of a playwright's works as a primary context of understanding (obviously not the only one).

And what of Shakespeare's *Romeo and Juliet?* Robert Demeger (Friar Laurence) viewed "this production as nodding in the direction of an adaptation rather than being a definitive production," but "the RSC's job, as well as doing the plays in a way that has reverence and respect and commitment to Shakespeare's intentions, is also to have a commitment to interpreting Shakespeare's intentions and putting on versions of the plays that challenge and discuss as much as they comfort."[5] He noted, too, that there were "more gimmicks in rehearsal than we ended up with," and that this *Romeo and Juliet* had a very strong effect on young people, school parties, and the like, sending some of them "absolutely over the moon."

Much of the vehicle that did the sending had been assembled by the director himself. According to Niamh Cusack (Juliet), the transposition of prologue to epilogue and the endplay cuts were "a fait accompli when the actors arrived." She said that Bogdanov believes Shakespeare should always be performed in modern dress, because that "helps the audience identify more quickly," and that he emphasized a "superficial coming together of the two families." He spoke of himself as "making the point more boldly than Shakespeare dared to. . . . He's just taken it one step further." Such changes as there had been in the course of the run from the beginning until August were minor improvements due to the actors; for example, the meeting sonnet of 1.5 was originally spoken—and inevitably thrown away—on the staircase. The actors sought the necessary approval of Bogdanov, which he gave.

This *Romeo and Juliet* was a certain though unacknowledged adaptation, with the script seemingly as heavily ideologized with supertext as is easily possible without rewriting the script. Whatever Bogdanov may have assumed about his audiences' knowledge of Shakespeare's *Romeo and Juliet*, John Barton could assume very little knowledge of Aphra Behn's *Rover*, first performed on 3 July 1986 in the new Swan Theatre in Stratford-upon-Avon, which itself had opened with the first performance of *The Two Noble Kinsmen* on 26 April 1986. It was perhaps all the more necessary to acknowledge his as "an adapted text, as established halfway through the rehearsals," ample caveat even though what went on the boards involved further alterations (transposed opening scenes, for example).[6] In fact, the title page itself identifies "An adaptation of THE ROVER (The Banished Cavaliers) by Aphra Behn." It is difficult not to suspect that the reason some directors do not so identify an adaptation is that they want it both ways: full credit for artistic originality at the playwright's expense when such a "production" is well received, and freedom from responsibility at the same expense when it is not.

Barton's adaptation seemed faithful to the spirit and much of the textual intentionality of Behn's play, and incorporating parts of one of her prime sources, Thomas Killigrew's *Thomaso, or the Wanderer,* is very much of her own turn of playwrighting. But Wells is surely right to find fault with Bogdanov's "production" of *Romeo and Juliet* as such. "Legitimate?" Robert Speaight said a decade ago that "the academic, poring over a text with the Variorum at his elbow, is bent on deciding what the play says and what the play means. The stage director must at all cost please, if possible surprise, and perhaps shock his audience."[7] As he also says, "the régis-seur," who has taken the place of the Victorian actor-manager, "is to be judged as [Granville] Barker would have asked to be judged, by the quality of his service to the play, which need not exclude the entertainment of the audience."[8] Today there is little enough agreement that "service to the play," in the form of high fidelity to the script, at any rate, is anything but unoriginal and slavish, if even possible. It is—and it is not—surprising to find so distinguished an actor as Ian McKellen remarking quite indepen-dently that "the only reason we work hard in the privacy of the rehearsal room is to be of service to the play. Not for the benefit of ourselves, but for the benefit of the audience."[9] But it is widely thought that, since the script of a play is inevitably "transformed" on the stage, the "best" should be made of it by wholesale transformation. Aside from the fact that a second-order work of dramatic art seldom improves upon a great first-order work unless it utterly takes leave of it, becoming a whole new thing, we are at the crossroads of theoretical crux here.

When and where ideological perspective is privileged over the script, Bogdanov's *Romeo and Juliet* has claims to special recognition and reward for what it does *not* give us of Shakespeare's, mostly in accordance with the post-Brechtian view that catharsis is to be eschewed as bourgeois massage in favor of Marxist message. "Alienation productions" have their place, but they are not less adaptive or reconstitutive than "exploitation productions" are. The difference is in the valorization of departures as-cribed to one kind of motive-and-effect and its opposite, respectively: service to society and the revolution, as it might be called, on the one hand, versus self-indulgence and/or capitalist commercialism on the other. It is hardly surprising, then, that I agree with Wells substantially on the overall departure of the "production" from the script but also differ over important particulars. This sort of variation is inevitable in responses to a production where the director seems to have it both ways, neither of them unmistakably the playwright's. And the potential tangible rewards of professing radical ideology in the West should not be underestimated.

Several questions that arise are these.

1. When is a "production" not a production? In theory an easy one, a riddle, even. Answer: when it's an adaptation, acknowledged or not.

2. What differentiates an "exploitation production" from an "alienation production?" This question overlaps with the preceding, obviously, owing to the ambiguity of *production* as (a) any stage presentation, a "show"; and (b) a stage-rendition, or performance, of a particular script.

What responsibility have producers and performers

3. to the playwright and the script?

4. to the particular audience(s) addressed?

5. to make money (for whomever)?

6. to serve the ultimate best interests of society, and/or to promote what they see as ideological imperatives?

It will be obvious that these are questions of importance for performance *criticism* as well as for stage performance; indeed, the answers to them, in terms of what a critic assumes, penetrate every pore of description, interpretation, and evaluation—or any kind of performance-related discourse, whether it admits the validity of interpretation and (explicit) evaluation or not, and some contemporary theories definitely do not. It is all a matter of what is allowed priority, or is "privileged," in a critical system. If ideology, then the responsibility both of performers and of critics is in one vital respect the same, mutatis mutandis: "to serve the revolution," reinforce the status quo, or whatever, a cause that virtually obviates special concern for the playwright and his or her script and "its" performance as such ("bourgeois individualism," "liberal humanism").

Identifying a theoretical position and its premises is important, but it will not in itself solve all problems. From one perspective, "exploitation theatre" and "alienation theatre" are the same, since neither practices special allegiance or duty to script or playwright, and many of their effects upon an audience will be similar if not the same: those of a performance in which the verbal-cognitive values of script qua script are "deprivileged" in favor of the values privileged in their place, either (1) novelty and entertainment, and profit, in the case of (quasi-capitalist) "exploitation theatre"; or (2) systematic didacticism—or merely "foregrounded" ideological values, as sometimes claimed—in the case of (quasi-Marxist) "alienation theatre" *lehrstücke*. By contrast, Robert Speaight's droll remark—it is worth repeating—neatly stresses a balance of relationships desirable from a perspective privileging playwright (implicitly), script, and audience: the *"régisseur"* is to be judged *"by the quality of his service to the play, which need not exclude the entertainment of the audience"*—for which Shakespeare's plays were in part if not entirely written, so far as we can penetrate to his intentions, a consideration-problematic that in no way excludes the presence of serious purposes and ideological operations, whether brought unconsciously or deliberately into place and play in his works.

Exploitation and alienation theatre, whether "capitalist" or "Marxist," may coexist in the same "production," with some audiences, general *and* critical, responding variously more to the one than to the other. In fact, the most effective alienation theatre may well be that in which the effect of entertainment is more in evidence than the didacticism (a Horatian commonplace), something not difficult of accomplishment. Even the constant metadramatic reminders that "it's only a play, not the Real World" may entertain; and Brecht's own extravaganzas affect audiences by pleasing them through their entertainment values—in Western production, at least—more than they arouse them through their transparent teachings. It is no coincidence that *Mack the Knife* alone could have made the late Bobby Darin rich on either side of many a curtain. And where many go from there is not the meeting hall but the pub.

A caveat lector seems in order here. The valorization implicit in the use of such a term as "exploitation theatre" or even "alienation theatre" should be taken to apply not necessarily to the deliberate intentions or motives of the professionals concerned, but to the practical effects of a production and the privileged intentionalities it implies. To take the notorious RSC *Merchant of Venice* of 1984, the set was so ineptly oppressive that the frustrated actors themselves freely commented to that effect in public. Its most memorable features were a huge oriental carpet shrouding the set, a pair of ceiling-high organs at right and left stage-rear with seated players reminiscent of Terry Jones as Monty Python's nude piano player, and a set of huge "caskets"—shaped like London postboxes on pedastals—on cantilevers, which tended to bounce about even when not being lowered into or raised above the action. The actors had done as well by the script as their abilities and the circumstances permitted, and I could be convinced that the (he)arts of even designer and director were pure according to their lights. But here a case of recognized theatrical failure might well be seen as a case of "exploitation theatre," whatever made it so: alienating, all right, but political "alienation theatre" it was not.

All such "productions" have in common that they contradict the script in "saying" things in parts or as a whole that the script demonstrably does not say or imply. Two examples given in the Performance Seminar at the

International Shakespeare Conference in August 1986 clearly illustrate a line legitimately drawn between departure and extension: the weird sisters of *Macbeth* as "three attractive young women in diaphanous robes" as opposed to a pregnant Lady Macduff. Can there be any doubt which better expresses the script? The second effect supplies a condition complementing the dialogue and stage directions. The first makes a wholesale reversal of script identities and appearances—in an adaptation, fine; in a production, distortive. In fact, one of the best musicals playing in London in late summer 1986, during a season glutted with them, was the National Youth Theatre's rock musical, *Nightshriek* (19 August–6 September), originally and better named *Rockbeth,* a brilliant adaptation by twenty-two-year-old Trisha Ward, who was responsible for the music, lyrics, and book—with plenty of unaltered Shakespearean dialogue in evidence in a skillful fusion of congenial elements.[10]

In "The Reviewer as Historian," leading up to the pointed bon mot that "today one reviews the designer," Ralph Berry writes that

> there is no question that recent Shakespearean productions of the RSC have shown increasing reliance on the auxiliaries of staging, on the technicians of lighting, sound, design, and special effects.
> History has changed, and with it the schema within which the reviewer submits his impressions. It so happens that we have a date with which to locate our sense of change: mid-1981. At that point the Governors of the RSC, the makers of manners, determined that there was an urgent need to increase investment in productions. So there was; box-office returns had fallen very substantially. More money, then, was allocated to productions, starting with the final production of the 1981–82 season, Trevor Nunn's *All's Well That Ends Well.* This change of policy coincided with much better business in 1982. It can be argued that the RSC's success in 1982 was attributable to the muscular U.S. dollar (which is reflected directly in visits to Stratford-upon-Avon) and the presence of Derek Jacobi in several major roles throughout that season. Such an argument does not modify the main thesis. The policy of higher investment in productions is now officially regarded as a success; it is the key fact of the Shakespeare we now see at the most influential contemporary stages.[11]

Money can corrupt and disfigure, but it is noteworthy that at least some of these productions had their means and ends in the right order, with wonderful productions resulting. I don't doubt that with the same casts and less extravagant staging they would have played to much the same, perhaps even greater, effect.

Not having had the good fortune to see Giorgio Strehler's famous Teatro Piccolo production of *The Tempest,* I have no way of knowing exactly what it meant for a participant in the Performance Seminar at the International Shakespeare Conference (20 August 1986) to say that it was probably the best production of the play he had ever seen, a sentiment consonant, however, with Bernard Beckerman's remarks about it referred to above. Nor could I "resonate" as readily as perhaps I should have done at the same session to the notion of the "Director as Visionary." One *can*—must?—value any theatrical performance that seems to show originality and genius, whatever its sources, including the exhumed remains of Shakespeare assembled in such a way that the Creator could scarcely recognize their owner. But when it comes to *production,* the nature and scope of originality and genius are bounded in a measure by the script and the intentionalities it embodies and transmits, as I assume that even Strehler's production is. Liviu Ciulei's monumental production at the Guthrie in 1981 definitely was.

Too much unprofitably innovative Shakespeare—intellectually, not box-officially, unprofitable Shakepeare—seems to result from asking and self-reflexively answering the questions, What can I do with—or to—this play (or part) that has never been done before? How can I make this play speak directly to "our" condition as it is right now (as on Saturday night, 11 October 1986)? And, a little worse, How can I make this play sufficiently Mine that shakespeare's subsidiary role is recognized, by suppression, for what it is?

More fruitful questions would seem to me to be, What can I find within this script's expression and significance that has not been found before, but seems on careful study and reflection to be "there"? What force and relevance can "our" condition recognize in this play when it is allowed to speak *for itself* first and to *"us"* second? How can I balance my own expressiveness and creativity with the playwright's in cooperation across the ages? And, in summary, What fresh, striking, yet congenial means can I use to help the script to speak for itself and to us, our condition, and the resources of *our* theatre (whatever it might be) at one and the same time?

It would be absurd to suggest that *all* lavish productions in large theatres should be discontinued. Even if that were economically feasible, it is undesirable as closing off an important avenue of exploring the plays and of entertaining and enlightening audiences, and provoking them to thought and even action. In fact, such productions also beget creative and constructive counterreaction—in smaller venues or in large—as a lively and welcome if inadvertent offspring. I shouldn't wish to see eliminated even grotesque and bizarre distortions, much less searching explorations like those of Ariane Mnouchkine, Giorgio Strehler, and Liviu Ciulei, and I find much in the theatrical work and theorizing of Charles Marowitz to be grateful for. Fortunately, there is little danger of any such reaction to the views and even the fulminations of critics. There will always be "experimental theatre," because experiment is of the very nature of theatre.

Down and across the history of the "audience reception" of Shakespeare's plays, it has been argued by turns they do not need to be performed to have their effect—this by the bookish but *not* fugitive and cloistered Samuel Johnson, for example—and (of course) by persons who make their living in the theatre that a "play" has no life until a script has come to performance. Such complementary advocates are surely right within the limits of what they assert and promise for delivery, whether a self-contained written text not much to be improved by being dressed up (and sometimes disguised) in performance, or bare words on a page that require miracles of mental production by a reader in order barely to approximate their three-dimensional life, enacted. All that is involved here, aside from a vocational tug-of-war, and usually differences of temperament and intellectual preference, is the respective cognitive/affective properties of reading (and perhaps hearing) versus "seeing" and hearing (in Shakespeare's day and until quite recently *audi*ences were said not to see but to hear a play). Different modes of mediation entail differences in cognition and effect/affect, no doubt, but it is only in part that performance qua performance is the cause; the primary cause is what-is-performed in and through and around the script. No script, no action, anywhere.

This kind of argument aside, for the critic as expositor or interpreter, the relationship between script and performance is symbiotic. Interpreters of bare texts constantly err, as every playgoing reader knows. And that is partly where performance criticism and one of its indefatigable and most illuminating practitioners, Marvin Rosenberg, came in. As he has shown in the published first three volumes of his tetralogy on the Bradleian Big Four tragedies, it is by the (im)possibilities of consonant performance that we know what a text must have "meant" and how it may signify when norms of language, production, and social value have changed "dramatically."

It remains the case, however, that critics and scholars, as well as daily reviewers and "general theatregoers," differ on the meaning and significance of scripts by themselves, as read, as well as in performance. Our views of the former are almost bound to be modified by the latter, unless we have been fixated upon some kind of reified and fetishized Platonic "ideal performance." But in practice it is seldom the case that the script is not the basis for the interpretation (and evaluation) of a production. And it is almost invariably the case that a critic likes a production according to its correspondence with what he or she thinks the play means and can of itself countenance in production. Perhaps only because I am guilty, I see no crime in that, but one hopes that any critic (even oneself) can appreciate the strengths of a compelling staging for what they are, as well as for what they seem not to be. An insurmountable difficulty here is that separable and potentially conflicting values are involved: aesthetic, theatrical, cognitive, ethical, sociopolitical—or (as some say) just one: ideological. Unless the script is assumed to be the enabling and authorizing norm, there can be no basis for resolving disagreements that are *not* essentially "ideological"; that is, adjudicated on the basis of individual or collective will per se.

3

Coriolanus is one of Shakespeare's primary Rorschach tests of all beholding and beheld by it, and perhaps also a prime example of what Stephen Booth in "The Shakespearean Actor as Kamikaze Pilot" calls Shakespeare's "experiments with setting audiences to attempt to see a play other than the one he gives them."[12] From the point early in the first scene when First and Second Citizen articulate the diametrical—and dialectical—opposition of both those within and those responding to the play's action, strong response after strong response is elicited—not without considerable critical disagreement over what these responses should be. One result is that many have had a "producer's" way with *Coriolanus* like Bogdanov's with *Romeo and Juliet,* except that where Bogdanov has "just taken it one step further," his counterparts with *Coriolanus* have gone from a leap to a league.

Yet, curiously enough, aside from adaptations by Brecht, Helene Weigel (after Brecht) for the Berliner Ensemble, Günter Grass, and John Osborne, *Coriolanus* has been produced in the twentieth century in greater accord with the 1623 Folio script, probably, than at any time since the earlier seventeenth century. After the Restoration Shakespeare's *Coriolanus* became Nahum Tate's *Ingratitude of a Commonweath* (1682); John Dennis's *Invader of His Country; or, The Fatal Resentment* (1720), an exploitation adaptation if ever there was one; and *Coriolanus: or, The Roman Matron* (1755), "a tragedy taken from" Shakespeare and James Thomson's own non-Shakespearean *Coriolanus* (1749) by adapter Thomas Sheridan. Of the various versions and hybrids in the eighteenth and nineteenth centuries, Garrick's (though drastically cut) and Macready's were nearest Shakespeare's *Coriolanus.* Theatregoers interested in seeing something resembling the play Shakespeare wrote have reason to recognize progress and be thankful. Still, the end tries all, and details of endplay in some recent and earlier productions afford matter testing the mettle of a production for fidelity to the spirit of the script, whatever it has done or not done to the letter of the ending.

Just how a play in performance "ends" is very much a matter of specific detail, as Bogdanov's *Romeo and Juliet* amply demonstrates; but the essential action, with or without dialogue, is the sine qua non, not the details as such. Kenneth Tynan remarked that "it is nobody's fault but Shakespeare's that the play ends with such casual abruptness,"[13] so it matters all the more, perhaps most of all, how Martius dies and with what entailed effects. In the Folio plenty is left to the imagination of performers (and readers), but there is prescription, too. Martius's being shot in the back by more than one conspirator (as in the productions directed by Michael Langham, Stratford, Ontario, 1961; and by Peter Hall, National-Olivier, 1984–85) corresponds closely with one crucial aspect, his assassination by treachery at the hands of conspirators: *"Draw both the Conspirators, and kils Martius, who falles, Auffidius stands on him"* (Hinman facsimile of the 1623 Folio, Through Line Numbers 3805–6; New Arden 5.6.130 and stage direction). The Folio stage direction does not specify the weapon, but we know that "draw" assumes Aufidius's "let him feele your Sword" (TLN 3715; 5.6.56). It is doubtful whether the spectacular (and auditory) effects of murder by swords or daggers at close quarters or by guns from a distance is a matter of "detail," but there are differences in the spectacle and potential effects, certainly. And the aftermath is scarcely less important than the killing itself, because that stamps an audience with the final impression of the cumulative effects and culmination of the action. A few examples suggest the range of possibilities, and perhaps also the limits of the "authentic" or, at least, the integral and consonant: what implicitly has been prepared for and is required in the round by the script.

Macready in the nineteenth century brought back Volumnia, Virgilia, Valeria, and Young Martius to mourn over Coriolanus, giving an epilogical focus that certainly is consonant with the importance of personal and familial relationships in the play, and the crucial part played by the family, not Volumnia alone, in winning a happy victory to Rome at the hands and to the mortal cost of Martius. The play *is* a case of all in the family, in one perspective. Such a conclusion invites the audience to join in the mourning for the dead Martius by weeping for those who are thus seen to grieve for him, acting in sympathy but with the appearance of empathy, as is typical of actual funerals. Despite the consonance, this conclusion substantially alters the direction and significance of the whole with the part: Shakespeare's Martius dies away from Rome with not a friend in place to bury him or mourn, so far as we can see.

With all the play's lines cut after his death, Richard Burton's Martius (Old Vic, 1953–54) was left alone on stage, another fitting enough conclusion, as far as it goes, for a loner and a stranger in a strange land, a man without peer in the play, unique and alone in death as in life. "Alone I did it" and alone he has been done and left: consider Martius and his worlds, together and apart, not without remembrance of ourselves.

Two other departures seem somewhat more questionable, by the measures of the script, one of them ingenious and powerful in its own right, the other striking enough but perhaps a little too au courant, if not a la mode, to deserve much credit even for invention.

In Peter Hall's 1959 production at the Shakespeare Memorial Theatre, as Kenneth Tynan describes it,

> "*Boy!*" shrieks the overmothered general, in an outburst of strangled fury, and leaps up a flight of precipitous steps to vent his rage. Arrived at the top, he relents and throws his sword away. After letting his voice fly high in the great, swingeing line about how he "flutter'd your Volscians in *Cor-i-o-li*," he allows a dozen spears to impale him. He is poised, now, on a promontory some twelve feet above the stage, from which he topples forward, to be caught by the ankles so that he dangles, inverted, like the slaughtered Mussolini.[14]

This horrifying business captured a parallel that was surely in mind when it was devised—late in the rehearsal period, apparently, according to Stanley Wells in *Royal Shakespeare* (1977). Wells also notes that Martius was "held dangling while Aufidius stabbed him in the belly,"[15] a ghastly act of mutilation reminiscent of the posthumous mutilation—there called for in the script—of one of Martius's antetypes and counterparts, Harry Hotspur, in *Henry IV, Part 1*.

In Tyrone Guthrie's production at the Nottingham Playhouse (1964), Aufidius, after killing Martius in the "rage" he claims in the script, stamped on Martius's groin, but then, realizing what he had done, gave a long moan as he flung himself on Martius's body—in accordance with Guthrie's director's note in the program, which stressed the play's contemporaneity and what he saw as the homosexual affinity between Martius and Aufidius, especially in Aufidius's attitude toward Martius.[16]

The first of these revisions is a stroke of genius, however dearly purchased. The second will vary according to the lights of the observer, from a "psychoanalytical approval," perhaps, to the view that this was a major diversion, in effect even a digressive flourish of fashionable perversity. Guthrie at any rate had given considerable thought to the matter and expresses his view in "Hidden Motives in Shakespeare's Plays," where he attends specifically to the meeting of Martius and Aufidius at Antium (4.5), which "cannot be truly regarded as other than a love scene."[17] Lines among those Guthrie refers to but doesn't quote are Aufidius's to Martius:

> Let me twine
> Mine armes about that body, where against
> My grained Ash an hundred times hath broke,
> And scarr'd the Moone with splinters: heere I cleep
> The Anuile of my Sword, and do contest
> As hotly, and as Nobly with thy Loue,

As euer in Ambitious strength, I did
Contend against thy Valour. Know thou first,
I lou'd the Maid I married: neuer man
Sigh'd truer breath. But that I see thee heere
Thou Noble thing, more dances my rapt heart,
Then when I first my wedded Mistris saw
Bestride my Threshold.

(TLN 2764–76; 4.5.107–19)

In both of these productions the endplay and therefore the wholes are radically altered, reduced, and in Guthrie's production arguably also trivialized in obliquity—not because homosexuality is unthinkable as a subtext of sorts but because it is *not* the be-all and the end-all of the play, and here because it focuses on *Aufidius*'s sense of loss, of all things, leaving us—worse—with the pop-song moral, "You always hurt the one you love." Macready's bringing back the family at the end is a much less unbalanced and more integral revision, nearer the heart of the play if not so close to the body of its hero.

The death of Martius in the Hall-Olivier production is a matter of degree that depends on the extent to which the mnemonic irrelevance of "another tyrannical Italian," as it were, and the historical *Duce* Benito Mussolini, is present to the mind of the beholder—the more, the worse, I should say. The brilliance, the shock value, and an apparent similarity in one dimension cannot be denied, but the effect also entails emphasis on the butcher butchered in a shambles, dehumanizing Martius and making him by alteration appear a justly executed tyrant like Mussolini. Some see Martius that way, but Shakespeare's own endplay as written is considerably less reductive.[18] This coup de théâtre of Olivier's was of course not repeated by Ian McKellen in Peter Hall's 1984–85 production at the National Theatre, where the promptbook says that

PG, DA, Guy W *shoot Cor* / Cor collapse C.S. face down / Auf X down seating to L of Cor / puts foot on him. . . . [At the very end, Coriolanus carried] in circle anticlockwise around stage [followed by one carrying a flag at half-mast]. DT picks up Cor helmet follows BK. RA picks up Cor sword follows DT out through centre door / doors close.[19]

PG, DA, and Guy W were Conspirators; BK, DT, RA Volscian Lords. Most reviewers made something or more of the fact that "Coriolanus himself saunters into a battle with a broadsword but is finally cut down by a hail of bullets" in the back.[20]

What follows Martius's death is no less important than what follows Brutus's, Antony's and an act later Cleopatra's, and Timon's. These Realpolitikal Roman (and Athenian) plays end with a world not only diminished but existentially sure of no better days to come for the better natures and the common lot, a Shakespearean *pax tragica* that retrospectively exalts as well as memorializes the heroes past, not only through the sealing speeches of those in the new ascendancy but by the irony of the contrast between the stuff and stature of the speaker (and other survivors present) and him or her lamented.

It was Aufidius who from 1.10 on would "potche at him some way" (TLN 873; 1.10.15), and his assassins finally did. He it was who ordered his soldier to "bring me word thither / *How the world goes:* that to the pace of it / I may spurre on my iourney" (TLN 891–93; 1.10.31–33; italics mine), revealing himself clearly to us while his terms also invoke a theme announced early in *Timon* ("how goes the world?" "It weares sir, as it growes," TLN 7–9) and of interest to Shakespeare throughout his play-wrighting—and sonnet-writing—career, seldom without suggestion that many a way of the world, including his own, is also the flesh's and the devil's.

It both is and is not fitting that Aufidius should have the last word in *Coriolanus*, beginning "My Rage is gone, / And I am strucke with sorrow" (TLN 3829–30; 5.6.146–47). In worlds like these—the Volsces' world sounds like Rome because it *is* like Rome, though in the course of history unsuccessful—Aufidius is the man of the hour and a hero for the times, friendly, even affectionate as occasion serves, but a ruthlessly ambitious hypocrite whose principles dissolve into expediency to serve his own occasion and his lords'. Or is it a case of psychopathic whimsy or a function of manic depression?[21] Like many in the play, he is a timeserver, "better" than most because he has undeniable skills, personal, political, and martial, and is in fact welcome partly *because* his principles are so pliant. In a world dominated by avaricious senators and conniving prag-matists, this is Aufidius the Volsce who could as well have been a Roman: duplicity bears not dual but universal citizenship.

In the script Martius falls to assassins without a fight, dying at the end in the optative and subjunctive moods of the beginning, a crucial charac-teristic rarely noticed of him, least of all by detractors. In the beginning,

> Would the Nobility lay aside their ruth,
> And *let me vse* my Sword, I'de make a Quarrie
> With thousands of these quarter'd slaues, as high
> As I could picke my Lance.
> (TLN 209–12; 1.1.196–99; italics mine)

A frightening speech, but in peace his bark is exponentially worse than his bite, like Harry's threatening before Harfleur, where grizzly threats of atrocity may serve to spare the very occasion that would elicit them. At the end, with "O that I had him, with six *Auffidiusses,* or more: / His Tribe, to vse my *lawfull* Sword" (TLN 3801–2; 5.6.127–29; italic *lawfull* mine), the wheel has come half, full, and double circle all at once. Rome or Corioli, what's to choose? *This* is the way of the world.

Whatever the ideological implications of the play are at present taken or made to be, the thrust and culmination of *Coriolanus* present a better Martius in retrospect and a worse Aufidius in his habit as he lives. A Martius not a paragon, certainly not "the Courtiers, souldiers, schollers, eye, tongue, sword" (*Hamlet*, Second Quarto, sig. Elv [not in First Quarto]; TLN 1807; 3.1.151), but one such that in some ways

> His nature *is* too noble for the World:
> He would not flatter *Neptune* for his Trident,
> Or *Iove,* for's power to Thunder: his Heart's his Mouth:
> What his Brest forges, that his Tongue must vent,
> And being angry, does forget that euer
> He heard the Name of Death.
>
> (TLN 1983–88; 3.1.253–58; italic *is* mine)

That would be the "tragic flaw"—as in another perspective cardinal vir-tue—of Martius, if there were such a thing as this post-Victorian invention imposed on Aristotle's *hamartia*. It is far from the whole story, but it is telling enough to suggest directions. The very telling it like it isn't by Aufidius at the end is a living reminder that not every incarnation of survival values has much to commend in him but his instinct, and that not every loss of life is a loss of the deserving a measure of immortality. Depending on who writes the script and how it is written. And rewritten. The lives of the past live only in the memory, historical as well as fictional, on which account, perhaps, the fictional great have not less claim to life than those they overarch. And what better venue than the stage for their continual rebirth?

What performance might be appropriate to give emphasis and ex-pression to some of the details and their significance as I have interpreted them here I do not propose to suggest, but I am of a mind that one of the most valid readings of *Coriolanus* as a script by Shakespeare would culminate with some such emphases and perspectives as these, and a Shakespearean stage might properly seek the means to let it show more often than it has been allowed to be seen.

4

It has been said that when news from within a discipline reaches the *Chronicle of Higher Education,* history has already passed away and been laid to rest. But if in "The Script's the Thing: Shakespeare in Performance Is New Area of Study" (30 April 1986) "Performance is New Area of

Study" would have been truer a quarter of a century ago, "The Script's the Thing" *is* (again) new. *Script* is an amphibious term, however, and what is new *now,* I think, is that *the text as transcription of potential action,* in conjunction with real and hypothetical performance, is receiving attention in many quarters both academic and theatrical. And not a day too soon, for such reasons as RSC actor Henry Goodman gave (22 August 1986) in remarking on directorial concepts and staging at the Royal Shakespeare Theatre: "We are teaching the audience to look and to expect the next thing that is lookable at. We're not teaching them to be excited about the language, even though our aspiration is to do that. . . . [There has been an ongoing tradition in the past eight or ten years] at the expense of listening to the poetry. With the media, television, cinema, all that's going to be increasingly hard to hold onto, anyway: the art of listening, the art of sharing."

Something emphatically in evidence in two of the three productions playing in repertory at the Swan in August 1986 was that language had assumed an emphasis and center-staging rarely to be seen—heard—in the main house, the Royal Shakespeare Theatre, in recent years, though emphatically in evidence in the productions at the much smaller Other Place in Stratford-upon-Avon and the Barbican-Pit in London. The result was that *verbal* drama displayed its character in relief, in oral-aural form, and expressed its range and depths in a way that may well be called rejuvenated. Probably some special stress in preparation and rehearsal was laid on understanding and delivering the dialogue in this set-spare space, but the proximity of actors to audience, together with the sparing sets, would have had the same result: audience and actors brought into community through "the art of listening, the art of sharing." Gorgeous costumes and their antitypes themselves may help to achieve this community, by strongly attracting or repelling, as they do in the working of their counterpart signs in Real Life. But the real compound medium is the message: script, actors, audience; shared experience and cognition. Goodman it was, too, who spoke of a "tide in the affairs"—of Avon?—and said that the Swan has "given the theatre back to the actors, where it belongs. . . . We've had an era of exploiting wonderful conceptual and brilliant design ideas, but perhaps now the balance can be" restored, directors too seeking that "more organic relationship. . . . Why is it you remember the *Macbeth* in The Other Place more than other things? Time after time I hear that from group after group after group. . . . It's because there's nothing on the stage, just people going through the motions of what acting is all about." He wondered, too, whether in transferring to a bigger house like the Royal Shakespeare Theatre one couldn't "turn up the gas" and achieve that "elusive thing called style" that would enable "sharing" there.

Robert Speaight said Granville Barker "realized that in the matter of

Shakespeare production the way forward was the way back,"[22] as seems true not only of Shakespeare in production but also, in some vital ways, of performance criticism. The history of theatrical space in the twentieth century has impelled us ahead in this direction, first to a greater intimacy between actors and audience, and now to more of the same with the growth of shrinking spaces; here as with other architecture, often less is more. For a long time the fringe in Edinburgh, London, New York, the Twin Cities, and many other places has become the heart of living theatre, and something of that vital fire has spread to national and equivalent studio theatres like The Other Place and the Pit. All these have promoted community through proximity and fueled a demand that the Swan has further helped to meet: a theatre of sharing primarily through the script and its enacting in a space that makes that not only possible but inescapable. The Swan itself has broken both old and new ground in Stratford-upon-Avon, and it is devoutly to be wished that the Bankside Globe now abuilding, with completion hoped for by 1991, will do likewise. Could it be better situated in space and concentration, even time?

It is no coincidence that this essay ends in Bernard Beckerman's territory, *Shakespeare at the Globe*. If one takes the view that there's sap in't yet, in Shakespeare and his works as such, then there is much to rejoice at in the developments in progress and in prospect, no archaizing movement or pilgrimage of bardolatry, but a potential revival of major proportions with social value that is cultural not merely with a capital *c* and swallowed *r*, as in Cultchah, but in many of the best affective and cognitive modes that verbal dramatic art in action is uniquely capable of achieving. That way lies Aristotle, in part, but so does it Freud and far beyond. If we are not ciphers, but citizens by the ones and twos and multiples as Shakespeare found them, he may be all the better seen and felt to be, as even his ambivalent admirer found him, not of an age, but for our time. *All* time as may be, but now and in the foreseeable future, very much alive.

Notes

1. *Shakespeare Quarterly (Reviewing Shakespeare)* 36, no. 5 (1985): 588–93.
2. Ibid., 588–89.
3. *New Literary History* 17 (1986): 511–38.
4. *Script* has become a word of magical transforming power in some performance-critical discourse of the past two decades. Cf. Cary M. Mazer ("Shakespeare, the Reviewer, and the Theatre historian," *Reviewing Shakespeare,* 650): "Whether the script is a precisely notated and strictly delimited score, or else a pretext for an infinite range of possible realizations (the truth, of course, lies somewhere in between), the very assumption that Shakespeare's plays are scripts implies that the scripts themselves are incomplete, or at least unrealized, until they exist in the act of performance. This assumption in turn acknowledges the contribution of the artists of the theatre," etc.

By *script* in the present essay I mean "dramatic text" or "theatrical text," the written or printed form of a play, in which by definition dialogue, and actions implied in dialogue or explicitly called for in stage directions, are the "manner of imitation" (Butcher's nonpejorative phrase in his translation of Aristotle's *Poetics*).

5. The actors participating in the panel discussion held at the Shakespeare Institute in Stratford-upon-Avon on 22 August 1986 (and the plays they were in at the time) were Niamh Cusack (*Art of Success, Rom.*), Robert Demeger (*MND, Rom., TNK*), Henry Goodman (*Every Man in His Humor, WT*), and Imogen Stubbs (*Rover, TNK*).

6. It perhaps should have opened on 23 April, since the date of Shakespeare's birthday is as uncertain as the authorship of parts of *TNK*. Ironically enough, most of the cuts in Barry Kyle's production were from Shakespeare's parts. Kyle tried to improve the play "by cutting about 350 lines, and striking a new balance. The longer scenes are not always saying more, so I've cut. Act one contains a lot of clotted language—I've tried to make it more speakable by editing. Undramatic repetitions have gone." N. W. Bawcutt is doubtless right to say that "if Shakespeare had gone on to write the whole of *The Two Noble Kinsmen* the first act would probably have received more attention than it has" (New York: Penguin, 1977, 27). One can understand trimming in performance, and the result, with settings and costumes from many periods and cultures, was not unspeakable, but it was not very coherent or prepossessing, either; in the event, Kyle went mostly for performance values, one of the most spectacular of which was an entrance by the gifted actress Imogen Stubbs singing while walking on her hands.

Kyle is quoted from the Director's Note in the Swan Theatre Plays "programme/ text" with commentary by Simon Trussler (London: Methuen, 1986), 5. Methuen deserves commendation for publishing these production texts and including much useful information—including an invaluable Director's Note in the first three, at least—at the very nominal cost of £1.80 at the theatres.

7. *Reviewing Shakespeare*, 534.

8. Ibid., 536.

9. In John Barton, *Playing Shakespeare* (London and New York: Methuen, 1984), the book based on Barton's video series (187).

10. For a wholly integrated production others deserve credit, too, including director Edward Wilson, designer Brian Lee, and Judy Brown, the understudy who stepped into the role of Lady Macbeth for the performance I saw and blew us all away (4 September 1986).

11. *Reviewing Shakespeare*, 595.

12. Ibid., 570.

13. *Curtains: Selections from the Drama Criticism and Related Writings* (New York: Atheneum, 1961), 35.

14. Tynan, *Curtains*, 241.

15. *Royal Shakespeare: Four Major Productions at Stratford-upon-Avon* (Manchester: Manchester University Press, 1977), 21: "it is said that not even his [Olivier's] fellow actors knew how he would perform this scene until a very late stage in the proceedings; and this is borne out by the fact that the pencilled directions in the promptbook overlay others that have been erased."

16. See Geoffrey Reeves's discussion of "Guthrie's *Coriolanus* in Nottingham's New Playhouse" in *Encore* 11 (March–April 1964): 43–49.

17. Tyrone Guthrie, "Hidden Motives in Five Shakespearean Plays: *Coriolanus*," in *Various Directions: A View of the Theatre* (New York: Macmillan, 1965), 90.

18. In his consideration of a "trade-off" in "the final scene of *Coriolanus*, a moment especially vulnerable to such alterations" ("Reviewing Shakespeare for the Record," *Reviewing Shakespeare*, 606–7), Alan C. Dessen "focus[es] upon the 1980 Oregon Rendition directed by Jerry Turner," with some concentration on "the Folio stage direction for Coriolanus' death" and on "the three groups of figures for this final confrontation," on which he has acute remarks on the significance of parallels with earlier action. He concludes that

> to include the same elements in the final scene in the Volscian City (again, with one of the groups—the lords of the city—supportive) is to emphasize the obvious fact that there is no world elsewhere, that the hero's second confrontation with such a city leads to a second defeat, this time his death (and an ignominious death for the conquering war machine of Act 1). The ironies and deflation of the Folio ending (at least as I read it) were therefore traded off for a herioc climax guaranteed to appeal to a modern audience—at the risk of rewriting the play or translating it into a new language or idiom.

There are ample grounds in the play for arguing—as I think—that "the ironies and deflation" are largely inventions of twentieth-century critics like O. J. Campbell, and it is possible accordingly to conclude that Jerry Turner's production ended substantially in the spirit of Shakespeare's play. If so, the standing ovation was entailed by a not only well-performed but authentic production.

19. I am grateful to the National Theatre, South Bank, London, for access to the promptbook and press cuttings, and to Liz Page, in particular, for seeing me to work with dispatch and good cheer.

20. Benedict Nightingale, *New Statesman*, 21 December 1984; quoted from the *London Theatre Record*, 2–31 December 1984, 1135.

21. Some suggestion of a motivating manic-depressive temperament was in the air of the Kick Theatre Company's production of *Coriolanus* (17 September–11 October 1986) due to open at the Almeida Theatre, Islington, on the day after I had to leave London. What I saw in five hours of rehearsal on the 15th made me the more regreat having to miss the production as a whole, which was directed by Deborah Warner, the Kick's founder. I am most grateful to her and to Fiona Gaunt, the Kick's agent, for permission to sit in on the rehearsals, and to them and other members of the company for much information and stimulating discussion.

Martius was to die at the hands of the conspirators by gestures only, no physical swords or other weapons, in keeping with a spare, stylized, individual, but for the most part textually faithful production in which the director tried to present the play objectively for theatregoers to make up their own minds. Costumes were "vaguely Oriental baggy trousers" (as Michael Billington described them), and there were few props except for twelve orange crates, arranged in a circle around the primary playing space, which twelve actors knelt beside—and sometimes used for drums—when not playing a part. George W. Williams writes me from London (6 October 1986) that "the orange crates—of which one hears much—are left over from the tradition of the 1978 RSC *Macbeth* at The Other Place, the Warehouse, and the Young Vic. Ian McKellen and Judi Dench demonstrated what could be done with boxes."

In the *London Theatre Record* 6, no. 19 (1986): 1005–7, three reviews were strongly favorable and three unfavorable, and one review was mixed. The content even of the negative reviews amounted to praise-in-effect for a strenuous production that yet deliberately avoided a party line, in opposition to the demands of those minded like Michael Billington to the effect that the play "requires specific political decisions by the director. . . . This production . . . belongs in no particular period and takes no detectable line" (*Guardian,* 20 September 1986). Precisely as the director intended and perhaps Shakespeare himself at one time, if not for all time, in the spirit of Keith Nurse's observation that "in the absence of any elaborate distractions or visual luxuries, we are obliged to concentrate on the power of Shakespeare's words, and that is no bad thing because this production . . . is as vivid and vigorous as it is unclattered" (*Daily Telegraph,* 25 September 1986). The major departure from the script—widely commented on—is well expressed by Giles Gordon in *Punch* (1 October 1986): "it's a bit alarming when he [Martius] announces to the Roman mob in the Forum, 'I have wounds to show you, which shall be yours in private,' then flashes his privates in public," a regrettable open-raincoat extension of a wink-wink, nudge-nudge line that could lend unfortunate tags to an entire production which seems to have deserved much better: "after nearly four hours, the final overwhelming exhilarating impression is of a shared experience, often gruelling, always gripping, between actors and audience. Not to be missed" (Jane Edwardes, *Time Out,* 24 September 1986). Michael Coveney of the *Financial Times* (19 September 1986) put The Case forcefully and succinctly in his opening paragraph: "Deborah Warner's unfunded Kick Theatre Company unleashes this tremendous production at the Almeida to make a nonsense once again of how the Arts Council distributes its resources. I have only seen this *Coriolanus* and last year's *King Lear,* but it is high time this six-year-old enterprise was placed on a permanent footing." Amen.

Postscript (18 July 1987): in 1987 Deborah Warner traveled to Bangladesh in a new version of *The Tempest* with Bengali actors, and has directed the RSC Swan Theatre production of *Titus Andronicus.*

22. *Reviewing Shakespeare,* 535.

Bernard Beckerman, 1921–1985
A Memorial Tribute

On rare occasions life introduces us to a "compleat gentleman." As the Elizabethans realized, such an individual is no poseur who must instantly dazzle beholders with the full range of his extraordinary abilities. On the contrary, he is likely to be a man whose understated charm unfolds new virtues, unsuspected talents, remarkable achievements, and durable strengths year after year after year. Bernard Beckerman, in my judgment, was the complete gentleman.

I need hardly tell this gathering of his accomplishments as a scholar, and there are those here who can speak eloquently of Bernie's gifts as a teacher. Some of you will recall his work as a director, sensitive to the full range of drama beyond Shakespeare. Yet professional pursuits mark only one side of a man, and it is for his thoroughly decent humanity that everyone loved Bernard Beckerman. I never saw him try to impress or humiliate or avoid anyone, no matter how tiresome. His patient good humor, combined with a certain diffident modesty about his own importance, made him the most comfortable of companions.

Moreover, Bernie really cared about widening his—and our—circle of possible companions. Instead of limiting his interests and friendships to the academy, he always maintained a lively dialogue with people in the theatre, prefiguring this healthy interchange long before it became popular with most Shakespeare scholars. And in his year as president, Bernie reminded us of the "public, receptive to Shakespeare, a public not in school, but out in the world, a public intrigued by his mind and heart, whatever the statistics tell us of the decline of the humanities. "How can we speak to these people?" he asked. "Or do we leave them to the multimediasts, the idiosyncratic, odd-ball introducers of televised performances, the users rather than the cherishers of 'our fellow Shakespeare'?" The question Bernard Beckerman posed in 1982 and the example he set throughout a lifetime challenge each of us not to narrow the parameters of our professional responsibility.

This eulogy was presented at the annual meeting of the Shakespeare Association meeting in Montreal, March 1986, by Ann Jennalie Cook, executive director of the association.

But besides being one of us—maybe the best of us—Bernie fully experienced a life common to all men. He was a soldier in his youth, and a very brave one. He honored the faith of his Jewish fathers. He himself fathered two fine sons and loved the children of those sons. He was a teen-age bridegroom, who still held hands with Gloria after forty years of marriage. And he had lots of fun. Last year in Nashville at our annual meeting, after munching Goo-Goos at the Grand Ole Opry, he and Gloria gathered a motley crew of other Shakespeareans who ate and danced and laughed the night away at the Stockyard Restaurant. How he relished the telling of it the next day in my home, the last time I would ever see him.

Bernie was always so solidly *there* that it is hard to realize he is gone. But he is. And I ask you now to stand a moment in silence to remember and honor a complete gentleman—Bernard Beckerman.

Appendix
Suggested Readings in Performance Criticism

The Playhouse

Adams, John Cranford. *The Globe Playhouse: Its Design and Equipment*. New York: Barnes & Noble, 1942, 2d ed. 1961.

Gurr, Andrew. *The Shakespearean Stage, 1574–1642*. Cambridge: Cambridge University Press, 1970.

Hodges, C. Walter. *The Globe Restored: a Study of Elizabethan Theatre*. 2d ed. London: Oxford University Press, 1968.

Nagler, A. M. *Shakespeare's Stage*. Translated by Ralph Manheim. New Haven: Yale University Press, 1958.

Orrell, John. *The Quest for Shakespeare's Globe*. Cambridge: Cambridge University Press, 1983.

Smith, Irwin. *Shakespeare's Blackfriars Playhouse: Its History and Its Design*. New York: New York University Press, 1964.

Speaight, Robert. *William Poel and the Elizabethan Revival*. London: Heinmann, 1954.

Thomson, Peter. *Shakespeare's Theatre*. London: Routledge & Kegan Paul, 1983.

Wickham, Glynne. *Early English Stages, 1300–1660*. 3 vols. London: Routledge & Kegan Paul, 1959–81.

The Stagecraft

Beckerman, Bernard. *Shakespeare at the Globe, 1599–1609*. New York: Macmillan, 1962.

Bevington, David. *Action is Eloquence: Shakespeare's Language of Gesture*. Cambridge: Harvard University Press, 1984.

Coghill, Nevile. *Shakespeare's Professional Skills*. Cambridge: Cambridge University Press, 1964.

Flatter, Richard. *Shakespeare's Producing Hand, A Study of His Marks of Expression to be Found in the First Folio*. New York: Norton, 1948.

Hasler, Jörg. *Shakespeare's Theatrical Notation: the Comedies*. The Cooper Monographs on English and American Language and Literature, vol. 21. Bern: Francke, 1974.

Homan, Sydney, ed. *Shakespeare's More Than Words Can Witness: Essays on*

Visual and Nonverbal Enactment in the Plays. Lewisburg: Bucknell University Press, 1980.

Howard, Jean Elizabeth. *Shakespeare's Art of Orchestration: Stage Technique and Audience Response.* Urbana: University of Illinois Press, 1984.

King, Thomas James. *Shakespearean Staging, 1599–1642.* Cambridge: Harvard University Press, 1971.

McGuire, Philip C. *Speechless Dialect: Shakespeare's Open Silences.* Berkeley: University of California Press, 1985.

Slater, Ann Pasternak. *Shakespeare the Director.* Totowa, N.J.: Barnes & Noble Books, 1982.

Styan, J. L. *Shakespeare's Stagecraft.* Cambridge: Cambridge University Press, 1967.

Watkins, Ronald. *On Producing Shakespeare.* 2d ed. New York: B. Blom, 1964.

The Conventions

Bethell, S. L. *Shakespeare and the Popular Dramatic Tradition.* Westminster, London: P. S. King and Staples, 1944.

Booth, Stephen. *"King Lear," "Macbeth," Indefinition, and Tragedy.* New Haven: Yale University Press, 1983.

Bradbrook, Muriel C. *Elizabethan Stage Conventions, a Study of Their Place in the Interpretation of Shakespeare's Plays.* Cambridge: Cambridge University Press, 1932.

———. *Themes and Conventions of Elizabethan Tragedy.* Cambridge: Cambridge University Press, 1935, 2d ed. 1980.

Charney, Maurice. *Shakespeare's Roman Plays: The Function of Imagery in the Drama.* Cambridge: Harvard University Press, 1961.

Dessen, Alan C. *Elizabethan Drama and the Viewer's Eye.* Chapel Hill: University of North Carolina Press, 1977.

———. *Elizabethan Stage Conventions and Modern Interpreters.* Cambridge: Cambridge University Press, 1984.

Hartwig, Joan. *Shakespeare's Analogical Scene: Parody as Structural Syntax.* Lincoln: University of Nebraska Press, 1983.

Poel, William. *Shakespeare in the Theatre.* 1913. Reprint. New York: B. Blom, 1968.

Styan, J. L. *Drama, Stage, and Audience.* London: Cambridge University Press, 1975.

Audience Manipulation

Berry, Ralph. *Shakespeare and the Awareness of the Audience.* New York: St. Martin's Press, 1985.

Brown, John Russell. *Shakespeare's Plays in Performance.* New York: St. Martin's Press, 1967.

———. *Shakespeare's Dramatic Style: "Romeo and Juliet," "As You Like It,"*

"Julius Caesar," "Twelfth Night," "Macbeth." New York: Barnes & Noble, 1971.

Honigmann, E. A. J. *Shakespeare: Seven Tragedies: The Dramatist's Manipulation of Response.* New York: Barnes & Noble, 1976.

Jochum, Klaus Peter. *Discrepant Awareness: Studies in English Renaissance Drama.* Neue Studien zur Anglistik und Amerikanistik, vol. 13. Frankfurt am Main: Lang, 1979.

Rabkin, Norman. *Shakespeare and the Problem of Meaning.* Chicago: University of Chicago Press, 1981.

Performance Criticism and Theory

Garber, Marjorie B. *Drama in Shakespeare: From Metaphor to Metamorphosis.* New Haven: Yale University Press, 1974.

Granville-Barker, Harley. *Prefaces to Shakespeare.* 6 vols. Princeton: Princeton University Press, 1927–74.

McGuire, Philip C. and Samuelson, David A., eds. *Shakespeare: The Theatrical Dimension.* AMS Studies in the Renaissance, vol. 3. New York: AMS Press, 1979.

Styan, J. L. *The Shakespeare Revolution: Criticism and Performance in the Twentieth Century.* Cambridge: Cambridge University Press, 1977.

Van Laan, Thomas F. *Role-Playing in Shakespeare.* Toronto: University of Toronto Press, 1978.

Metatheatre

Abel, Lionel. *Metatheatre.* New York: Hill and Wang, 1963.

Burckhardt, Sigurd. *Shakespearean Meanings.* Princeton: Princeton University Press, 1968.

Calderwood, James L. *Shakespearean Metadrama: The Argument of the Play in "Titus Andronicus," "Love's Labour's Lost," "Romeo and Juliet," "A Midsummer Night's Dream," and "Richard II."* Minneapolis: University of Minnesota Press, 1971.

———. *Metadrama in Shakespeare's Henriad: "Richard II" to "Henry V."* Berkeley: University of California Press, 1979.

———. *To Be and Not to Be: Negation and Metadrama in "Hamlet."* New York: Columbia University Press, 1986.

———. *If It Were Done: "Macbeth" and Tragic Action.* Amherst: University of Massachusetts Press, 1983.

Dawson, Anthony B. *Indirections: Shakespeare and the Art of Illusion.* Toronto: University of Toronto Press, 1978.

Edwards, Philip. *Shakespeare and the Confines of Art.* London: Methuen, 1968.

Egan, Robert. *Drama within Drama: Shakespeare's Sense of His Art in "King Lear," "The Winter's Tale," and "The Tempest."* New York: Columbia University Press, 1975.

Farrell, Kirby. *Shakespeare's Creation: The Language of Magic and Play.* Amherst: University of Massachusetts Press, 1975.

Goldman, Michael. *Shakespeare and the Energies of Drama.* Princeton: Princeton University Press, 1972.

Homan, Sidney. *When the Theater Turns to Itself: The Aesthetic Metaphor in Shakespeare.* Lewisburg: Bucknell University Press, 1981.

Huston, J. Dennis. *Shakespeare's Comedies of Play.* New York: Columbia University Press, 1981.

Righter, Anne. *Shakespeare and the Idea of the Play.* London: Chatto & Windus, 1962.

Production History

Bartholomeusz, Dennis. *Macbeth and the Players.* Cambridge: Cambridge University Press, 1969.

——. *"The Winter's Tale" in Performance in England and America.* Cambridge: Cambridge University Press, 1982.

Berry, Ralph. *Changing Styles in Shakespeare.* London: Allen & Unwin, 1981.

Carlisle, Carol Jone. *Shakespeare from the Greenroom: Actors' Criticisms of Four Major Tragedies.* Chapel Hill: University of North Carolina Press, 1969.

David, Richard. *Shakespeare in the Theatre.* Cambridge: Cambridge University Press, 1978.

Halstead, William P. *Shakespeare as Spoken: a Collation of 5000 Acting Editions and Promptbooks for Shakespeare.* 12 vols. Ann Arbor, Mich.: University Microfilms International for American Theatre Association, 1977–79.

Odell, G. C. D. *Shakespeare: from Betterton to Irving.* 2 vols. New York: Charles Scribner's Sons, 1920.

Price, Joseph G., ed. *The Triple Bond: Plays, Mainly Shakespearean in Performance.* University Park: Pennsylvania State University Press, 1975.

Ripley, John. *"Julius Caesar" on Stage in England and America.* Cambridge: Cambridge University Press, 1980.

Rosenberg, Marvin. *The Masks of Othello.* Berkeley: University of California Press, 1961.

——. *The Masks of King Lear.* Berkeley: University of California Press, 1972.

——. *The Masks of Macbeth.* Berkeley: University of California Press, 1978.

Shattuck, Charles Harlen. *Shakespeare on the American Stage: From the Hallams to Edwin Booth.* Washington, D.C.: Folger Shakespeare Library, 1976.

Sprague, Arthur Colby. *Shakespearian Players and Performers.* 1953. Reprint with a new preface by the author. New York: Greenwood Press, 1969.

—— and Trewin, J. C. *Shakespeare's Plays Today: Some Customs and Conventions of the Stage.* Columbia: University of South Carolina Press, 1970.

Trewin, J. C. *Shakespeare on the English Stage, 1900–1964; A Survey of Productions Illustrated from the Raymond Mander and Joe Mitchenson Theatre Collection.* London: Barrie and Rockliff, 1964.

Wells, Stanley. *Royal Shakespeare: Four Major Productions at Stratford-upon-*

Avon. Reprinted from *Furman Studies,* n.s., vol. 23. Manchester: Manchester University Press, 1977.

Editions

Brockbank, Philip, gen. ed. *The New Cambridge Shakespeare.* Cambridge: Cambridge University Press, 1984–. Each volume has a special editor and includes production history materials.

Wells, Stanley, gen. ed. *The Oxford Shakespeare.* Oxford: Clarendon, 1982–. Each volume has a special editor and includes production history materials.

Mulryne, J. R. gen. ed. *Shakespeare in Performance.* Dover, N. H.: Manchester University Press, 1984–. Each volume has a special editor: the first volume in this play-by-play series is *All's Well That Ends Well,* edited by J. L. Styan, 1984.

A Bibliography of Bernard Beckerman's Publications

Books

Shakespeare at the Globe. New York: Macmillan, 1962.

Dynamics of Drama: Theory and Method of Analysis. New York: Knopf, 1970.

With Joseph Papp, eds. *Troilus and Cressida.* New York: Macmillan, 1967.

With Joseph Papp, eds. *Love's Labor's Lost.* New York: Macmillan, 1968.

With Howard Siegman, eds. *On Stage: Selected Theatre Reviews from the "New York Times" 1920–1970.* New York: Quadrangle; New York: New York Times Books, 1973.

Ed. *Five Plays of the English Renaissance.* New York: New American Library, 1983.

Articles

"The Globe Playhouse: Notes for Direction." *Educational Theatre Journal* 5 (March 1953): 6–11.

"Shakespearean Production in New York, 1906–1956." *Speech Association of Eastern States Fifty Year Publication* (1959).

"Shakespearean Production in America." *Enciclopedia della Spectacollo,* 8:1191–93.

"Shakespeare's Theatre." In *The Complete Pelican Shakespeare,* edited by Alfred Harbage, 21–29. New York: Penguin, 1969.

"Dramatic Theory and Stage Practice." In *Papers in Dramatic Theory and Criticism,* edited by D. M. Knauf, 24–36. Iowa City: University of Iowa Press, 1969.

"A Shakespearean Experiment: The Dramaturgy of *Measure for Measure.*" In *The Elizabethan Theatre, II,* 108–133. Toronto: Macmillan, 1970.

"The University Accepts the Theatre." In *The American Theatre: A Sum of Its Parts,* 339–55. New York: Samuel French, 1971.

"Philip Henslowe." In *The Theatrical Manager in England and America,* edited by Joseph W. Donohue, Jr., 3–62. Princeton: Princeton University Press, 1971.

"Dramatic Analysis and Literary Interpretation: *The Cherry Orchard* as Exemplum." *New Literary History* 2 (Spring 1971): 391–406.

"Theatre." *Encyclopedia Americana,* 1972.

"The Flowers of Fancy, the Jerks of Invention: Directorial Approaches to Shakespeare." In *Shakespeare 1971.* Proceedings of the World Shakespeare Congress, 200–214. Toronto: University of Toronto Press, 1972.

"Theatrical Production." *Encyclopedia Britannica,* 15th ed.

"Explorations in Shakespeare's Drama." *Shakespeare Quarterly* 24 (1973): 128–37.

"Shakespeare and the Life of the Scene." In *English Renaissance Drama: Essays in Honor of Madeleine Doran and Mark Eccles,* edited by Standish Henning, Robert Kimbrough, and Richard Knowles, 36–45. Carbondale: Southern Illinois University Press, 1976.

"Past the Size of Dreaming." In *Twentieth Century Interpretations of "Antony and Cleopatra,"* edited by Mark Rose, 99–112. Englewood Cliffs, N.J.: Prentice-Hall, 1976.

"Some Problems in Teaching Shakespeare's Plays as Works of Drama." In *Teaching Shakespeare,* edited by Walter Edens et al., 305–16. Princeton: Princeton University Press, 1977.

"The Artifice of 'Reality' in Chekhov and Pinter." *Modern Drama* 21 (June 1978): 154–61.

"Past the Size of Dreaming." In *Shakespeare: The Theatrical Dimension,* edited by Philip McGuire and David Samuelson, 209–223. New York: AMS Press, 1979.

"Shakespeare's Industrious Scenes." *Shakespeare Quarterly* 30 (1979): 138–50.

"Theatrical Perception." *Theatre Research International,* n.s., 4 (May 1979): 1957–71.

"The Persons Personated: Character Lists in English Renaissance Play Texts." In *Poetry and Drama in the English Renaissance Play Texts, In Honour of Professor Jiro Ozu,* edited by Yasuo Tamaizuni, 61–69. Tokyo: Kinokuniya, 1980.

"The Use and Management of the Elizabethan Stage." In *The Third Globe,* edited by C. Walter Hodges, et al., 151–63. Detroit: Wayne State University Press, 1980.

"Schemes of Show: A Search for Critical Norms." In *The Stage and the Page: London's "Whole Show" in the Eighteenth-Century,* edited by George Winchester Stone, Jr., 209–28. Berkeley: University of California Press, 1981.

"Shakespeare's Dramaturgy and Binary Form." *Theatre Journal* 33 (March 1981): 5–17.

"Historic and Iconic Time in Late Tudor Drama." In *Shakespeare, Man of the Theater,* edited by Kenneth Muir, Jay L. Halio, and D. J. Palmer, 47–54. Newark: University of Delaware Press, 1983.

"Playing the Crowd: Structure and Soliloquy in *Tide Tarrieth No Man.*" In *The Mirror up to Shakespeare: Essays in Honour of G. R. Hibbard,* edited by J. C. Gray, 133–45. Toronto: University of Toronto Press, 1983.

"Shakespeare and 'The Purpose of Playing.' " New Orleans, La.: Graduate School of Tulane University, 1983.

"Acts of Truth and Wonder." *Mask und Kothurn* 29 (1983): 179–88.

"Spectacle in the Theatre." *Theatre Survey* 25 (May 1984): 1–13.

"Shakespeare Closing." *Kenyon Review,* n.s., 7 (Summer 1985): 79–95.

"The Odd Business of Play Reviewing." *Shakespeare Quarterly* 36 (Summer 1985): 588–93.

"Selling Shakespeare Short." *American Theatre* 2 (October 1985): 13–17, 44–45.

"Shakespeare's Dramatic Methods." In *William Shakespeare: His World, His*

Work, His Influence, vol. 2, edited by John F. Andrews, 397–416. New York: Scribners, 1985.

"The American Shakespearean Actor—An Endangered Species." In *Shakespeare Study Today,* edited by Georgianna Ziegler, 71–92. New York: AMS Press, 1986.

"Scene Patterns in *Doctor Faustus* and *Richard III.*" In *Shakespeare and His Contemporaries,* edited by E. A. J. Honigmann, 31–41. Manchester: Manchester University Press, 1986.

"Beckett and the Act of Listening." In *Beckett at 80 / Beckett in Context,* edited by Enoch Brater, 149–67. New York, Oxford: Oxford University Press, 1986.

"The Dynamics of Peter Shaffer's Drama." In *The Play and Its Critic: Essays for Eric Bentley,* edited by Michael Bertin, 199–209. Lanham, Maryland: University Press of America, 1986.

"Theatrical Plots and Elizabethan Stage Practice." In *Shakespeare and Dramatic Tradition: Essays in Honor of S. F. Johnson,* edited by W. R. Elton and William Long. Newark: University of Delaware Press, 1988.

"The Play's the Thing—But What's a Play?: Dramatic Literature at the University." In *Master Teachers of Theatre,* edited by Burnet M. Hobgood. Carbondale: Southern Illinois University Press, 1988.